ALEXANDRE KOJÈVE

Also by Shadia B. Drury

THE POLITICAL IDEAS OF LEO STRAUSS

ALEXANDRE KOJÈVE

THE ROOTS OF POSTMODERN POLITICS

SHADIA B. DRURY

ST. MARTIN'S PRESS
NEW YORK

Scholarly and Reference Division,
St. Martin's Press, Inc., 175 Fifth Avenue,
New York, N.Y. 10010

First published in the United States of America in 1994

Printed in the United States of America

ISBN 0-312-12089-3 (cloth)
ISBN 0-312-12092-3 (paper)

Library of Congress Cataloging-in-Publication Data

Drury, Shadia B., 1950–
    Alexandre Kojève : the roots of postmodern politics / Shadia B.
Drury.
        p. cm.
    Includes bibliographical references (p.   ) and index.
    ISBN 0-312-12089-3 (cloth). — ISBN 0-312-12092-3 (paper)
    1. Kojève, Alexandre, 1902–1968—Contributions in political
science. 2. Postmodernism—Political aspects. 3. History–
–Philosophy. 4. Ideology. I. Title.
JC273.K57D78   1994
320'.01—dc20   94-18531
                                                              CIP

Interior design by Digital Type & Design

To my parents
Nazli and Anwar Basilious

C·O·N·T·E·N·T·S

A·C·K·N·O·W·L·E·D·G·M·E·N·T·S

I am indebted to the Social Science and Humanities Research Council of Canada for providing me with funds in support of this work. I am also indebted to the Calgary Institute for the Humanities for a fellowship that released me from teaching for one semester.

I would like to thank my graduate students, Stefan LaBranche, Len Wilson, Giles Norman, and Stephen Haigh, for all their help. Thanks also to my daughter, Kelly Drury, for helping with the project. Special thanks to my colleague Carol Prager for her careful reading of the manuscript and for her impeccable stylistic and substantive advice. Thanks also to my colleague Hugo Meynell for reading and commenting on the chapters on Foucault and Bataille. As always, John W. Yolton provided continued support and encouragement. My greatest debt is to my husband, Dennis Drury, whose help and support made the whole enterprise worthwhile.

P·R·E·F·A·C·E

The far-reaching intellectual influence of Alexandre Vladimirovitch Kojèvnikov (1902-1968), known simply as "Kojève," is better known than it is understood. Kojève was a Russian émigré who settled in Paris where he gave a series of lectures on Hegel's *Phenomenology* at the École Pratique des Hautes Études from 1933 to 1939. These lectures are believed to have "dramatically shaped the French intellectual landscape of this century."[1] They were attended by a remarkable group of French intellectuals that included Raymond Queneau, a leader in surrealist literature; Georges Bataille, a novelist, sociologist and literary critic; Maurice Merleau-Ponty, a philosopher; André Breton, founder of the surrealist movement; Jacques Lacan, a psychoanalyst; and Raymond Aron, a political theorist.[2] But Kojève's influence was not limited to those who attended his lectures. Leading figures of postmodernism such as Michel Foucault and Jacques Derrida also pay tribute to him and are deeply indebted to his reading of Hegel. Nor was Kojève's influence confined to fashionable intellectuals in France. He also had a considerable impact on American followers of Leo Strauss such as Allan Bloom and Francis Fukuyama, whose books have received enormous attention, not only in American intellectual circles, but also in the popular press. Two American commentators have recently noted that Kojève's work is of such "uncommon brilliance and penetration" that "its influence on philosophical thought in France, in the rest of Europe, and in America, cannot be exaggerated."[3]

Long before the end of the Cold War, Kojève announced the inevitable triumph of Washington over Moscow. And he was prescient enough to declare in the late 1950's that the conflict between the two superpowers will be resolved by economic rather than military means. He believed that the Americans were bound to triumph over the Soviets because the technocratic culture of the West has proven itself to be the most successful in ministering to universal human needs and desires. Kojève believed that twentieth-century capitalism has overcome the difficulties or "contradictions" that plagued it in the nineteenth century and that Marx described so well. In the industrial world, capitalism has succeeded in conquering nature, ending scarcity, and distributing wealth. The same miracle will soon be accomplished in the Third World. Since capitalism will also undermine national boundaries and homogenize culture around the globe, Kojève anticipated that history will culminate in the final and unsurpassable triumph of a global capitalist order. Soon we will be living in what Kojève called a universal and homogeneous state. After the Second World War and until his death in 1968, Kojève worked in the French Ministry of Economic Affairs. He was one of the earliest architects of the European Union, and the General Agreement on Tariffs and Trade (GATT). Apparently, Kojève was the *éminence grise*, the power behind the throne, at the Ministry of Economic Affairs. He exerted a great deal of influence on Olivier Wormser and Valéry Giscard d'Estaing. He took his work very seriously and was often angry when his suggestions were not adopted.[4] Clearly, he believed that he was presiding over the development of the final shape of the world.

Kojève arouses interest because he is an enigmatic and contradictory figure. On one hand, he is an indefatigable optimist, a modern knight, championing the cause of modernity—rationality, efficiency, a global economy, universal peace, equality, and prosperity. On the other hand, he is a postmodern nihilist—gloomy, pessimistic, melancholic, and just plain bleak. This book is the story of the metamorphosis of Kojève's Marxist conception of the "realm of freedom" into the world of Nietzsche's "last man." It is the story of how Kojève turned the "end of history" into a symbol of the despair that grips those who are convinced that history, understood as the domain of significant events and glorious actions, is a casualty of the modern world.

For some reason, Kojève began to regard the modern project to which he had devoted most of his life as an object of aversion. He came to believe that the unabashed triumph of reason in the world has created a global tyranny of hitherto unimaginable proportions. He thought that modernity has emasculated the world, feminized it, and robbed it of all its enchantments. Kojève did not become disillusioned because he believed that history had been derailed, or had failed to achieve its goals. On the contrary, it was the very success of the modern project that was the source of his unhappiness. As a result, Kojève echoed the fashionable *Kulturpessimismus* that has become the hallmark of the European highbrow.

It is my contention that Kojève is a pivotal figure in understanding the nature of the postmodern disenchantment with modernity. Kojève's postmodern admirers regarded him as the living embodiment of the fatal logic of Enlightenment rationalism. They saw his work as proof that reason is homogenizing, totalizing, oppressive, and totalitarian. And in this light, the postmodern repudiation of reason is quite understandable.

Kojève's end of history is reminiscent of the end of ideology that so gripped American political science in the 1950's. The circumstances in which both of these theories emerged are similar. At the beginning of the Cold War, political scientists such as Seymour Martin Lipset and Daniel Bell observed that within the advanced industrialized countries political ideologies of the Right and the Left had become exhausted. Instead of an irrational and irreconcilable clash of ideologies, a new consensus had emerged as the foundation of democratic politics. This new consensus was based on the realization that neither the unhampered capitalism of the Right nor the totally planned economy of the Left was a viable alternative. Instead, a combination of planning and free enterprise (i.e., a mixed economy), a welfare state and political pluralism were the most workable. Accordingly, they declared that a rational politics has replaced the irrational fervor of ideologies. This model of democratic life was the yardstick against which every political order around the globe was to be measured by the science of comparative politics. The disappearance of ideology also meant the disappearance of rationally unfounded value commitments. Now, politics can be a true science unhampered by ideological bias. Of course, the science of politics that emerged was far from neutral. In the name of science and neutrality it enshrined the values of the status quo, the values of American liberal democracy.

The similarities notwithstanding, the differences between the end of history and the end of ideology are more significant. Whereas the end of ideology was grounded in science, the end of history has its foundation in historicism; whereas the former was rooted in American pragmatism, the latter is shrouded in Hegelian philosophy; whereas the former tended to be optimistic and relatively free of self-doubt, the latter comes complete with its own brand of nihilism.

In Part I, I give an account of Kojève's brand of Hegelianism. His commentary on Hegel's *Phenomenology of Mind* is such a hypnotic blend of the ideas of Hegel, Marx, Heidegger, and Nietzsche that all those who listened to his seminar were completely spellbound. What is appealing about Kojève's thought is not the lucidity of his ideas, the sharpness of his arguments, or the systematic clarity of his analysis, but the way he was able to weave Hegel's *Phenomenology of Mind* into a tale with a tragic ending. Kojève was a great storyteller. Although his work is dense and poorly edited, I will try to present it in a way that is faithful to the narrative form that Kojève's listeners found so compelling.

In Part II, I examine Kojève's influence on French intellectuals such as Raymond Queneau, Georges Bataille, and Michel Foucault. The influence of Kojève sheds new light on postmodernism: it reveals the source of its dark romanticism; it explains why the self-refuting character of post-modernism is integral to a deep understanding of its motivations and aspirations; and it shows why postmodernism is not concerned with liberty in any ordinary sense of the term.

Part III focuses on Kojève's influence in America. This influence was largely the result of Kojève's lifelong friendship with Leo Strauss. I examine the colossally misunderstood debate between Kojève and Strauss, as well as the influence of Kojève on Straussians such as Allan Bloom and Francis Fukuyama. I believe that Kojève's view of America as the embodiment of modernity has imbued the American conservative psyche with such disdain, abhorrence, and contempt for America that conservatives are hard-pressed to find something to conserve. I regard the American admirers of Kojève, no less than his French admirers, as post-moderns. I hope to show that postmodern politics is as radical in its right-wing as well as in its left-wing manifestations. A tamer version of the chapter on the debate between Kojève and Strauss was delivered at the University of Chicago in April of 1991. Part of the chapter on Allan Bloom was previously published in Robert L. Stone (ed.), *Essays on the Closing of the American Mind* (Chicago: Chicago Review Press, 1989), as "Allan Bloom on the Charms of Culture," pp. 158-165. A short version of the chapter on Francis Fukuyama was published in *International Journal*, Vol. XLVIII, No. 1 (Winter 1992-1993), pp. 80-99, as "The End of History and the New World Order."

I believe that Kojève's demonization of reason, his glorification of the past, and his understanding of freedom have contributed to the radical-ism of postmodern politics, its dark romanticism, its despair, its impo-tence, and its glorification of gratuitous violence. Nevertheless, I do not reject the Kojèvean sensibility *tout court*, for there is much in our world that fuels it. But there are better ways to understand our afflictions and less cowardly ways to deal with our troubles.

Part I

KOJÈVE'S HEGELIANISM

CHAPTER

▪ 1 ▫

Introduction

Born to a wealthy Russian family in 1902, Kojève was fifteen when the Russian Revolution broke out in 1917. The hardships of the time led Kojève to peddle soap on the black market, which in turn led to his arrest and then to a narrow escape from execution. These events had a remarkable effect on the young Alexandre. Instead of making him hostile to communism, he became a convert.[1] Long after he left Russia in 1920, he continued to describe himself as a communist and a Stalinist.[2] Kojève eventually went to Heidelberg, where he studied with Karl Jaspers—he wrote a thesis on Vladimir Soloviev, a Russian mystic very much influenced by Hegel. Later he settled in Paris where he took over his friend Alexandre Koyré's seminar on Hegel in 1933 when Koyré left for Egypt. The seminar came to an end in 1939 when the Second World War broke out. After the war Kojève was influenced by former students to take a job in the French Foreign Ministry of Economic Affairs, which he held until his death in 1968. A recent biography of Kojève focuses on his life as a high-ranking bureaucrat and reveals the extent of his influence on French foreign policy during those years.[3] He was one of the earliest architects of the European Union, and was also instrumental in establishing the GATT talks (General Agreement on Tariffs and Trade). But even during his life in the French ministry, Kojève continued to write and to teach, especially those Americans who were sent by Leo Strauss to study with him.[4] And even though he might have become more ironic about the "end of history," Kojève continued to be serious about it and regarded himself as a Hegelian to the end.

Kojève's fame in the intellectual world is the result of his ingenious interpretation of Hegel's *Phenomenology of Mind.* And, along with Jean

Hyppolite, he is responsible for having introduced French intellectuals to Hegel. The overwhelming interest in Hegel and Marx during the 1930's was connected to the Russian Revolution and to the success of the Red Armies under Lenin and Trotsky after the end of the First World War. In the 1940's, interest in Hegel continued to intensify in France because of the active role of the French Communist Party in the French Resistance, as well as their subsequent participation in De Gaulle's government at the end of the Second World War. Socialism and its intellectual heritage were of utmost significance to the political life of the time. French intellectuals did not see themselves as transcending politics or philosophizing in a domain beyond the political. To take the intellectual high ground, to proclaim one's detachment, to declare oneself above the political fray, were all pretenses. Worse, they were the routes of cowards who would stand by in the face of unspeakable atrocities. All claims to impartiality were suspect; they were tantamount to collusion with the powers that be. In short, neutrality was not an option. The question was not so much whether or not to be *engagé*, but which side to take and why.

Kojève shared this sense of political engagement. And it was in this highly politicized atmosphere that he embarked on his interpretation of Hegel. For him, interpreting Hegel was not just an academic matter; on the contrary, he considered it a work of "political propaganda" intended to influence action and determine the shape of the future.[5]

Even though it was Hyppolite who ended up holding a full-time academic position, and who was the teacher of Michel Foucault, Gilles Deleuze, Louis Althusser, and Jacques Derrida, Kojève was by far the brighter star, and his influence on his generation, including his influence on Hyppolite, was unmistakable.[6]

Before embarking on an analysis of Kojève's Hegelianism, it behooves us to outline a few of the basic elements of Hegel's philosophy of history. The point is not to give an exhaustive interpretation of Hegel's philosophy, but merely to sketch those aspects of his work that shed light on the idiosyncratic nature of Kojève's interpretation. That Kojève's interpretation of Hegel is singularly flawed is a fact that is already well-known to Hegelian scholars—even if the magnitude of the difference has not yet been fully grasped.[7] Although Hegel is at times a very fanciful thinker, his thought contains a certain sobriety that is altogether lacking in Kojève's work. My intention is not to criticize Kojève for being untrue to Hegel. But since I am sympathetic to Hegel, I will occasionally use Hegel's ideas to criticize Kojève.

HEGEL'S PROJECT

There are several aspects of Hegel's philosophy of history that are relevant for our purposes. First, Hegel's philosophy is dialectical; second, it is optimistic without necessarily being progressive or deterministic; third, it is preoccupied with the moral life of the spirit; and fourth, it has a sober view of the role of philosophy in the history of the world. As we shall see, all of these elements of Hegel's philosophy are overturned by Kojève.

Hegel does not believe that history is simply about isolated individuals and their actions. He thinks that it is also a manifestation of the forms that the historical consciousness or Spirit assumes in the lives of a people or *Volk*. Individuals are heirs to this world spirit and do not "grow out of the earth like a mushroom."[8] Hegel did not think that this universal mind or spirit was an alien God in a distant heaven. It is not a "motionless statue" but a "mighty river" to which we are heir—not as passive recipients, but as active participants.[9] Our inheritance of principles, beliefs, prejudices, and possessions is something that we act upon and transform. To describe the transformations of this inheritance is not simply to describe change, but development. And unlike simple change, development builds on what has gone before. It "enriches and preserves at the same time."[10] Of course, Hegel is famous for preserving that which he transcends. *Aufheben*, the hallmark of the Hegelian dialectical movement, means both to cancel and preserve. It is therefore not surprising to find all sorts of philosophies in Hegel—philosophies that he enriches only to transcend.

Hegel's project is nothing less than an attempt to grasp the various historical shapes that the world spirit assumes in its quest of self-discovery and fulfillment. The *Phenomenology* is a study of phenomena understood as the diversity and multiplicity of shapes and forms which Spirit assumes in the course of its development from rudimentary to more sophisticated levels of self-understanding. Hegel has a clear idea of what a deep self-understanding would entail, but nowhere does he find this manifested in historical life. Nevertheless, he does clearly indicate higher and lower levels of such actualizations. But Hegel's general optimism leads him to think that Spirit is constantly struggling toward completion, self-fulfillment, and self-understanding. At the intellectual level, this elevated self-understanding would transcend the usual dualism of subject and object, the mind and the world.

Hegel's unique brand of idealism dissolves the rift between consciousness and the world, between Being-for-itself and Being-in-itself.[11]

However, this reconciliation of consciousness and the world of sense experience is not to be accomplished by making the actual world, the world of sense experience, a mere figment of the mind; nor is it to be accomplished by reducing the mind to an epiphenomenon of the world. Hegel insists on a unity of both in a relation of mutual dependence and independence. Hegel describes a consciousness for whom the world is not alien—for it finds the other in itself and itself in the other. Consciousness can achieve this level of self-understanding only when it is genuinely dialectical—which is to say when it involves a dynamic unity of opposites each completing the other, being completed by the other, and finding itself in the other.

At the practical level, the exalted Hegelian conception of self-understanding refers to a genuinely fulfilling moral life that combines freedom and oneness, individuality and community, transcendence and immanence, God and man, in a moral life that is as deep as it is wide, and as all-inclusive as it is intimate. All this may sound too incredible to be believed. Yet there are so many simple levels on which it makes perfect sense. At the moral level, Hegel is talking about a life in which individuals live according to the moral law, not out of fear, or habit, or unquestioning obedience, but with a glad heart because the recognized law is the same law that springs out of their own hearts and that conforms to their own conscience. Hegel believed that such a rich moral life was the gift of Christianity. He had a definite antipathy toward the Catholic Church because he thought that it subverted the unique dignity of Christianity. According to Hegel, the Christian legacy was connected to the emergence of conscience, and with it, the free ethical personality that follows the moral law not as an external and alien thing, but recognizes itself, its identity and its very being, in that law. Hegel describes a moral life in which the spirit is at home. In contrast, the Church was autocratic, hypocritical, and Pharisaic. Cynics may dismiss Hegel's project as fiction, but even they cannot deny the beauty of his moral vision. And even if it is unattainable, Hegel may be right in thinking that it is the sort of homecoming that every spirit longs for.

Even though Hegel holds out the hope of this self-actualization of the spirit, he does not find such fulfillment in the historical world. Nor does he give us any reason for thinking that the history of the world is progressive in any simple meaning of the term. Hegel's use of ancient Rome and eighteenth-century Europe as examples of the estrangement and alienation of the spirit trapped in a soulless community devoid of warmth, depth, or intimacy indicates that the *Phenomenology* is not a reconstruction of history.[12]

There is no doubt that Hegel's view of history is optimistic. But this does not mean that every historical development that comes after is necessarily superior to the one that came before. And as Judith Shklar has noted, Hegel's account of history can be quite regressive.[13] In her view, Hegel's conception of history begins with the golden age of the Greeks and their moral community and degenerates into the alienation of the eighteenth-century European civilization and its supposed Age of Enlightenment that finally culminates in the Reign of Terror of the French Revolution. The Greeks were at home in their world; they lived a truly communal life and did not suffer from the modern sickness of alienation and its corresponding unhappy consciousness. The rise of individualism put an end to this primal happiness. In Shklar's view, Hegel regarded history as a long tale of woe—the result of the experiments of individualistic consciousness from Socrates to the present. The rise of this individualistic consciousness has been the ruin of mankind and has precluded the possibility of any future happiness or of the return to the blessedness of Greek life. Shklar's argument is brilliant but incomplete. What makes it seem plausible is that Hegel is deeply disturbed by the conditions of his own time. He thinks of the Terror as the logical outcome of the demand for absolute freedom of alienated individualities. Shklar's work is a good antidote to so many interpreters, including Kojève, who portray Hegel's view of history as radically progressive and rigidly deterministic. For Kojève, history is a series of regimes that pass away only to be followed by better ones, with the whole process culminating in a definitive world order that is destined to last for all eternity. The value of Shklar's work is that it alerts us to the fact that these interpretations are quite misleading.

Even if we abandon the idea that Hegel's view of history is progressive, it is impossible to deny that his view is optimistic. Hegel's optimism consists in his ability to find the rose in every cross. Even if Shklar is right that in the whole history of the world Hegel could not find a human condition that compares to the blessedness of the Greeks in its beauty, happiness, and homeliness, it is nevertheless the case that he not only thinks a return to that happy time is impossible, but undesirable. No matter how wretched adult life may get, Hegel does not think anyone would choose to return to the puerility of youth.[14] And much of what Hegel says about the Greeks clearly indicates that he thought of them as a manifestation of moral consciousness in its infancy. Despite the beauty and homeliness of their moral life, Hegel thought it consisted of little more than blind obedience to conventional morality—a *Sittlichkeit* as distinct from a *Moralität*.[15] The difference is critical. *Sittlichkeit* is intimate and cozy, but unconscious and uncritical. It is a simple, almost instinctive obedience to established law and custom. In this sort of moral community people live unreflectively by tradition and not by their own lights. But there always comes a time when the traditions are questioned; this is an age of enlightenment or *Aufklärung*, as a result of which *Sittlichkeit* gives way to *Moralität*.[16] The latter is an individualistic morality that has its source in individual conscience. And even though Hegel regards this morality of conscience to be far more sophisticated and enriching than a merely conventional morality, he also thinks that this enlightened morality has its dangers, as the case of Socrates illustrates. Liberated from the shackles of conventional morality, individuals may wreak havoc on their communities as Critias and Alcibiades did. The latter was an Athenian general and a traitor who contributed to the defeat of Athens in the Peloponnesian wars, while the former was one of the thirty tyrants who ruled Athens after the Peloponnesian wars. Both were students of Socrates. In Hegel's view, Socrates did not encourage their treacheries, but he is responsible for having opened the Athenians up to the dangers of a subjective or reflective morality. Yet in doing so, Hegel is certain that Socrates discovered a higher morality. The latter is the fruit of knowledge of good and evil; and even though this knowledge is linked to the Fall, Hegel reminds us that it also "contains the principle of redemption."[17]

Hegel's profound analysis of Socrates as both the "ruin" of Athens as well as the "great historic turning point" of the West sheds light on the project of the Spirit that he believed was seeking actualization in history. In the Hegelian view, the Greek world was animated by a collective "we" that personified a spontaneous harmony of ideas and feelings. Those who were part of this collectivity were at home in the world because their personal feelings and inclinations were in complete concord with the social order. They did not suffer from the alienation, isolation, and estrangement so characteristic of men in modern society. The Greeks created a world in which order and liberty existed side by side in perfect harmony. Hegel envied them this harmony, but by the same token, he thought that they were morally infantile. Their freedom and harmony was the product of thoughtless conformity to conventional morality. It was Socrates who broke the spell of this happy coincidence of freedom and order. Socrates represented a new sensibility that was richer, deeper, and more introspective. He taught his fellow citizens to listen to the voice of conscience that had for so long been silenced by their collective mania. Socrates did not destroy the public morality in the name of private caprice or will to power. Socrates discovered an "I" deep in his soul that was not just a private or personal voice.[18] It was the voice of the universal, the transcendent, the beyond that is higher than the collective concord of the Athenian "we." By introducing this universal and transcendent standard, Socrates created a rift between heaven and earth, nature and convention, the political and the good. When consciousness wrenches itself from the public morality and gains an awareness of its own independence, then it no longer acknowledges unquestioningly and immediately what is put before it. The result is that law is no longer the "unbroken continuity" of a collective consciousness. A rift occurs between the subjective and the objective, the reflective consciousness and the community, the individual and the state, the truth of society and the truth of the soul. As a result, the state loses its power and the positive morality is shaken.[19] There is no doubt that Socrates is guilty of having destroyed the Greek world. But he did not accomplish this single-handedly. The Greek sensibility was already in decline and a new consciousness was already emerging, which Socrates merely articulated. The fact that the Athenians repented the condemnation of Socrates is not an indication that he was guiltless, but that he personified what Hegel called the tragic "innocence which is guilty and atones for its guilt."[20]

Socrates is a tragic figure (and not just an unfortunate one) because he is both innocent and guilty.[21] He is innocent because the principles he represented are valid and good, yet he is guilty because what he stood for was destructive of Greek life. Tragedy consists of a clash of two principles that have legitimacy, validity, and value, but that are mutually exclusive. The Socratic "I" came into conflict with the collective "we" of the Athenians. Because their coexistence was impossible, one had to destroy the other. Yet, it was through this tragic sacrifice of Socrates that the West got its glimpse of the "universal Idea" or the "true good."[22]

According to Hegel, Socrates discovered a superior morality that springs from the heart—a morality that is rooted in the universal and is therefore inclusive—unlike the Athenian morality, which excluded slaves and non-Athenians from its collective "we." The trouble is that Socratic consciousness has a way of getting mired in subjectivity, and a terrible subjectivity at that; for it is a subjectivity that tends to absolutize itself and to make demands in the name of the universal. This is the sort of subjectivity that can be the ruin of all collective life, order, and happiness. It is the same subjectivity that was responsible for the Reign of Terror of the French Revolution. So, while Socratic consciousness represents a higher level of development, it is also a very dangerous thing. It would be easy to say that the emergence of this new subjectivity is a watershed after which all happiness was irretrievably lost, but Hegel does not say so. Even though he is painfully aware of the hazardous road that Socratic consciousness has traveled, he never doubts that it is a definite advance. And if it ever reaches maturity, Hegel thinks that it will achieve a harmony of the moral law with passion, desire, and inclination— which have been categorically excluded from all accounts of the ethical life from Socrates to Kant. The Romantics of Hegel's time certainly affirmed the passions, but they did so in a revolt against reason and in opposition to all its claims. The postmoderns of our time have also succumbed to the same romantic aversion to reason. In contrast, Hegel's project consisted in discovering a harmony between reason and the passions, duty and desire, discipline and freedom.

What Hegel means is not as mystical as is often believed. I once heard Canadian prima ballerina Karen Kain describe the development of her dancing in perfectly Hegelian terms. Even though Karen Kain has probably not read Hegel, her description of the three phases in the development of her art is a testimony to the richness as well as the reality of the Hegelian synthesis. When Karen Kain was young, she danced with complete abandon; her body was at one with the music, her limbs were indistinguishable from the notes, and her spirit was the melody itself. But as she matured, she became more self-conscious, more reflective, and more preoccupied with technique. In this period of her development she acquired a proficiency and virtuosity that made her a technically flawless dancer, but she was also less natural, less spontaneous, more mechanical and more deliberate. One could say, as Hegel says of Socrates, that something rare and beautiful was shattered by the emergence of self-consciousness. But one must add, with Hegel, that the new awareness had the potential of giving birth to something that far surpasses the primal oneness from which it originated. Karen Kain would agree. In the third and final stage of her development she returns to her earlier abandon and spontaneity; but she preserves the technique she acquired while transcending its mechanical, deliberate, and artificial dimension. As a result, her dancing reaches a new height in which it combines the self-consciousness of flawless technique with youthful exuberance, self-abandon, and spontaneity. This is the highest stage of her development, which is a genuinely dialectical movement beginning with a simple unity and proceeding through self-consciousness and alienation toward a synthesis of opposites that is superior to the original and unconscious unity from which it began. Karen Kain is a microcosm of the Hegelian dialectic, and a testimony to both the actuality and the richness of life that it describes.

What is significant about the Hegelian project is that it is dialectical in the sense of being a genuine synthesis of opposites. In the case of Karen Kain, the opposites combined in the highest stage of her development were spontaneity and deliberation, self-abandon and self-consciousness. In the case of the moral life, the synthesis is between duty and inclination, reason and desire, the objective and the subjective, the universal and the individual. There is no denying that at its deepest level, the moral life does not consist of blind obedience to unquestioned traditions and conventions; nor is it compliance with law out of fear of punishment either here and now or in the beyond. There is good reason for thinking that the man who is motivated to be just out of fear, or who is righteous by convention and unthinkingly, like Cephalus in Plato's *Republic*, is one whose righteousness has no depth and is easily swept away when put to the test. And this is precisely what led Plato to believe that any genuine virtue requires knowledge and love of the good. Hegel goes even further by insisting that the good one loves should not be a distant and alien thing, but should spring from one's own heart. For Hegel, the deep ethical life belongs to one who knows "that the law of his own heart is the law of all hearts."[23] One need not believe that such a life can be realized on a mass scale or that it is the goal of the historical process, in order to endorse the beauty and richness of the Hegelian vision.

In contrast to the depth and intimacy of this Hegelian vision, we will find Kojève's inexorable march of history to be cold, soulless, and altogether indifferent to the moral life of the spirit. And even though Hegel's view of history is optimistic, it is far from being radically progressive and rigidly deterministic. Moreover, Hegel's view of history is dialectical in the sense of providing a dynamic unity of opposites that is not as mysterious as is often believed. In comparison, we will find that there is absolutely nothing dialectical about Kojève's vision. Indeed, I will show how Kojève replaces the Hegelian dialectic with a rigid dualism.

One more aspect of Hegel's philosophy is important for our purposes: Hegel's understanding of the role of philosophy itself in the world. Hegel does not believe that ideas make history; nor does he think that philosophers shape the world. On the contrary, philosophy always arrives too late:

When philosophy paints grey in grey, then has a shape of life
grown old. By philosophy's grey in grey it cannot be rejuve-
nated but only understood. The owl of Minerva spreads its
wings only with the falling dusk.[24]

Philosophy can only describe the shapes that Spirit assumes in its quest
for greater self-understanding, but it cannot lead or direct its course. In
contrast, we will find Kojève giving the philosopher a most exalted role
in the history of mankind.

The attraction of Hegel is undeniable. His philosophy is rich, boun-
tiful, and robust. It combines what appear to be conflicting elements—
idealism with realism, communitarianism with individualism,
conservatism with radicalism. His attempt to reconcile these apparently
conflicting elements into a coherent whole is the reason for both his
greatness and his mystery. My simple account of his thought is meant to
highlight aspects of his philosophy that are altogether missing in Kojève's
interpretation.

Unfaithfulness to Hegel is not the sort of criticism that would disturb
Kojève. In contrast to Hyppolite, Kojève had a certain disdain for schol-
arship. He was interested in Hegel because he believed that the problems addressed by Hegel were the most pressing problems of the time.
Although he is generally regarded as the most influential interpreter of
Hegel, Kojève certainly did not consider himself to be a mere com-
mentator on Hegel's work. Instead, he saw Hegel as the source of his
own philosophical reflections. And for the most part, I will regard
Kojève as he regarded himself—namely as a thinker in his own right.

THROUGH THE LENSES OF MARX AND HEIDEGGER

The clue to understanding Kojève's Hegelianism is to recognize the fact
that he reads Hegel through the lenses of Marx and Heidegger simultaneously. Like Marx, he believes that man is the moving force of history.
And like Heidegger, he understands man in terms of Being-toward-
death. The result is a wild, if not hypnotic, mélange of ideas.

Like Marx, Kojève's reading of Hegel is secular, humanistic, and anti-
theological. In the conflict between the anthropocentric and the theological interpretations of Hegel, Kojève comes down decidedly on the
secular, humanistic side. Kojève follows Marx in thinking that history is
made by man and not by *Geist* or Spirit. The theological interpretation of
Hegel, often called the Right or Old Hegelian interpretation, regards

man's unhappiness and alienation to have their foundation in his separation from God after the Fall of Adam and Eve. In this view, the historical dialectic is a process of reconciliation between man and God. The history of man's sin, division, alienation, separation, loneliness, and torment ends in harmony and beatitude. History is the story of the relationship between man and God. The moving force of the historical process is Hegel's Spirit understood as God or the Holy Spirit. Hegel's Universal represents the Church, the earthly mediator between man and God. Hegel's Absolute represents the final reconciliation of man and God in beatitude. In this view, Spirit is the moving force of history. Man's salvation depends on God; man must be resigned to his lot and wait patiently for his savior. And even though man believes or knows that salvation comes at the end of the process, the ways of God remain inscrutable. This is what Hegel must have meant by the "cunning of Reason."[25]

In contrast to the Right Hegelian interpretation. Kojève followed Feuerbach and Marx in considering God a mere projection of man's own idealized conception of himself. In this view, the dualism between man and himself (projected as God) is transcended in the course of the historical process. At the "end of history," man recognizes God as his own creation, and is no longer alienated from himself because he has become one with himself, or his own idealized view of himself. So understood, history is man's own self-making project. This is the reason that Kojève's interpretation is often characterized as a "Marxist humanism."

Having replaced *Geist* with man, Kojève follows Marx in thinking that man makes history, and pays less attention to the other half of Marx's proclamation—namely, that history makes man. Kojève encounters familiar difficulties. Who is this abstraction called *man* who makes history? Is it or is it not the ghost of the banished God? If by *man*, Kojève means real live individuals, then if they are to make history according to a plan, they must all agree on the same plan. If they disagree, then history will be nothing more than a struggle between competing visions of the good society. And if these visions are not satisfied with small local manifestations, but insist on being globally realized, then a grand struggle will ensue. The triumphant one will then rule the world. On the other hand, *man* could refer to a given human nature with universal needs and desires that operates mysteriously behind the activities of individuals who, in pursuing different ends, eventually converge on a single outcome. In this way, Hegel's "cunning of Reason" is replaced by Engels's "cunning of History." Kojève writes as if the latter is the case. He writes as if there is a single set of human needs, desires, hopes, and aspirations that are eventually realized in the course of the historical process. But I suspect that this latter view necessarily collapses into the former view. In other words, in the absence of common hopes, purposes, and aspirations, history remains a conflict between individuals who are bent on mutually exclusive ends. If history comes to an end in a single universal and homogeneous state, that state must be a tyranny achieved by force. In this way, the abstraction, *man*, necessarily becomes the basis of a tyranny of some men over others—a tyranny justified in the name of a common and universal humanity. This explains why the radical political projects inspired by Marx in our century have been mired in irrationalism and tyranny. Kojève anticipates this sort of criticism and tailors his philosophy accordingly. And as we shall see, this admirer of Stalin did not shrink from the prospects of a global tyranny.

Kojève has a fixed conception of human nature. Unlike Marx, he does not think that human nature is shaped by the social and material conditions of life. For Marx, human nature under the conditions of capitalism is aggressive, materialistic, and competitive; but with the conquest of scarcity and the advent of communism, the aggressive and competitive inclinations are bound to give way to social and cooperative ones. But for Kojève, human nature is given—it has fixed desires and inclinations, even if some of these desires are regarded as more genuinely human than others. History is the project of transforming the world so that it can satisfy man's given nature and its desires. Once the world is so transformed as to furnish the complete satisfaction of human desires and aspirations, then the historical project is complete.

The whole question of *man* is further complicated by the fact that Kojève's conception of man, the protagonist of history, is inspired primarily by Heideggerian existentialism. According to the latter, man is radically distinct from the rest of the world. He alone is conscious, he alone is free, he alone is aware of his existence and of his impending death. Human freedom and authenticity can be achieved only by living in the face of one's death and finitude. Indeed, the whole of Kojève's philosophical project can be understood as an effort to historicize Heideggerian existentialism. Kojève defines man as a being who flirts with death. Only by risking his life and by facing his death, understood as complete annihilation, can man attain his freedom. The quest for freedom is intimately linked to the transcendence of the fear of death, and is believed by Kojève to be the goal of the historical process. The end of history is reached when man shuffles off his comforting religions and other childish illusions and faces his mortality without fear and trembling.

Kojève attempts to blend a Marxist view of history with an existential view of man that emphasizes his radical freedom. This may leave Kojève tangled in an irreconcilable clash of ideas. But he insists that the historical consciousness of Hegel and Marx must be supplemented by the existentialism of Heidegger and vice versa.

By reading Hegel through the lenses of Heidegger as well as Marx, Kojève gave birth to that curious phenomenon known as existential Marxism, which is epitomized by the works of Jean-Paul Sartre.[26] Starting from the same premises, Sartre arrived at different conclusions. It may be argued that Sartre's rejection of any end to history is more commensurate with Kojève's premises and that Kojève's conclusions are ultimately defeated by his existentialism. However, I will argue that Kojève managed to reconcile his conception of man with his end of history thesis in surprising ways.

In conclusion, I have highlighted certain aspects of Hegel's philosophy that are not found in Kojève's interpretation. It is necessary to belabor the simple point that the Hegelian dialectic always involves a dynamic unity of opposites. I have tried to illustrate how Karen Kain exemplifies the unity of spontaneity and discipline and how the moral life combines freedom and reason, inclination and duty. As a result of this dialectical union, Hegel's philosophy is rationalistic without being cold, soulless, and indifferent. Hegel's rationalism has an emotional or passionate dimension. In contrast, Kojève's thinking is not only materialistic and anthropocentric but also dualistic, romantic, and irrational. In what follows, I will argue that Kojève replaces the dialectic with an extreme dualism between reason and passion, femininity and masculinity, necessity and freedom, discipline and spontaneity. And while he follows Hegel in thinking that reason is bound to triumph in history, it is a cold, soulless, instrumental, and heartless rationalism that conquers the world. Kojève's despotic portrait of reason has become the cornerstone of postmodern thought. Indeed, the postmodern repudiation of reason can be fully appreciated only in light of Kojève's depiction of the modern world in terms of the tyrannical embrace of a cold rationalism that has completely and mercilessly banished all its enemies. I will argue that Kojève's philosophy gives birth to a deep nostalgia for what has been banished—unreason, disorder, spontaneity, passion, instinct, and masculinity. It is my contention that the same dreary nostalgia accounts for the dark romanticism of postmodernity.

In telling the story of man, Kojève identifies three significant historical eras: the age of mastery, the age of slavery, and the end of history. I will examine each in turn.

▪ 2 ▫

The Age of Mastery

K ojève reads Hegel's *Phenomenology* as if it were a linear account of the history of human civilization culminating in a "universal and homogeneous state" that is supposedly the unsurpassable embodiment of human wisdom, satisfaction, completion, and self-understanding. In Kojève's account, history has a clear beginning and a definite end. The center of the Hegelian edifice and the motor of history is Hegel's master-slave dialectic.

In his *Phenomenology of Spirit* Hegel gives an enigmatic account of a dialectic between master and slave intended to explain and vindicate the transcendence of mastery.[1] Hegel's account can be read at many levels, but at the simplest level it is safe to say that Hegel wanted to show that mastery as a psychological frame of mind and as a social relationship was pathological and needed to be transcended. The reason he gives is that mastery and slavery are two aspects of a single human consciousness—one dependent and existing only for another (the slave), the other independent and existing only for itself (the master). In Hegel's view, consciousness is in truth both dependent and independent, both lord and serf. Hegel expects that consciousness will ultimately discover this unity and find itself in what it regards as its "other." Once the differentiation of consciousness from its primal oneness has occurred, mastery tends to be the predominant feature of self-consciousness. However, once consciousness is at home with itself, once it reaches a higher level of self-understanding, it will realize that its completion and fulfillment are linked to being for another and not just being for self. What Hegel means by mutual recognition is to find oneself in the other and the other in oneself. For Hegel, to renounce mastery is wisdom, for individuals as much as for civilizations. And to the extent that human history has moved away from despotism, toward more civilized forms of political association, it can be said to have progressed.

Kojève regards Hegel's master-slave dialectic as an account of human history.[2] The master-slave dialectic is also the clue to history because it explains what it is about man that sets him apart from animals and makes him a historical being, or a creature with a history. In his account of the master-slave dialectic, Kojève is preoccupied above all else with discovering what is uniquely human. He surmises that man's humanity is intimately linked with this unprecedented act of conquest that begins with one man's attempt to enslave another and reduce the other to a thing to use for his own purposes and satisfaction. But what makes him do it? Kojève identifies two qualities of man that make him a creature with a history: self-consciousness and desire.

Self-consciousness consists in an awareness of the self, or of the I, as something that is different from, even radically opposed to, the rest of the world or the non-I.[3] To be self-conscious is to be a subject reflecting on oneself as an object. A self-conscious being is characterized by an internal duality of subject and object. Self-consciousness reveals to man his true self—it makes him conscious of the fact that he is altogether unlike the rest of the world of nature. He is not a thing or an animal—given, fixed, defined. Self-consciousness makes man human because it prevents him from becoming submerged in the "extension of animal-life."[4] In contrast to the world of nature and animals, man has the capacity for self-transformation or self-creation, simply because he is a profound emptiness, or nothingness, called desire. Kojève does not describe this desire as a desire to improve oneself or to make more of oneself; rather, he maintains that it is simply the desire to be *perceived* by others as a subject, and to be valued as a subject for oneself or one's very being (*sein*).[5]

According to Kojève, the certainty of oneself as a subject has the quality of a mirage unless it is acknowledged by others. If the recognition of the self as a subject—that is, as a nonnatural object that is not a thing—is to become more than just a self-flattering illusion, it must be recognized by others. Only then can it become a reality, or assume the status of truth. In other words, truth is collective and intersubjective; what is not intersubjectively affirmed is either madness or crime.[6] Self-consciousness is linked to the peculiarly human desire for recognition.

Desire is what disquiets man and moves him to action, especially to "action negating the given."[7] Desire is a nothingness, or emptiness, filled only by action that destroys, negates, or assimilates. So understood, desire is much like hunger, which is to say that animals also experience it. But Kojève distinguishes sharply between genuinely human desires and mere animal desires. Animal desires are directed toward natural things like food, or the body of another as a sexual object. But a genuinely human or "anthropogenetic Desire" is a desire for recognition by another self-consciousness; Kojève uses the relationship between a man and a woman as an example.[8] If the parties desire only one another's bodies, then it is a purely biological or animal relationship. The relationship between a man and a woman is genuinely human only if or only because what they desire is to be loved for their value as human subjects. Kojève thinks that such amorous desire can be satisfied by love alone, without any "materialization."[9]

The desire to be loved is only one instance of the uniquely human desire to be recognized. What is uniquely human about this desire is that it is not directed toward a natural object that has biological utility. Human desire must be "non-natural."[10] It must be a desire for that which is "useless from a biological point of view."[11]

Animal desires are biological: they are desires for life or for what is useful for life. In contrast, human desires are desires for what is useless from a biological point of view: love, admiration, honor, and their symbolic manifestations in biologically worthless objects such as a medal or the enemy's flag.[12]

Desire is an awareness of the absence of a reality—in particular, the awareness of the absence of admiration, honor, respect, or recognition.[13] Human desire moves man to action; it moves him to transform the given and to create a new reality in which he is recognized as a subject. However, this desire is strictly one-sided. It is a desire to be recognized as a subject without reciprocally recognizing the other. On the contrary, it reduces the other to a thing or a means to one's own quest for recognition.

Kojève defines man as desire or nothingness that is "greedy for content."[14] Man's nothingness moves him to "annihilate Being," and through this act of negation, to make himself the creator and shaper of reality. Man realizes himself "at the expense of Being."[15] History is the story of human action negating the given, and creating a new reality that satisfies the all-consuming desire for recognition.

Man's very essence is action negating nature. But, insofar as man is also an animal in nature, nature is inseparable from his being. So, to be fully human, he must negate the nature that dwells within him. In other words, to satisfy the genuinely human desire for recognition, he must negate the natural or animal desire for self-preservation. The latter is a powerful obstacle to the genuinely human desire for recognition. To be human, man must triumph over his animal desire.[16] He must overcome the fear of death, and risk his life to gain recognition in the "fight for pure prestige." This is the fight that sets history in motion.[17]

In a totally unprecedented and daring action, man stakes his life in a fight to the death for supremacy and prestige. In this "fight for pure prestige" one man forces another to recognize him as a superior.[18] The loser in the fight must recognize his superior without being recognized in turn.

In the fight for pure prestige, the winner becomes the master and superior, while the loser becomes his slave and inferior. The master is superior to the slave not just because he won the fight, but because he was strong enough or man enough to have conquered the enemy within—the fear of death and the natural instinct for self-preservation. He won the fight because he was able to live by the motto: *conquer or die*. In contrast, the slave gives way to the natural love of life. Unable to conquer his animal instinct, the slave gives up his freedom in exchange for his life. The master's superiority over the slave has its source in his superiority over nature—the master triumphs over his own animality— therein lies his humanity. In contrast, the slave, like animals and "primitive men," continues to live in the "bosom of Nature."[19]

From the beginning of history in the fight for pure prestige, to its culmination in the universal and homogeneous state, Kojève conceives of man as being opposed to nature. Man is the unnatural, or antinatural being par excellence. The fight is proof of man's unnaturalness, for it has *no biological purpose*. It is, therefore, a supremely *human* action, a truly free action.[20]

So important is the fight for pure prestige that Kojève is led to declare that "the human being is begotten only in and by the fight that ends in the relation between Master and Slave."[21] For it is only in and through the fight that man's humanity is manifest.

For Kojève, nothing manifests this distinctive quality of the human being more than the master's conscious risk of life in the battle for pure prestige. For in so doing, the master displays his "Nothingness," his "Negate-ivity" or his capacity to negate given nature, including his own given nature. Man is "*Negativity* incarnate."[22] Only through his negativity does man manifest his freedom as a self-creative being. For it is in man's "negate-ive" action that man's freedom is actualized. Freedom is inseparable from his negativity, his nothingness and his death. It may seem paradoxical to think that death is the ultimate manifestation of freedom. But the premise with which Kojève begins compels him to reach this conclusion. If man's freedom is manifest in the act of negating the given, and if what is given is life and the instinct for its self-preservation, then it follows that the negation of life through the choice of death is the ultimate act of freedom. As Kojève puts it, "a death that is voluntary" is the "supreme manifestation of freedom."[23] And this is why "man is truly historical or human only to the extent that he is a warrior."[24] Kojève's admiration for the master is unmistakable.

Although he would like to avoid this conclusion, Kojève's reasoning leads him to intimate that the slave is not fully human. Overwhelmed by his instinct for self-preservation, the slave shrinks from death. By choosing life, the slave binds himself "completely to his animal life," he becomes "one with the natural world of things." In short, "he does not rise above the level of animals."[25] We can say that he becomes the master's slave only because he was already a "Slave of Nature." He is thereby inferior to the master (one is tempted to say, by nature); and he recognizes this inferiority as much as he recognizes the master's superiority. In reading Kojève's account of the master-slave dialectic, one cannot help but conclude that the slave *deserves* to be the master's slave, even though Kojève does not say so.

If Kojève were true to his own reasoning, his story would end with the pagan state as he understands it. But it does not. Kojève tries to follow Hegel in denying that the master is happy, or that mastery is satisfying. He insists, with Hegel, that mastery ends in an "impasse." Kojève provides three arguments to establish his case. In what follows I will show that these arguments are altogether feeble, and that no one who accepts Kojève's premises would join him in concluding that mastery is unsatisfying, or that the state of mastery must be negated. On Kojève's account, there is no reason for history to proceed beyond the pagan state of mastery to something better—because Kojève's premises lead to the conclusion that mastery is the best life for man.

First, Kojève follows Hegel in maintaining that the master's situation is "tragic." This is so because the recognition he fought and risked his life for is not worth having, since the slave is but a thing. The master apparently discovers that only "mutual and reciprocal recognition" can satisfy him.[26]

This argument is altogether unconvincing because, unlike Hegel, Kojève associates the world of the polis with the age of mastery. For example, he writes:

> On commence par étudier le Monde du Maître. C'est le Monde antique grec. Car le Maître n'est pas seulement le Maître d'un Esclave. Il est aussi citoyen d'un État (aristocratique; la polis).[27]

The pagan state in which mastery thrives is also a state of mutual recognition and equality among masters. This mutual regard of masters for one another has its source in their willingness to risk their lives in the fight for recognition which Kojève simply refers to as "la Lutte."

It is important to note that for Hegel, mastery was not a social condition. He insists that in the context of mastery, recognition is altogether lacking.[28] The sad thing about the master is that he embarks on the project of mastery for the sake of recognition, but then he discovers that he cannot get recognition from slaves who depend on him and fear him. Genuine recognition must be given freely and voluntarily; only an equal is up to that task. This is why mastery is a dead end for an intensely social being in search of recognition. The mutual recognition of one master by another is no part of Hegel's *Phenomenology*. There can only be one master, not a society of masters. This is why Hegel does not discuss Greek life in the context of the master-slave dialectic. A life that involves any degree of mutual recognition is for Hegel an ethical life. But a psyche in the grip of the pathological condition of mastery is incapable of according such recognition, even to the few.

By equating mastery with the pagan state and with the conditions of social life and mutual recognition, Kojève undermines his claim that mastery ends in an "impasse." In other words, the master's situation loses the sorry quality it had in the Hegelian account. Even though the admiration of his slaves is not enough for him, the master is recognized by his fellow masters.[29] Moreover, the act of conquest satisfies his negativity and affirms his freedom as a creative being. As a result, Kojève's claim that the pagan state does not yield the satisfaction that man seeks is unconvincing.

The second argument that Kojève advances against the state of mastery is that it is boring. The master finds himself with nothing to do; "he is fixed in his mastery."[30] Kojève complains that the master no longer has any need to *act* in the genuinely human sense of *negating* the existing state of affairs, and creating a new human reality. As we shall see, this objection is identical to Kojève's objection to the end of history. While it may be a legitimate reason to object to the end of history, it is not a plausible objection to pagan mastery. It presupposes that mastery is a cozy and comfortable affair—that once won, it is secure, unchallenged, and irreversible. But surely, this is unrealistic; as long as slavery exists, the master's position is insecure. For slaves can decide at any time to renew the fight, and there is no telling what the outcome of the next fight will be. It is also the case that, because of his mentality, the master perpetually seeks new conquests, and lusts for the subjugation of others. Masters must therefore continually train for war. This is precisely what the pagans did. It may be boring, but it is not the boredom of one who has nothing left to do. Besides, Kojève makes it clear that war and its accompanying risk of death is an essential component of man's being without which he cannot manifest his negativity—the hallmark of his humanity, freedom, uniqueness, and creativity.

Kojève's third and final account of why the pagan state of mastery cannot satisfy man is that it fails to give recognition to the *sein*—the being, or "particularity" of the individual.[31] The pagan society of masters values its citizens only insofar as they continue to fight battles for pure prestige. Kojève portrays the pagan state as a macrocosm of the master's psyche: it must continue to conquer others, and to impress its supremacy on their consciousness. As such, it attributes value to its citizens only to the extent to which they contribute to its goals. In other words, it values its citizens only for what they do, not for what they are. It values what Kojève calls their "universality," not their "particularity." The latter is valued only within the family, where the citizen is father, husband, or son.

Kojève maintains that the family places supreme value on the *sein* or being of the person. As a result, the family comes into conflict with the state. This is how Kojève accounts for the nature of tragedy: it is a conflict between the demands made by the family on one hand, and those of the state on the other. Kojève believes that in the final analysis, the pagan state perishes because it cannot withstand the enmity of woman: the agent of the family, particularity, and femininity.[32]

The conflict between the family and the pagan state is a conflict between two ruling principles: one operating in the family, the other in the state. Even though Kojève does not use these terms, I will call these two principles the *feminine* and *masculine* principles respectively. In Kojève's view, the feminine principle involves the recognition of a person simply for the sake of his being, which Kojève defines in terms of the "biological *life*" of the person.[33] Conversely, the masculine principle consists in recognition only on the basis of merit—specifically, as demonstrated by success in battle.

The opposition between the two principles is stark. Neither seems altogether believable. Even mothers cannot be said to love their offspring purely for their being. When interviewed on national television, the mothers of monstrous criminals do not usually acknowledge loving them. By the same token, the most splendid achievements in battle, music, science, or philosophy pale in the face of flaws of character like treachery, malice, and dishonesty. Alcibiades was a case in point.

Kojève never tires of repeating that it is the natural and biological that must be transcended if man is to be fully human, if he is to be more than just an animal living in the "bosom of nature." It is therefore puzzling why biological life, in and of itself, should be a thing of value.

In light of Kojève's premises about humanity and animality, one would expect him to reject any attempt on behalf of the feminine principle to seek actualization beyond the limited domain of the family. Instead, Kojève identifies what I have called the feminine principle with Christianity, and he regards its historical triumph as the supreme goal of history. At the end of history, the feminine morality prevails since everyone's being is recognized as having equal worth. So understood, the feminine morality is an egalitarian nightmare that is totally blind to merit, excellence, accomplishment, or achievement. It is puzzling, to say the least, why Kojève would champion a conception of history characterized above all else by the triumph of this blind principle. Had he been more properly dialectical, he would surely have championed a synthesis of the masculine and feminine principles. I am not suggesting an androgynous society, but simply an ethic that transcends both principles, and cancels their opposition by containing elements of each. Such an ethic would not only be more genuinely Hegelian, but more balanced and moderate.

Hegel understood Greek tragedy as a clash between two competing but equally valid moralities. One was the morality of the family, the other was the morality of the community. One was governed by the divine law, the other by the human law. One was feminine and was manifest in the sister, the other was masculine and was manifest in the brother. The relation between the two corresponds to the perfect relation between brother and sister, a relation of mutual recognition and love unpolluted by desire and its contingencies. For Hegel, the brother and sister relation was the most perfect moral relation between man and woman because it had a "universal" aspect free of the particularities and contingencies of desire.[34] In Hegel's estimation, the brother and the sister, the feminine and the masculine, are two equally necessary components of the moral life. The feminine component is deep, unconscious, and undifferentiated. This is not because it is based on natural instinct or sexual desire, but because the family is a single substance, a living whole. The feminine spirit of the ethical life is deep and unconscious because it does not distinguish between the particular and the universal, the individual and the family. In the family one's existence as a particular individual is in total harmony with one's existence as a member of this micro-community.

In contrast to the feminine dimension, the masculine dimension of ethical life is conscious, more widely dispersed, and more differentiated. The brother leaves the "immediate and elemental" ethic of the family to contribute to the moral life of the greater community.[35] Unlike the moral life of the family, the moral life of the political community has its foundation in consciously crafted human law. Unlike the divine law, the human law does not belong to the mysterious darkness of the "nether world," but is exposed to the "daylight" of consciousness. In being a member of the greater community, the brother achieves a higher, more differentiated stage of consciousness. But by the same token, it is also a consciousness that is more divided against itself. Unlike the sister, the brother is aware of having two identities—one particular and the other universal; one as an individual, the other as a citizen.

Tragedy is the coming into conflict of the two moralities. What makes the conflict *tragic*, and not just sad, is that the two moralities are equally valid. By the same token, neither of the two is by itself absolutely valid.[36] They need to complement and to complete one another. For they are in truth two integral components of the complete moral life. The latter requires the union of the feminine and the masculine principles, the harmony of divine and human law.[37]

In following the historical adventures of the ethical spirit, Hegel finds that it is the masculine spirit that triumphs temporarily over the feminine. The historical movement is in the direction of greater and greater universality—from the family to the Greek city-state to the Roman Empire. But the Roman Empire turns out to be a hollow empire, totally soulless, devoid of all intimacy, depth, and warmth. For Hegel, Christianity fills the void of the hollow empire with a morality that is as wide as it is deep, as masculine as it is feminine.

Unlike Hegel's account, Kojève's account is dualistic rather than dialectical. The masculine and the feminine principles are absolute dualities—any reconciliation or compromise between them is impossible. In the conflict between the two principles, only one emerges triumphant. The other is totally defeated. In Kojève's account, it is the feminine principle that triumphs, while the masculine one is utterly defeated. Kojève regards Christianity as the "feminine morality" or "slave morality." And even though he thinks that the theism of Christianity is eventually transcended by the historical process, the slavish femininity at the heart of Christianity is preserved in its secular form. The end of history therefore marks the eclipse of the masculine principle and its corresponding capacity for mastery. And since Kojève links mastery and masculinity with humanity, it should not surprise us when Kojève concludes that the end of history signals the end of our humanity and our return to animality. It is my contention that the dualism at the heart of Kojève's way of thinking is connected to his existentialism, and it has the effect of defeating his historicism. For there is in the Kojèvean account of the nature of man a decidedly existential element. The close resemblance between Kojève's view of man and the view later developed by Jean-Paul Sartre is unmistakable. Like Kojève, Sartre also developed a dualistic ontology that divides reality into two radically different types of beings, the static and the historical, the human and the nonhuman, the self-conscious and the one devoid of consciousness, the subject and the object, Being-for-itself and Being-in-itself. In this Cartesianism gone mad, we find man defined in terms of his not being a thing, in terms of his no-thingness or his nothingness.[38] For Sartre as for Kojève, man endeavors to make his no-thingness recognized by others by reducing the other to a thing before one is reduced to a thing by the other. To live as a thing, to live for another and as the other expects, is to live unauthentically or in *bad faith*.[39] To be true to oneself, one must reduce others to thingness and resist being so reduced. A fight to the death is not necessary: the "look" or "gaze" of the other often suffices to plunge the ego into the humiliation of being reduced to a thing. This explains why human relations are for Sartre always relations of masters and slaves.

Like Kojève, Sartre believes that man's nothingness is not mere absence of thingness; it indicates the presence of a definite negative capacity or a capacity for negation, a capacity with which, needless to say, things are not endowed. This capacity for negation is the sine qua non of man's freedom. All of these aspects of Kojève's reading of Hegel are well-known features of Sartre's philosophy. There is no doubt that Kojève's existential reading of Hegel exerted a significant influence on Sartre. However, Sartre reaches very different conclusions about history: he does not believe that there can be such a thing as the end of history. He thinks that the idea is preposterous since it is neither possible nor desirable. The end of history is not possible because it precludes the negate-ive activity of man. And it is not desirable because it would amount to reducing man to thingness and this would mean the *death of man*. In contrast, Kojève clings to the idea of the end of history, but he is compelled by the logic of his premises to announce the *death of man*. This ominous pronouncement was to be repeated again and again by French intellectuals from Claude Lévi-Strauss to Michel Foucault.

For Kojève and Sartre, the full self-understanding of man as a free historical actor is possible only if man faces death understood as total annihilation. This means a recognition of the truth of atheism and an
acceptance of life without God. But Kojève is not simply an existentialist. Kojève tries to historicize existentialism by maintaining that this
authentic self-understanding of man comes only at the end of history.
History is largely the story of the slave and the ideologies he invents to
cope with his fear of death. I will examine the age of slavery in the next
chapter, but suffice it to say here that there is no reason to insist that
authenticity so defined can become manifest only at the end of history.

For all its repudiation of classical philosophy and its essentialism,
Kojève's position is a parody of essentialism. It identifies certain capacities as distinctively human—the capacity to negate the given, to gen-
erate a new reality, to demand recognition, to risk life, to strive for
prestige. And as we have seen, the pagan state as Kojève portrays it provides the conditions for the satisfaction of man's humanity.

In view of the satisfactions of the pagan state as understood by Kojève,
there seems to be no reason for history to go on. Kojève's master-slave
dialectic gives no impetus to the historical process. Of course, history has
gone on. But Kojève would have displayed more self-understanding
were he to have looked back nostalgically to the age of pagan mastery.
Instead, he looks forward to the grim triumph of the feminine principle.

▪ 3 ▫

The Age of Slavery

Kojève asserts that the slave is the key to history and that it is in and through the work of the slave that history progresses. Even though the master initiates the "anthropogenetic movement" or history, he does not continue to be the catalyst of the historical process. The master does not work and has no reason to work, since the slave provides him with all his needs. Moreover, not being a slave, he has no reason to change the world, or to change himself. The master is therefore not an agent of change—he is eternally the same, forever "fixed" in his mastery. In contrast, the slave is dissatisfied with his slavery, so he has every reason to change the world—he has every reason to dream about a world in which he is free and in which his being is valued or recognized.

For all his animality, or bondage to nature, the slave nevertheless manages to *act* in the human sense of *negating the given* or nature. Motivated to work by "absolute primordial terror," the slave becomes aware of his capacity to negate the given, to act on nature, and to conquer her.[1] In other words, work arouses in the slave a sense of his lost humanity, his freedom, his nothingness. However, his freedom is not yet actual; it exists only on the level of subjectivity, and is not a social reality.

Through work, the slave negates the given and transforms the world. By working, the slave manages to live humanly despite his servitude. In contrast, the master can die like a man on the battlefield, but he lives like an animal because he merely consumes and does not work. Ironically, the slave lives more humanly than the master because his daily life involves negating the given, and transforming the world. The activity of the slave is therefore the moving force of history; and it is in and through the work of the slave that mankind progresses. History is therefore the story of the slave, his work, his conquest of nature, his ideologies and his struggle to liberate himself from his servitude. And in the final analysis, history is the triumph of the slave.[2]

The slave is better situated to be the agent of historical change not just because he works and changes the world, but because he is in the best position to understand the truth about humanity. Having experienced the terror of annihilation (or *Angst*), the slave has caught a glimpse of his nothingness.[3] He is therefore fully aware of the fact that he is a nothingness that is sustained in being, a nothingness whose action is a negation of being in the name of a concept, an idea or an ideal that does not yet exist. By fathoming his nothingness, the slave understands his own being as a *project*, as that which is not yet.

Work will not automatically liberate the slave from his servitude. It is not enough for the slave to conquer nature through work; the slave must also conquer himself. He must conquer the nature that dwells within him in the form of the fear of death and the instinct for life. He must remember that he became the master's slave only because he was already the slave of nature. To liberate himself he must conquer his own fear of death. He must recognize that his servitude is connected to his own shortcomings. He must overcome his fear and risk his life in order to be free.

The historical narrative, the drama of the slave's struggle for self-liberation, unfolds on two levels simultaneously—one material, the other ideological. On the material level, the slave conquers nature through work. In the fullness of time, he achieves the complete technological mastery over nature that brings an end to scarcity. On the ideological level, the slave must conquer the fear of death, which is the voice of nature within him. The two processes go hand in hand. Kojève does not have much to say about the technological mastery of nature. He is more interested in the ideological or psychological transformation of the slave's attitude toward death.

Despite his consciousness of his freedom, the slave still does not have the courage to risk his life in a fight against the master. Nevertheless, awareness of freedom makes slavery difficult to bear; as a result, the age of slavery generates a plethora of ideologies intended to help the slave live with his slavery.[4] Kojève identifies Stoicism, skepticism, and Christianity as slave ideologies. They all endeavor to reconcile the conflict between the subjective feeling of freedom and the objective fact of slavery.

Kojève maintains that ideologies are the products of "intellectuals." The latter do not actually participate in the historical process. Somehow, they manage to live above the fray, "above the battle."[5] Intellectuals are content to talk about the world in which they live—a world that is not of their own making, a world made by others. Nevertheless, intellectuals are not entirely passive, since they produce ideologies that justify the existing conditions of life. Their ideas are the "superstructures" of social life, as Marx would say. However, they are not aware of the fact that their ideas are mere ideologies. They are unaware of the fact that their ideas are just a slice of time, a moment in the evolution of the world. They believe their ideologies to be philosophies that describe the eternal and unchanging essence of the world, and pass them off as such. They are convinced that they are describing the totality of being. But in reality, ideologies minister to the age of slavery, and once the latter is surpassed, they will become superfluous.

Stoicism is one of the slave ideologies. It allows the slave to convince himself that he is free simply by thinking that he is free, or by having the abstract idea of freedom. In this way, the slave becomes convinced that the fact of slavery is unimportant.[6] Stoicism tries to deny the conflict between the ideal of freedom and the reality of slavery by relegating the actual world to the status of nonbeing. In this way, Stoicism becomes an excuse for inaction. It convinces people that there is no need to change the world or the state in order to realize the abstract idea of freedom. It insists that man is free even though he is everywhere in chains.[7]

Eventually, the "chatter" of Stoicism becomes tiresome. Not only are its deceptions transparent, but the life of inaction it promotes ultimately becomes "boring." Man needs to *act* and to *negate* in order not to be a thing or an animal. As a result, Stoicism bores man; and man is the only animal capable of being bored.[8]

Stoicism therefore gives way to skepticism, solipsism, and nihilism. These ideologies deny the very reality of the world and of other human beings. Only the "I" is true; only the "I" is real; only the "I" is free. Everything that is not "I" is but a mirage or chimera. In this way, skepticism merely affirms or brings to the level of consciousness what is already implicit in Stoicism. But skepticism cannot be sustained for long. Life itself reveals it for the lie that it is. Skepticism therefore fails to remove the contradiction in Stoicism between the subjective certainty of freedom and the objective reality of slavery.

The third and final slave ideology is Christianity.[9] In contrast to Stoicism, Christianity does not deny the conflict between the ideal of freedom and the reality of slavery. Instead, it justifies the condition of bondage in this world by positing another world, or a beyond that transcends the world of the here and now. The conflict is interpreted as a conflict between this world and the next. Freedom is real only in the beyond; in this world, all is slavery.[10]

Christianity is the most ingenious of all the slave ideologies. But it is also a philosophy of inaction. Like all the slave ideologies, it is meant to reconcile the slave to his slavery since the slave is not yet ready to risk his life in a fight for recognition. Christianity teaches the slave that there is no need to fight in order to be recognized, since one is recognized by God, in the only world that has any real significance.[11]

The Christian replaces the earthly master with a divine one. But nothing much has changed. He accepts the divine master for the same reason he accepted the earthly one—because he fears death. He accepted his first master to save his biological life, he accepts his divine master in the hope of saving his eternal life. Kojève believes that Christianity has its source in the "Slave's terror in the face of Nothingness, his nothingness."[12] It has its source in the same inability to face the truth about human existence, to face death. The foundation of Christianity is the "slavish desire for life at any price."[13] What is worse, Christianity drives the slavishness to new heights. Unlike the earthly master, the divine master is an absolute master and this makes the Christian a total slave; Kojève describes him as the "pure essence of slavery."[14]

In Kojève's view, the slave cannot hope to free himself unless he can conquer his fear of death. And he cannot do so unless he abandons the religious crutches and faces his mortality squarely and without illusions about the beyond. For that, a pure and unadulterated atheism is necessary. Only the latter can "overcome" the Christian theology and open the way to the actual realization of freedom in the here and now.[15]

Despite its shortcomings, Kojève thinks of Christianity as absolutely critical in the historical realization of a world in which the equal freedom of all is universally recognized. For Christianity provides the ideal whose realization is inaugurated by the Enlightenment and the French Revolution. The ideal of Christianity therefore serves as the model according to which man makes history.

First, Christianity introduces the idea of a universal or global society. It proclaims that its God is not just the God of a particular city, or of a people, but of all mankind. It poses as a universal religion valid for all times and places. Second, Christianity affirms the "particularity" of the individual. In the world of mastery, only the master's "universality" was recognized by the state, and it was recognized only to the extent that he fought and risked his life. But the master's "particularity" was recognized only in the family, and it was the conflict between the state and the family that ultimately led to the demise of the pagan state. In contrast, Christianity sets an absolute value on the *sein*, or being, or biological life of the individual person, and it regards this particularity to be recognized by God, an absolute and universal being. Nothing illustrates this premium of particularity more than the incarnation of God in the person of Jesus Christ. This is the ultimate reconciliation of universality and particularity and it is the reason, Kojève suspects, that tragedy no longer exists in the post-Christian world.[16] Christianity therefore achieves a dialectical union between the universal and the particular.

What seems absolutely startling in the development of Christianity is that the Christian slave manages to convert the pagan master to his religion. Kojève explains this enigma as follows. The logic of perpetual war is such that the stronger will always defeat the weaker. The Greek city-state was therefore usurped by the empire. But as was the case with the Roman Empire, the masters were too few to defend it, so they had to hire mercenaries. As a result, the citizens became soft and no longer made war. And those who do not make war are, by definition, slaves. In this way, the citizens of the empire lost their freedom and became mere subjects of the emperor. But since they never worked, they could not be considered real slaves, but merely pseudo-slaves. In any case, they were not real masters. This is how the pagan world of mastery gave way to the Christian world of slavery.[17] In that world there were no masters, everyone was a slave. Naturally this was the ideal setting for the success of Christianity, the slave morality par excellence.

Roman law, Rome's only original contribution to civilization, displays elements of the Christian emphasis on particularity. In Roman law, the individual is recognized by law as a juridical person. Kojève understands Roman civil law to be placing an absolute value on the *sein* or the particularity of the person, independent of his actions.[18]

We can now see the emerging rudiments of a state that is ready and willing to give its recognition to the particularity of the person. Only in a world where the particularity of the individual is recognized by the state (i.e., the "concrete universal") can man be truly satisfied. But before this can happen, the theological aspect of Christianity must be "overcome."

For all its progressivism, Christianity remains a slave ideology, since it has no intention of actualizing its ideal of universal freedom and recognition in this world. Kojève therefore surmises that only when "God is dead" will the ideal of Christianity become actual in this world. Only then will God's abstract and otherworldly recognition be exchanged for the real and universal recognition of the state. Only then will slavery be replaced by freedom. Atheism is the necessary condition of freedom, because atheism requires the acceptance of one's death and finitude.[19] And that is what it takes to transcend slavery.

The death of God is the responsibility of the intellectuals. Even though Kojève regards the intellectuals as people who do not take an active part in history, since they neither fight nor work, he nevertheless entrusts them with a momentous historical role. Apparently they are ideally suited for this role because they are neither masters nor slaves—they are *nothing*.[20] In view of Kojève's anthropology, describing the intellectuals as nothing amounts to bestowing on them the highest status possible, and it is therefore not surprising that he assigns them a historical task commensurate with their status. Not being slaves, they are able to dispense with the transcendental and slavish dimension of Christianity. And not being masters, they are able to affirm the synthesis of universality and particularity at the heart of Christianity. Hegel is Kojève's prototype of this intellectual.

In his early work on Vladimir Soloviev, Kojève shows how Christianity itself contributes to the task at hand. In other words, Christianity contains the seeds of its own destruction. The very minute difference between the theism of Soloviev and the atheism of Hegel illustrates what Kojève means.[21] With the exception of his later writings, Soloviev had a progressive, utopian, and apocalyptic view of history. Not atypical of a Christian mystic greatly influenced by Hegel, Schelling, Jacob Boehme, and Gnosticism, Soloviev imagined the possibility of the perfection of the world through its union with Sophia, the wisdom and spirit of God. His thought was partly based on three mystical experiences in which Sophia revealed herself to him. His mystical inclinations led him to believe that the duality between man and God (which is typical of Catholic theology) is based on a grave misunderstanding. He thought that the spirit of God was the true essence of man and that in the course of history man would become reunited with his essence and this would complete the perfection of humanity and the world.[22]

According to Kojève, Christianity is the only religion which could possibly have given birth to the idea that the world is perfectible. The Christian idea of the Incarnation is unique among religions.[23] It has allowed Christianity to breach the gulf between the mortals and the immortals, the earth and the heavens. No other religion could boast anything remotely resembling this. The idea that God is actually present in the world has the effect of sanctifying it, and this makes it possible to imagine the perfection of the world. Soloviev is a case in point. But

Kojève also links Christianity to Western science. He claims that the Copernican discovery that the earth is itself part of the heavens led to the discovery of mathematical laws and to the eventual development of modern science. However, Kojève is quick to add that science no longer needs Christianity. Modern science is now aware of the fact that chance is the foundation of the universe, and is quickly discovering order in the new disorder.[24]

By deifying and sanctifying the world, Christianity has made God superfluous, and has led to its own dissolution. Kojève believes that Hegel understood this. He insists that Hegel's metaphysics is totally atheistic. According to Kojève, Hegel's *Weltgeist* or World Spirit is nothing more than

> humanity in its historical evolution in the midst of the natural world. At the end of this evolution, in the person of Hegel, man grasps himself as absolute Spirit which was earlier called "God."[25]

In other words, theology has always been an unconscious anthropology in which

> Man projected into the beyond, without realizing it, the idea that he had of himself, or the ideal of his own perfection that he pursued. Now, at the end of history . . . the most sublime ideal implied in Christian theology is realized by man.[26]

All this is vintage Marx and Feuerbach, but Kojève believes that it was Hegel who drew the logical consequences of Christianity and proclaimed the "death of God."

The death of God makes it possible to conceive of the realization of the Christian ideal in history. For Kojève, history progresses toward the secular realization of the Christian ideal of the universal recognition of every individual. This ideal is actualized in history when God is replaced by the state as the concrete embodiment of the universal principle which recognizes the *sein* or biological being of every individual as having absolute value.[27] According to Kojève, Napoleon is the secular Christ who succeeds in establishing this Kingdom of Heaven on earth, and the "completion of history."[28] Kojève is certain that Hegel shares this view. Based on his reading of an obscure passage in the *Phenomenology*, Kojève argues that Hegel regarded himself and Napoleon as the "dyad" that completes the dialectic. When Hegel refers to Christ he means "Napoleon-Hegel."

The latter is the real Christ, the "Christ who empirically exists," the "Logos truly become flesh." Napoleon completes history through the "bloody battle" and Hegel reveals through his discourse the meaning of the evolution that has just been completed. Hegel is therefore Napoleon's consciousness. At the same time, Napoleon provides Hegel with "self-certainty" because, thanks to Napoleon, the reality that Hegel describes "is definitively completed."[29] It is therefore not surprising that Hegel was "grief-stricken" at the defeat of Napoleon. In the aftermath of that defeat, Hegel "pretended" that the "perfect and definitive State begun by Napoleon was realized by the kingdom of Prussia."[30]

What is interesting in Kojève's account of the relation between Hegel and Napoleon is the extent to which it mirrors Kojève's own feelings about Stalin. Stalin was to Kojève what he claims Napoleon was to Hegel. As Kojève told an interviewer, he used to think that Hegel had miscalculated the end of history by about one hundred and fifty years, and that it was his destiny to declare that it was not Napoleon but Stalin who marked the end of history. In other words, it was Kojève's destiny to be the consciousness of Stalin and to complete Stalin's work by his discourse. And being the sage he was, Kojève knew that Stalin's coming to power would be accompanied by unspeakable terror and that this would mean "trente années terribles." He did not leave Russia because he was opposed to Stalin.[31] After the war, Kojève came to believe that Hegel had been right all along, and that 1806 was the year that marked the end of history. This is not to say that Stalin was insignificant, but he was merely trying to complete the work started by Napoleon—which was to create a universal empire that is "homogeneous" in the sense of having no masters or slaves, and where everyone's being is equally recognized as having absolute value. When Stalin died in 1953, Kojève's biographer tells us that Kojève was grief-stricken. Needless to say, this puzzled his colleagues at the French Ministry of Economic Affairs.

It is important to realize that Kojève does not lament the terrors of revolution. On the contrary, he places special emphasis on terror as a necessary component of revolution. For Kojève, man cannot be liberated simply by having Hegel renounce God and introduce an age of atheism. The liberation of the slave is "not possible without a Fight."[32] Kojève explains that the reason for this is metaphysical—since the idea to be realized is a synthesis of mastery and slavery, the slave must be a worker as well as a warrior. This means that he must "introduce into himself the element of death" by risking his life while being fully conscious of his mortality.[33] But how is this possible in a world without masters, in a world where everyone is a slave? Kojève stumbles on an idea. Robespierre's Terror is the perfect vehicle for transcending slavery. In a dramatic departure from Hegel, Kojève applauds the Jacobin Terror that followed on the heels of the French Revolution. It is "only thanks to the Terror" he writes, "that the idea of the final Synthesis, which definitively 'satisfies' Man, is realized."[34]

Stalin understood the need for terror and did not shrink from crimes and atrocities—whatever their magnitude. This was integral to his greatness in Kojève's eyes. Kojève thought that the crimes of a Napoleon or a Stalin were absolved by their success and their achievements. This has led scholars to describe Kojève as having a "terrorist conception of history."[35] And while this is accurate, it is not complete. Kojève is not just a modern-day Machiavelli. Terror is not just the price of the "achievements" of a Napoleon or a Stalin, it is integral to the accomplishments themselves. In other words, terror is not just a means to an end, it is constitutive of the end itself—which is transcending the fear of death, accepting one's mortality by choosing death "voluntarily" and without any "biological necessity."[36] In short, terror is not necessary in the sense of being a necessary means to the end, it is rather a necessary component of the end itself.

Kojève is under the mistaken impression that Hegel also endorsed the Terror. But far from endorsing the Terror, Hegel thought that it represented the derailment of the revolution, nay of Enlightenment thought itself.[37] It was a classic illustration of what happens when individuality goes mad and insists on absolutizing itself. Far from being a dialectical union of "particularity" and "universality," of subjectivity and objectivity, of mastery and slavery, of the individual with the whole of humanity and with God, it was a desperate attempt on the part of the particular, isolated, singular will to universalize and absolutize itself by force. The Terror was the logical result of the pernicious demand for "absolute freedom," unhampered, unrestrained, arbitrary, and capricious. It was a desperate act of mastery that could not possibly create a world that transcends mastery and slavery in a genuine dialectical union of the two—a world in which everyone regards himself as everyone else's servant but is treated as if he were their master. Even though Hegel was not an enemy of the revolution, he was certainly not its unqualified admirer.[38]

Kojève is unaware of the rift between himself and Hegel. But he is aware of the fact that Marx tended to minimize the importance of violence in the making of the proletarian revolution. Kojève thinks that this is a serious error. He is critical of Marx's failure to take full cognizance of the importance of death in the revolution.[39] In Kojève's view, the revolution must be bloody in order to accomplish its purpose—which is the liberation of the proletariat (i.e., the slave) not just from the oppression of his master, but from the fear of death.

In conclusion, Kojève's account of the age of slavery displays the same preoccupation with conquest, mastery, negativity, death, terror, and nothingness that we encountered in the age of mastery. It seems that history is nothing more than the story of how the slave manages to accomplish laboriously what he failed to achieve in the "fight for pure prestige." Through his *conquest* of nature, through his *negative* action, he gains a sense of his humanity and his freedom. Once again, we find Kojève celebrating conquest and mastery as the route to freedom and the proof of man's humanity. But Kojève rejects this conclusion. He thinks that the slave accomplishes much more—he accomplishes what the master could not. In the course of the historical process, the slave manages to gain recognition of his *sein*, his biological being, his particularity. Through his work and struggle, he manages to bring into being a state— a concrete universal—that is willing to recognize his particularity as a thing of absolute value. In the pagan state of mastery, this sort of recognition was relegated to the domain of love and family; it is the feminine principle of recognition.[40] Kojève insists that nothing short of the politicization of this principle can satisfy man. Indeed, the historical realization of this sort of recognition completes the dialectic. This completion ends history because, having attained what he has always desired, man no longer wishes to negate the world:

> To be sure, the end of history is not a limit *imposed* on man *from without:* history is, if you please, unlimited. For man can negate all that he wants, and he only ceases to negate and to vary if he no longer *wants* to do so. He therefore does not complete his becoming unless he is perfectly *satisfied* . . . by what he is; or more precisely, by what he has done . . .[41]

It is possible to make at least three objections to this line of argument. First, Kojève's logic is elusive. Why should a being who thrives on conquest, mastery, negativity, death, terror, and nothingness ever be satisfied? Moreover, why should he be satisfied with something as paltry as the state's recognition of his biological being, his *sein*, as having absolute value. After all, it is not his biological being that he values; it is certainly not the core of what he is. Man is above all the unnatural being, the one who sets himself against nature. The triumph of the feminine principle of recognition can be nothing but a demotion, a relegation of man to his natural being, to his animality.

Second, Kojève's conception of the union of master and slave, universal and particular, that ends the historical dialectic consists of nothing more than the recognition by the state (i.e., the concrete universal) of the absolute value of the individual (i.e., the particular).[42] According to Kojève, this amounts to a dialectical union of mastery and slavery because mastery is linked to universality and slavery is linked to particularity. The recognition of one by the other therefore ends the struggle between masters and slaves in a dialectical union of the two. But surely, this is a dialectic of the most superficial variety. I contend that it is nothing more than the triumph of the slave morality and its feminine principle of recognition that is independent of any merit.[43] Kojève himself admits that the end of history is the secularization and politicization of Christianity understood as the slave morality. Meanwhile, the masculine principle of recognition, the sort of recognition linked to achievement, especially on the battlefield, is totally defeated. What we have here is a dualism in which one of the parties emerges victorious while the other is totally vanquished. This will prove significant in the end. As we shall see, Kojève and his followers will wax nostalgic for that which has been so utterly defeated—namely mastery, conquest, death, terror, and negativity.

Third, it is important to remember that for Marx the conquest of nature was a means to ending scarcity, which accounts for much, if not all, of man's inhumanity to man. Marx did not exalt the conquest of nature as an end in itself—men do not conquer nature for the sheer pleasure of negation and mastery, but for tangible goods, for food, territory, and the control of resources. In contrast, Kojève insists on the nonmaterial, nonbiological, and totally groundless character of mastery. Mastery is therefore at the very root of human fulfillment. In this light, it is far more reasonable to think that instead of liberating mankind from bondage, conquest over nature will augment the human capacity for mastery, and herald a new, hitherto unsurpassed age of mastery of man over man, not an age of freedom and mutual recognition.

CHAPTER

■ 4 □

The End of History

History is the "anthropogenetic" movement that starts with the fight for pure prestige and ends with the actualization of the Christian or feminine principle of recognition.[1] The "end of history" refers to the goal as well as the completion of history. At the end of history the Christian belief in the equal value of every human being before God becomes secularized into the equal recognition of every person before the law. At the end of history, men mutually recognize one another "without reservation," and no longer fight. And due to the conquest of nature, the condition of equal and mutual recognition is coupled with a life of leisure and prosperity in which men "work as little as possible."[2]

History is the story of man's search for satisfaction. It ends only when that satisfaction is finally achieved on every level—the economic, the psychological, and the political. *Economically* speaking, history ends with capitalism; the latter facilitates man's conquest over nature and inaugurates a world of global prosperity. *Politically* speaking, history ends in a universal and homogeneous state—a state that is universal in the sense that it encompasses the globe, and homogeneous in the sense that it is a classless society or a society without class structures, without masters or slaves—a state in which no one's "life prospects" (as John Rawls would say) are determined by their class. Politically speaking, great wars based on clashing visions and incommensurable goals give way to agreement, harmony, homogeneity in a universal society uniting all mankind. This is not to say that the state will vanish.[3] On the contrary, a strong state is needed if these political goals are to be achieved. Kojève claims that the end-state or universal state will require a universal tyrant.

Philosophically speaking, history ends with absolute knowledge. At the end of history, philosophy, understood as the love of knowledge, gives way to wisdom or knowledge itself. As ideology gives way to truth, so the philosopher is replaced by the sage. *Artistically* speaking, history ends with abstract art. The pictorial art of previous generations tended to portray culturally specific scenes, reflecting cultural differences. With the advent of the universal and homogeneous state, these differences become a thing of the past. Abstract art is therefore appropriate to the conditions of life at the end of history. *Psychologically* speaking, history ends when man accepts his own mortality and lives authentically in the face of death. History must end with atheism. I will discuss each of these aspects of the end of history in turn.

CAPITALISM

Economically speaking, history ends in capitalism. Like Marx, Kojève had immense faith in capitalism's transformative capacities. Not only did he believe that capitalism has unleashed hitherto unimaginable productive forces, and has produced hitherto unknown wealth, he thought that it has undermined the ideological differences between nations. Capitalism has created a homogeneous global culture of free, equal, and prosperous men and women. Marx expressed Kojève's sentiment perfectly when he wrote:

> National differences and antagonisms between peoples are daily more and more vanishing, owing to the development of the bourgeoisie, to freedom of commerce, to the world market, to uniformity in the mode of production and in the conditions of life corresponding thereto.[4]

Marx attributed the disappearance of nationalities to capitalism and not to the proletarian communist movement. Kojève followed Marx in this. However, Kojève argued that since capitalism has accomplished all this, communism is unnecessary.

Kojève did not share Marx's communist dream; for Kojève, history ends with capitalism.[5] Kojève believed that Marx's negative views of capitalism were based on an accurate understanding of nineteenth-century capitalism. The latter was indeed a system of production that exploited the working many, while allowing the nonworking few to prosper. In contrast, twentieth-century capitalism has demonstrated its capacity to spread the wealth it produces. In so doing, it has rendered the socialist revolution unnecessary. Having overcome its own internal "contradictions," capitalism has created the conditions in which the rule over men is replaced by the administration of things, to use Marx's famous phrase. Twentieth-century capitalism has succeeded in bringing about the very conditions of life for which Marx had hoped, and has therefore deprived the socialist revolution of its object—namely, ending the impoverishment of the masses. However, Kojève argues that Marx could not have anticipated these developments. Kojève goes so far as to compare Marx with God, and Henry Ford with his prophet.[6]

Unlike Marx's, Kojève's vision lacks revolutionary fervor and exhilaration. For Kojève, the age of revolution is already past. The necessary revolutions have already taken place. The end of history is already here. A global agreement has already been reached regarding the ends of historical struggle—freedom, prosperity, and equal recognition. All that is left is to work out the details. Civil servants like Kojève, not philosophers, are the order of the day. Kojève spent his life working in the French ministry believing that he was presiding over the development of the final shape of the world. As I mentioned earlier, he was instrumental in the GATT (General Agreement on Tariffs and Trade) talks, and was one of the earliest architects of the European Union.

In the spirit of Lenin it is possible to object that capitalism is congenitally incapable of overcoming its own internal contradictions. It has indeed shared the wealth with the workers of the developed world, but only because it has exploited the underdeveloped world. Imperialism is the final stage of capitalism, by which it contrives to postpone the revolution of its own workers. This is why Lenin expected the Third World to become the focal point of the genuinely Marxist revolution.[7] But Kojève is certain that the age of revolution is past, and that prosperity will soon overtake the globe. It may be objected to both Lenin and Kojève that the earth cannot sustain a prosperous technological existence for mankind on a global scale, and that the prosperity of some will always be purchased at the expense of others. However, such sobering thoughts are no part of either Lenin's or Kojève's way of thinking.

As early as 1948, Kojève believed that the United States was the model of economic life at the end of history. Long before the Cold War came to an end, Kojève anticipated the triumph of America over the Soviet Union. He also anticipated that it would not be a military triumph, but an economic one.[8] He believed that the American economy was the model for the post-historical world precisely because it has proven itself to be more efficient and more successful than the Soviet model. It seemed to Kojève that the Americans had attained the goal of history—namely, the conquest over nature.

Kojève did not consider the differences between Washington and Moscow significant. As far as he was concerned, the conflict between the two superpowers was not a political or ideological one. It was primarily an economic rivalry about whose methods would be more effective in attaining the ends in view. It was a contest about means, not ends. The two superpowers had the same goals and values—they wanted to create a universal society of equal and prosperous men and women. The ends of history have long been settled—ever since Napoleon's battle of Jena in 1806.[9] From that date on, the nations around the globe have shared the same principles, hopes, and aspirations. Everything since the battle of Jena, everything that ordinary men have mistaken for history, has simply been a matter of eliminating the "anachronistic sequels" of Europe's prerevolutionary past—a matter of working out the residual snags of post-history. All wars between nations since that date have been nothing more than post-historical skirmishes intended to iron out the technicalities.[10] It was in this light that Kojève was inclined to regard the last two world wars: nothing significant has happened since 1806.[11] Even Hitlerism was no more than history's way of democratizing imperial Germany. By the same token, the Chinese revolution was nothing more than the introduction of the Napoleonic Code into China.[12] What are today mistaken for ideological, political, and historical battles are merely disputes about economic means to achieve the ends in view. This was Kojève's mature position. Earlier he thought that it was Stalin who was destined to bring history to its close. But later he decided that Hegel was right after all and that history ended with Napoleon.

All this led Kojève to claim that the only relevant political philosophy in the post-historical world is Hegel's. As a result, all post-historical politics is a conflict between right and left Hegelians. This is why Kojève claimed that all interpretations of Hegel, including his own, are works of "propaganda," or contests between the Right Hegelians (Americans, liberals and capitalists) and the Left Hegelians (Russians, Marxists and communists) about the best means to attain the universally recognized ends of history.[13] And even though the Left Hegelians have won numerous victories earlier in this century, Kojève was prescient enough to realize that these victories were not necessarily decisive. Long before the end of the Cold War, Kojève anticipated the triumph of the American way.

THE UNIVERSAL TYRANT

Politically speaking, history ends in a universal and homogeneous state, where the globe is no longer divided into hostile territories committed to mutually incompatible ideologies. Ideology has given way to a single human truth—human beings now live in a state of perpetual peace, equal dignity, and mutual recognition.[14] Despite his apparent optimism, Kojève was a hardheaded thinker who did not romanticize the end of history too much. Far from anticipating the withering away of the state, Kojève believed that the end-state needs a universal tyrant to keep order and to insure that the goals of history are achieved. Even though the end-state embodies the deepest hopes and dreams of mankind, Kojève did not assume that everyone would be wise enough to submit willingly to the principles of the universal and homogeneous state. He assumed that there were bound to be people who were recalcitrant, obstinate, and irrational enough to pit themselves against the universal order. The universal tyrant is therefore necessary to coerce or imprison those who constitute *inconveniences* to the rational order of the end-state. Nevertheless, it is important to keep in mind that this is no ordinary tyranny. The universal tyrant is but a "cog in the machine," an incarnation of the rationality of the final order of things. This modern tyranny, Kojève assures us, is unlike any other hitherto known to man—it is an egalitarian, rational tyranny, guided by philosophic wisdom and grounded in the nature of man, his needs, his deepest desires, and his genuine satisfactions. People therefore *ought to be satisfied*, and if they are not, then they are "sick" and should be locked up.[15]

Kojève's depiction of the tyranny of reason is daunting. The end of history is the apotheosis of the Gulag parading as the victory of reason. And what is worse, Kojève is convinced that the tyrannical embrace of this arid rationality is irrevocable. Remarkably, Kojève has managed to convince many of his devotees that we already live under the yoke of this rational tyranny. This despotism of reason has become so indelibly fixed in the postmodern imagination that the postmodern repudiation of reason can be fully appreciated only in light of Kojève's depiction of reason as the universal tyrant at the end of history. It is no wonder that postmodernism tends to revile reason and its claim to universality as a sham that conceals a thirst for global despotism.

THE SAGE

Philosophically speaking, history ends in the *absolute knowledge* of the sage. At the end of history, the bumbling philosopher, the mere lover of wisdom, is replaced by the sage or wise man. As Kojève puts it, "les philosophes ne m'intéressent pas, je cherche des sages."[16] Philosophers are much too *"graalesque"* for Kojève's liking; they are inclined to focus on the grail and ignore the end in view.[17]

Kojève thinks that philosophers cannot reach wisdom because they mistake particular and momentary aspects of history or being for the whole of being. In contrast, the sage reveals the totality of being, including the "anthropogenetic historical process, which ends with Napoleon."[18] Since being includes history, absolute knowledge is possible only when the historical movement of being is complete. Kojève compares Being to an edifice in which men are the bricks out of which the edifice is made, the masons who construct it, and the architects who devise the plan. And in the process of construction the bricks change, and even the plan is "progressively elaborated during the construction itself."[19] Something so historical cannot be understood in the middle of the process of its construction. Only when the edifice is fully complete is knowledge of it possible. The edifice is built in stages. History is a series of worlds created by man. The totality of being can only be comprehended at "the *end* of History, in the *last* world created by Man."[20] Hegel was the first philosopher who could possibly become a sage because

> . . . in and by Napoleon the *real* process of historical evolution, in the course of which man *created* new Worlds and *transformed* himself by creating them, came to its end. To reveal *this* World, therefore, is to reveal *the* World—that is, to reveal being in the *completed* totality of its spatial-temporal existence.[21]

At the end of history the sage is content to travel in thought over and over again through the completed historical process. Kojève explains that the end of history is an "eternal return" of thought since there is nothing to do but think and rethink the historical process that has been completed (by Napoleon) and understood (by Hegel).[22]

The "eternal return" of the thinking sage is not one of those frivolous activities with which people fill their time at the end of history. At the end of history, contemplation is particularly rewarding because absolute knowledge is possible. Kojève believes that this is the wisdom that the philosopher has long sought; the sage is therefore the *satisfied* philosopher who is conscious of the fact that history has ended and knows that he is satisfied. The absolute knowledge of the sage is a matter of knowing everything that has happened in history as well as everything that will ever happen. In effect, it is having the omniscience previously reserved for God. As Kojève tells Leo Strauss in a letter, the end of history and the absolute knowledge it affords transfigures the philosopher into a "god."[23] Of course, Strauss has no objection to philosophers being gods; his only worry is that these mortal gods might be crushed or locked up by the universal tyrant if they say anything that might offend the end-state's egalitarian creed.[24]

It certainly seems that history is intended solely for the satisfaction of the sage. There is something satisfying about being fully conscious in a world of "automata," as Kojève calls the citizens of the universal and homogeneous state. There is something delicious about being the only one conscious when everyone else is in a stupor. The only obstacle to the sage's total satisfaction is the problem of recognition. Will there be anyone to recognize this self-proclaimed god? Presumably he will cultivate slavish acolytes who will acknowledge his divinity. No doubt they will be flattered by the prospect of being demigods (Kojève reportedly nominated Merleau-Ponty to be his Apollo, seeing that he was handsome).[25] But even when the demigods are taken into account, it does not seem that the sage is any better off than the master in the master-slave dialectic. Like the master, the sage is recognized only by inferiors (even if they are demigods). But the master was also recognized by his fellow masters. So, if the sage is to be at least as satisfied as the master, he must find other sages to recognize him. That will be difficult since no one could be a sage who does not acknowledge that we live at the end of history. Anyone who dissents from the end of history thesis must be dismissed as unwise or unworthy. It is therefore very lonely being a sage. And if sages were different from other people, if they had no need for recognition, as Strauss thinks, then they would be content. However, Kojève argued against Strauss that even sages need recognition. Yet, far from achieving the recognition hoped for, the sage who announces that we live at the end of history and that he is a god possessed of absolute knowledge is likely to be dismissed as a lunatic. Apparently Kojève used to tell his secretary that he was a god; she laughed and that disturbed him.[26]

It may be objected that the whole idea of absolute knowledge is an exquisite exercise in self-deception. If all philosophers merely describe a particular and momentary aspect of being, what makes Kojève an exception? Kojève's answer is that we have reached a world that cannot be surpassed because it is the world that definitively satisfies man. But in light of the fact that everyone who is not "satisfied" has been labeled "sick" and has been locked up, the finality of this last world seems to depend largely on terror. Is this not a rather desperate measure to insure the "truth" of the end of history?

The idea that no one will want to negate the given or make significant changes in the world is not credible, except maybe for the sage. It is conceivable that the philosopher cum sage is so eager to cling to his absolute knowledge and the godly status that goes with it, that he will do everything in his power to uphold the tyranny of the universal and homogeneous state. Kojève certainly acknowledges the alliance of wisdom with tyranny.[27] For the sake of humanity, it behooves us to convince the sage that the recognition he longed for is not worth having—only then can we hope to undermine this deadly alliance.

KANDINSKY'S ART

Artistically speaking, history ends with the non-pictorial art inaugurated by Wassily Kandinsky's 1910 watercolor, which is generally regarded as the first abstract work of art. Kandinsky was Kojève's uncle and a giant among modern artists—the father of what is called abstract expressionism. Although Kandinsky died in 1944, this style became extremely popular in the United States in the 1950's and continues to be the dominant style in art to this day. Kandinsky's early work was for the most part traditional and figurative. Then he began to experiment with abstraction. The inspiration behind Kandinsky's experiments was music. The idea was to use art not to represent objects or scenes, but to express the moods and feelings of the spirit.[28] Kandinsky is often described as the man who discovered the power of line and color.

Kandinsky used his art to transcend particularity in favor of a universal aesthetic. The style of the Bauhaus school of design in Germany, with which Kandinsky was associated, is also called the International Style. This style is characterized by an absence of ornamentation or ostentation as well as by an attempt to combine aesthetics with the functional needs of a modern industrial world. When the Bauhaus school was closed down by the Nazis in 1933, many of the artists at the school left for the United States, where their architectural and artistic styles still flourish in the form of the starkly rectangular glass and concrete buildings so familiar to us today.

Kandinsky's universalistic aesthetic was a conscious reaction against the narrow racism of Bavaria in 1919.[29] Kandinsky's goal was nothing less than the rejuvenation of the human spirit, which he thought had become degraded by the modern world. He used millenarian themes such as Saint George's slaying of the dragon (illustrated on the cover of this book) to portray a new spiritual awakening that would reestablish community on a cosmopolitan, transnational, and universalistic scale. Abstraction was meant to purify art so that it would communicate directly to human feelings, and so contribute to the rejuvenation of the spirit in the coming "epoch of great spirituality."

It is easy to see why Kojève was keenly interested in Kandinsky's art and thought. At his uncle's request, Kojève wrote an article on Kandinsky's art in which he argued that far from being abstract and sub-jective, Kandinsky's art was altogether concrete and objective. Kojève maintained that every genre of pictorial art, whether expressionist, impressionist, realist, or symbolic, was abstract in the sense that it abstracted some element or other from the object it was depicting, or the attitude of the artist to the object or the impression which the object made on the artist, or the symbol represented by the object. All these forms of art take something from the world and portray it artisti-cally; but what is presented is not real, it is abstracted from the real world. Moreover, pictorial art is always fragmentary because it can only reproduce fragments of the world, but cannot reproduce the whole of reality. In contrast, Kojève argues that Kandinsky's art, insofar as it is not a pictorial representation of anything, abstracts nothing from the real world. Far from being an abstraction taken out of reality, it is absolutely concrete. It represents nothing other than itself. It is as real as nature itself. If it is beautiful, that beauty belongs to it alone; it is not a repre-sentation of the beauty of something else. Nor does it depict a fragment of the world; it is a whole that is as complete as it is concrete.[30]

It is easy to see how Kandinsky's art, with its antinationalist and uni-versalistic inspiration, is the sort of art that is particularly suitable for a post-historical age, even though Kojève does not mention this in his essay. It is also interesting to note that Kojève's conception of Kandinsky's art vis à vis all previous art resembles the distinction he makes between the absolute knowledge of the sage and all philosophical knowledge that pre-ceded it. Like pictorial or representational art, philosophical knowledge was fragmentary and incomplete—it was but a moment in the totality of being. In contrast, absolute knowledge, like Kandinsky's art, is not frag-mentary and partial, but objective, complete, and altogether concrete.

I, for one, have never found abstract art to be rejuvenating to the spirit. Far from being a remedy for the degradation of man in the modern world, I have always regarded its emptiness to be symptomatic of that very degradation. On discovering Kandinsky's intentions, I was touched by the loftiness of his hopes and saddened by his failure to move me. And I wonder if this failure is not in some ironic way connected to the shortcomings of the end of history thesis itself.

ATHEISM AND AUTHENTICITY

Psychologically speaking, history ends with atheism. The latter is a necessary condition of man's liberation from slavery, which Kojève identifies with the fear of death. It is not sufficient for man to conquer nature through his work, man must also conquer the nature that dwells within him in the form of the fear of death and the instinct for life and self-preservation. As we have seen, God is the symbol of the fear of death. Only when man has killed God will he be free. At the end of history, man no longer shrinks from death; he no longer needs religion or ideologies to help him conceal his own mortality; he willingly accepts his mortality and lives in a condition of Heideggerian authenticity.[31] In the end-state, atheism is triumphant. One would hope that people who cling to their religions at the end of history will be considered relics of man's historical past, maybe even a tourist attraction. This would certainly be preferable to defining them as "sick" and locking them up.

THE DEATH OF MAN

In a famous footnote, Kojève reflects on the life of man at the end of history.[32] He wonders what will become of man when the dialectic comes to an end. What is man to do? Kojève worries that man will have no reason to *act* in the peculiarly human sense of negating the given, since it would be irrational, or senseless, to negate the embodiment of truth. Will man be happy in the presence of truth? Or will life be dull and boring?

Kojève's first reaction is typically Marxist. He is quick to reassure the reader that the end of history will not be a "cosmic catastrophe." He explains that it will simply mean

> . . . the disappearance of wars and bloody revolutions. And also the disappearance of Philosophy; for since man himself no longer changes essentially, there is no longer any reason to change the (true) principles which are the basis of his understanding of the World and of himself. But all the rest can be preserved indefinitely; art, love, play, etc., etc., etc.; in short, everything that makes Man happy.[33]

Good riddance, the *bloody* dialectic is over. The world can breathe a sigh of relief; there will be no more wars, revolutions, or pretentious philosophers. The nasty dialectic is over, but the sporting, scientific, artistic, literary, and cultural dialectic will continue. Man will devote himself to the preoccupations that are genuinely rewarding and fulfilling. Time will not stand still; life will not be stagnant or consumed by apathy. On the contrary, discoveries will still be made, and innovations introduced. The dialectic that makes man happy, or displays his creative potentialities, will be in full swing. In Marx's words, the "realm of necessity" will give way to the "realm of freedom." Unlike Marx, Kojève does not mention hunting and fishing; apparently, his tastes were too urban for that.[34] Otherwise, his response is classic.

But on second thought, in a footnote added to the second edition of the book, Kojève seems to have a change of heart. In a mood of unmistakable gloom, Kojève declares that the end of history marks the animalization or reanimalization of man. If man is understood as "Action that negates given Being," then the end of history spells the *"definitive annihilation* of Man *properly so-called."*[35] This cannot be taken lightly, for it signals man's return to animality. In view of this, art, love, and play cannot remain what they were before. The things that "make Man *happy"* cannot be preserved.

Kojève surmises that the consequences of man's return to animality are much more far-reaching than he originally conceived:

> If man becomes an animal again, his arts, his loves, and his play must also become purely "natural" again. Hence it would have to be admitted that after the end of History, men would construct their edifices and works of art as birds build their nests and spiders spin their webs, would perform musical concerts after the fashion of frogs and cicadas, would play like young animals, and would indulge in love like adult beasts.[36]

It is not just bloody battles and pretentious philosophers that are destined to disappear, discourse itself will vanish:

> animals of the species *Homo sapiens* would react by conditioned reflexes to vocal signals or sign "language," and thus their so-called "discourses" would be like what is supposed to be the language of bees.[37]

Every shred of man's humanity will vanish. In the absence of discourse, love will be impossible. In this world of pure animality, all that will endure is the babble of post-history (probably called social science), coupled with plain animal sexuality.

In light of the animalization or reanimalization of man, the whole idea of happiness is brought into question. Kojève declares that it is meaningless to talk of the happiness of man at the end of history. It is even meaningless to talk of man at the end of history. Instead, we would have to say that the "post-historical animals" will be "*content*" with their erotic behavior in a post-historical world of abundance and security.[38]

The end of history marks the end of discourse, the impossibility of love, the absurdity of faith, the disappearance of war, and the eclipse of glory. All that is left are the relics of man's humanity. These curious remnants of man's glorious past are now the commodities of the tourist industry. As Raymond Queneau's novels illustrate, post-historical man is an insatiable tourist—history is his entertainment and the world is his museum.

For Kojève, America personifies the animalization of man. It provides ample evidence that "the return to animality" is "already present."[39] Nowhere is the post-historical process of animalization more advanced than in the United States. Kojève declares that the "American way of life" is the "eternal present" of mankind, the way of life "specific to the post-historical period."[40] Kojève finds America repellent. But there is no stopping her. Despite her pluralistic rhetoric, America is actively creating the world in her post-historical image: she is leading the world process of animalization. Sadly, American writers who were influenced by Kojève expressed the same sentiments about their native America.[41]

According to Kojève, Americans live in a "classless society," where everyone has "equal worth," and where anyone can "appropriate" whatever seems good to him "without working too hard." The Russians and the Chinese are eager to become just like the Americans.[42] They envy the equality and prosperity, and are determined to emulate it. And even though a universal society of equal and prosperous men and women has always been the goal of history, it now begins to look like animal farm. It is a pity that the owl of Minerva spreads her wings only at dusk!

The question is, what is to be done? One thing is clear: there is no retreat. And in light of *that*, there is no sense in despairing. The reasonable thing to do is to make the best of it. A trip to Japan provides Kojève with an inspiration. There may be a way to humanize the end of history after all.

DISCOVERING JAPAN

When Kojève visited Japan in 1959, he observed a society that was more post-historically advanced than any he had encountered. Japan "alone has for three centuries experienced life at the 'end of History'—that is, in the absence of civil or external war."[43] History had ended in Japan with the abolition of feudalism by Hideyoshi. We must surmise that everything that has happened since has been a post-historical technicality. Yet, Kojève was surprised to find that the lives of the Japanese nobles, who neither worked nor risked their lives, were "anything but animal."[44] He was struck by the fact that post-historical Japanese civilization developed in "ways diametrically opposed to the American way" (i.e., the way of animalism).[45] In other words, Japan had no religion, morality, or politics in the historical sense. However, by some miracle, it was saved from the return to animality illustrated by the "American way." Kojève ventures the following explanation:

> *Snobbery* in its pure form created disciplines negating the "natural" or "animal" given which in effectiveness surpassed those that arose, in Japan or elsewhere, from "historical" Action—that is, from warlike and revolutionary Fights or from forced Work.[46]

In Japan, Kojève came to the realization that snobbery is post-historical man's highest virtue. For "no animal can be a snob."[47] Therefore, snobbery is the way to rescue post-historical man from a descent into unadulterated animality.

Kojève was impressed by Japan's Noh theater, ceremonies of tea, and art of flower arranging because these arts were the legacy of Japan's warrior class, the *samurai*. What impressed Kojève about Japan was the living presence of the military ethic of the samurai. As he observed, every Japanese was "in principle capable of committing, from pure snobbery, a perfectly 'gratuitous' *suicide*."[48] With an airplane or a torpedo, a Japanese could simulate, at least in form, the life of the samurai. Kojève therefore concluded that Japan's post-historical society was rich in human form. In contrast, America was bereft of humanity altogether.

After his visit to Japan, Kojève decided that history need not culminate in the "definitive annihilation of Man properly so-called."[49] The Japanization of the world may enable post-historical society to avoid animality. What is needed is to replace the Americanization of the world with its Japanization. All this may seem very enigmatic, but it was an important discovery for Kojève, and to my mind, it rescues his position from incoherence, and clarifies his attitude toward the end of history.[50]

Some explanations are in order. The samurai were to Japan what the medieval knights were to Europe. They were professional warriors who fought for their lords in a feudal system headed by the emperor, followed by his *shogun* (commander-in-chief), *daimyos* (feudal lords or landowners), samurai, farmers, craftsmen, merchants, and peasants. In the twelfth century, Japan disintegrated into warring clans supported by armies of samurai warriors. This state of affairs continued until 1590 when Toyotomi Hideyoshi (1539-1598) succeeded in unifying Japan. By 1638, during the regime of Tokugawa Ieyasu, known as the Tokugawa Shogunate, all large-scale warrior conflicts were brought to an end, the feudal class lost their power, and a new age of peace and prosperity brought the merchant class to the fore as Japan began to trade with Europeans. This meant that the samurai were no longer needed. Their austere ideals began to lose their sense of relevance and immediacy. Kojève considers this to be the end of history because he understands history in terms of the supremacy of the warrior ethic.

It is easy to see why the samurai captured Kojève's imagination. The warrior ethic according to which the samurai lived had a certain resemblance to the motto of the master in the master-slave dialectic: conquer or die. This code of honor is described in the famous *Hagakure: The Book of the Samurai*.[51] It requires the warrior not only to have absolute loyalty to his lord, but also to commit suicide if in danger of being captured, if defeated, or if the master commands something contrary to his conscience. The samurai committed suicide by disemboweling himself in a ritual called *seppuku* (known incorrectly as hara-kiri), and if he was lucky enough, he would have a best friend standing by who would quickly cut his head off with a sharp sword, not so much to minimize the pain, but to prevent him from disgracing himself by screaming out. This meant that the samurai had to be prepared for death at all times, and this is why the *Hagakure* tells us that "the way of the Samurai is found in death."[52] Death was to be preferred to dishonor or defeat. Like the master in the master-slave dialectic, the samurai must prefer death to disgrace, humiliation, or slavery. The samurai was therefore supposed to set his "heart right every morning and every night" so as to think of his body as already dead, and this would supposedly give him "freedom in the Way."[53] Zen or the art of meditation was useful for achieving this inner peace and self-control that allowed the samurai to act without hesitation in battle or in suicide.

The samurai placed great emphasis on the arts—the tea ceremony, the art of flower arranging, and the Noh theater are all legacies of their class.

A samurai was not just a professional warrior, he was expected to understand poetry and to perform graceful dances. According to legend, the fierce General Oda Nobunaga performed a graceful dance with a fan for his troops before leading them into battle. And even though the samurai no longer exist as a class, Japanese life and culture is still reminiscent of their arts, their temperament, and their values. Some observers claim that Japanese workers have the same loyalty to their companies as the samurai had to their lords. Tea ceremonies are still performed at teahouses, and they are no doubt useful for relaxing the frazzled nerves of men who work in a modern society. Still seen on Japanese television are Noh dramas—solemn plays with music and poetry focusing on the living and the dead, the ghosts of warriors, and tragic destinies.

All these reminders of the age of the samurai clearly made a great impression on Kojève. He thought of the Japanese as living according to the old warrior ethic even in post-historical society. For Kojève, this meant that the warrior ethic was now severed from any connection it might have had with necessity; it was now completely devoid of purpose or utility; it existed simply as an end in itself. To Kojève's way of thinking, this indicated that the ethic had been refined even beyond its historical dimensions and this was simply exquisite!

What Kojève discovered in Japan was what he later called *la négativité gratuite*.[54] In Japan, Kojève came to the realization that "si l'histoire ne parle plus, alors, on fabrique soi-même la négativité."[55] If history cannot inspire man to negate the given, then he must rely entirely on his own resources to invent that "négativité qui est essentielle à l'humain."[56] It is no exaggeration to say that for Kojève, this rediscovered negativity, this altogether gratuitous negativity, became the indispensable means without which man could not escape from the post-historical descent into animality.

One of Kojève's modern Japanese admirers, Yukio Mishima, committed suicide according to seppuku rituals in 1967 at the Self-Defense Force Headquarters in Tokyo. The suicide was partially a protest against the pro-Western defense policies that prohibited the rearming of Japan. But it was also a more general protest against modernity's devotion to life. Three years before his suicide, Mishima wrote a book about the status of the *Hagakure* in the modern world.[57] The book is filled with disgust for "modernity," which Mishima associates with the Americanization of Japan. Mishima rails against materialism, hedonism, and the attachment to life. He complains that modern life is as meaningless as the death that follows it. He contrasts this love of life with the "way of the samurai," which is death. He juxtaposes modern materialism with the spirituality, austerity, and asceticism of the samurai. He bemoans the carnal condition of love practiced in America, where a man declares himself, presses his suit, and makes the catch. Apparently, this does not give the energy generated by love a chance to build up. Mishima contrasts these deplorable practices with the romantic ways of the samurai. The latter idealized the "secret love" because they believed that a love that was declared or confessed shrank in stature. They did not seek the satisfaction of love because they knew that "the voltage of love is dissipated the instant it is transmitted."[58] Mishima also deplores the "feminization" of the Japanese male which he also blames on the Americanization of Japan. He laments the fact that Japanese men are now preoccupied with their appearance and the "Cardin Look." Mishima admits that the *Hagakure* recommends the use of rouge (especially after waking up from a hangover) and teaches all sorts of meticulous habits of grooming. But he insists that these were not motivated by the desire to cut a dashing figure but by the manly desire to look good when you are dead—in order not to lose face. And since no man knows the hour of his death, he must be well groomed at all times.

Despite the fact that the American way has triumphed over the way of the samurai and the *Hagakure* has been radically denigrated by contemporary society, Mishima is confident that the *Hagakure* still "radiates its true light" in the midst of the darkness of the time, and that it will eventually "cure the peaceful character of modern society by the potent medicine of death."[59] By committing a public and altogether "gratuitous suicide," Mishima was demonstrating how the warrior ethic can still survive in a modern society even after it has been totally deprived of its historical mission. This explains Kojève's fascination with Japan, as the "human" model of a post-historical society—a society that has rediscovered negativity in the form of "*la négativité gratuite.*"

In fairness to the samurai, it should be noted that Kojève's and Mishima's post-historical reinvention of "the way of death" in the form of the "gratuitous suicide" introduces into the old ethic a very foreign element—it introduces an existential dimension that is absent from the "way of death" described in the *Hagakure*. The original ethic of the samurai is concerned with honor, courage, honesty, loyalty, and spiritual depth in life and in love. The original samurai is not an existential warrior who thinks he is "negativity incarnate," affirming struggle for the sake of struggle, and courting death because nothingness is the core of his being. I will return to this point in the next section.

THE ECLIPSE OF MANHOOD

Kojève and Mishima were no doubt nostalgic for the warriors of old, which they associated with virility and manliness. For Kojève, the death of man (properly so-called) is connected to the disappearance of virility. In Kojève's opinion, no one has described the eclipse of manhood more vividly than the young French novelist Françoise Sagan. In "Le Dernier monde nouveau," a satirical essay written after his trip to Japan, Kojève reviews two of Sagan's novels.[60]

Françoise Sagan was a great literary success whose first novel, *Bonjour Tristesse*, won her instant fame. She was a very chic Parisian—her signatures were the little black dress, the string of pearls, nightclubs, drinking, gambling, fast cars, and a high life in Saint-Tropez.[61] Her novels are very "modern" in the sense that they portray the loneliness, isolation, and "throwness," as Heidegger would say, of human beings in the world. Her female protagonists are generally aimless characters who are not particularly principled or strong-minded. Nevertheless, there is something heroic in Sagan's portrayal of women who are able to face a totally disenchanted world without despairing. There is something lionhearted about women who have absolutely no illusions or expectations of love. Love does not move the core of their being, it is just something they do, and even enjoy, like eating, drinking, or watching a sunset.

Sagan's characters are post-historical men and women who make love like adult beasts. There is no doubt that Sagan accepts this state of affairs; in my reading, she even celebrates it. In *A Certain Smile*, the main character, Dominique, tells us that her handsome young lover is nothing more than a "combination of muscles, reflexes and brown skin," and that his hair is "warm and thick, like that of an animal."[62] She finds him sexually satisfying, but otherwise a bore. Later, Dominique finds herself attracted to a middle-aged man. Even though he cannot compare physically to her young lover, he is intellectually cultivated (he reads Sartre) and is therefore more interesting company. Besides, he can afford to pay for the luxury hotels at Cannes. But what makes the relationship interesting is that the two are attracted to each other because they share the same "absence of morals" and lack of "genuine feeling." They enjoy a life without deep emotions and attachments, and consider it perfectly natural. They regard themselves as free, while others are in bondage. They enjoy each other's company precisely because they can be truthful, and need not feign love. They think that nothing is very serious, but they don't consider themselves cynical—they regard themselves as having a realistic rather than an indulgent view of life. The novel is about Dominique's failure—alas, she becomes emotionally attached to her middle-aged lover, longs for his presence, and can take no interest in other men. Far from celebrating the appearance of love in this nihilistic universe, the novel considers it a defeat. Now, Dominique is dependent and defenseless. The message of the novel is undeniably true: love makes one vulnerable because it means that one's life and happiness are in the hands of another. But, in my view, the issue is whether the risk is one worth taking. Sagan thinks that the odds are stacked against it. But some of us may prefer to live dangerously.

There is a certain similarity between Sagan's message and the feminist literature that bids women cultivate a harder and more callous approach to love, which will supposedly make them more like men, and therefore better able to escape the latter's clutches.[63] But these novels are hardly able to deny that they have a cynical view of men. However, this cynical view of the male sex cannot be sustained even by the novels themselves. Indeed, the only thing that makes these novels interesting is the encounters between these newly liberated women and the gentlemanly characters who fall hopelessly in love with them only to be sexually exploited, then callously rebuffed. Needless to say, these men are left bewildered. Kojève is right in thinking that these novels involve a certain reversal of roles—but not because it is manly to conquer and plunder as he intimates, or because women have always been pure and innocent and have never taken advantage of men. On the contrary, women have exploited men from time immemorial—but they have rarely exploited them simply as objects of sexual gratification. And it is this sexual depravity of the female protagonists that accounts for the newness and the shock value of these novels.

In *Bonjour tristesse*, Cecil, fresh out of her convent school, begins a carefree life with her widowed father and his steady stream of mistresses. She quickly adopts her father's casual attitude to life. What was shocking about the novel in the 1950's is that this young woman meets a physically attractive young man, and decides to have a sexual relationship with him even though she does not love him. She is annoyed by his silly declarations of undying love, his proposals of marriage, and his fear that she might get pregnant. Cecil and her father continue their carefree life until Anne, a very different, strangely serious woman who is respectable and principled, becomes romantically involved with the father. And this is when Cecil and her father first discover the meaning of *tristesse*.

It is easy to give this novel a Kojèvean interpretation: Cecil and her father are post-historical figures who live a life that is totally frivolous and gay, free of guilt and introspection, totally unencumbered by religion, illusions, or sentimentality (except about each other). Then Anne, a strange relic from history, enters their life. Only a woman still stuck in history could take sex so seriously that she would commit suicide just because her lover was unfaithful. Needless to say, sexuality is not such a big deal in post-history. On the other hand, if we take the *tristesse* at the end of the novel seriously, we might want to compare Anne with Socrates, and blame her, as Nietzsche blames Socrates, for destroying the carefree and happy life of the Greeks, a life lived according to instinct without introspection and guilt. In this case, history would be the process of overcoming this *tristesse* in a brave new world free of religion, illusions, and ideologies. In either case, it is easy to see why the novel was of interest to Kojève.

Kojève is impressed, maybe a little unnerved, by Sagan's own lack of sentimentality in the face of this brave new world. He is totally preoccupied with what is *absent* in these novels. He is convinced that the world of Sagan is totally devoid of manhood and virility.[64] Although he tries to be farcical, it is clear that he finds the male characters embarrassing. He finds the abundance of naked men in Sagan's novels somewhat disconcerting. He recalls the days of old when men were men and would not be caught dead naked, since nudity was associated with beautiful girls. In virile times, men's bodies were hidden by armor, and getting them to shed their clothes was a very difficult matter. Moreover, these virile men of days gone by thought of sex as a form of conquest: they used to "take" their women. Kojève maintains that in those days, women had to be raped several times before they could make love properly.[65] Then came a time when women offered themselves instead of being taken. But in our *"monde émasculé,"* the roles are reversed. Now, it is the females who do the conquering. Meanwhile, the males (we cannot call them men) parade in the nude and offer themselves. And, as he adds, these women are not even awed by these muscular bodies. It seems to Kojève that in Sagan's *"monde nouveau"* the old order has been turned upside down; the men are now relegated to their sexual roles of being husbands and fathering children. For Kojève, this is a far cry from the real business of men, which is *death*, not life.[66] Nevertheless, Kojève makes a valiant effort to put up a brave front to match Sagan's own boldness and lack of sentimentality; but he cannot conceal a certain *tristesse* when recalling the virile heroism of old. He ends up suggesting that the absence of manhood might account for the existential melancholy of Sagan's female protagonists. In the absence of real men—men who slay dragons, men who fight battles, men who go valiantly to their death, men who make history, men who rape and plunder—what are women to do? With the disappearance of these real men, women have nothing to fantasize about!

Contrary to Kojève's claims, what is absent from Sagan's world is not virility, but love. Kojève understands the novels in his own terms—as the triumph of the feminine principle and the eclipse of the masculine one; the men have been emasculated, softened, and effeminized. The result is the death of man "properly so-called." Sagan's post-historical world of adult beasts has replaced Kojève's historical world of virile conquerors. The end of history is therefore a crisis of manliness of monumental proportions.

FREEDOM AND THE *ACTE GRATUIT*

Kojève's *négativité gratuite* has its source in the idea of the *acte gratuit* of existential fame. The term is generally associated with André Gide, who gave it one of its most poignant expressions in *Les Caves du Vatican*. In this novel, Lafcadio, the main character, commits a senseless and altogether gratuitous murder. He kills a man he does not know—he pushes him out of the train on the spur of the moment apparently without any reason. When the police find the dead man's coat containing six thousand francs in cash, they naturally dismiss theft as a motive for the murder. But not being able to find a motive, they are unable to solve the crime.[67] Lafcadio's *acte gratuit* had no motive in the narrow sense of the term, but this is not to say that it was inscrutable. On the contrary, it followed logically from his character and the philosophy by which he lived. Lafcadio thinks of his crime as an "adventure." In my view, he deludes himself into thinking that he is noble and refined, unlike Protos, who is a mafioso, a garden-variety criminal. But on closer inspection, the difference between Protos and Lafcadio is not as great as Lafcadio likes to think. Lafcadio may be beautiful, impeccably dressed, and well monied, but the philosophy according to which he lives hardly differs at all from that of Protos. The latter believed that there are two types of people in the world, the "slims," who are superior, and the "crusted" who are inferior.[68] The slims are clever dissemblers who do not "present to all persons and in all places the same appearance."[69] There are many categories of slims and a definite hierarchy among them, but they always recognize each other through their disguises. In contrast, the crusted do not recognize the slims. The crusted are the dupes who are preyed upon by the slims. The crusted come from every walk of life and among them there is no hierarchy. Lafcadio's philosophy was a variation on the same theme. Like Protos, he divided humanity into two types: those who were like himself—beautiful, carefree, dashing, and well dressed, and the rest of humanity—ugly, clumsy, and incompetent worry-warts. While the latter suffered through life as if it were a burden, Lafcadio regarded life as an adventure, an experiment, a game, free from any purpose, ennui, suffering, and all the things that plague ordinary humanity. Lafcadio's murder of Fleurissoire was motivated by hatred, contempt, and disgust at the ugliness and clumsiness of commonplace humanity which Fleurissoire, with his disheveled appearance and ennui, represented. And how Lafcadio hated ennui, especially in himself! His *acte gratuit* was intended to separate him from the herd of humanity. Lafcadio wanted to live like an immortal god in the midst of mortal playthings.

There is something peculiarly modern about Lafcadio's brand of criminality (he would prefer the word "adventure," no doubt). It is certainly not foreign to those of us who live in a world filled with gratuitous terror and motiveless crimes directed against totally anonymous victims. These crimes do not have the usual motivations—greed, hunger, poverty, or sexual jealousy. The usual motivations, the kind that police are trained to look for, have some material, biological, or practical roots. But the new brand of criminality is motivated by boredom, a desire for adventure, and a quest for "pure prestige."

It is worth noting that the idea of a totally gratuitous act has roots within the Western tradition that are much older than existentialism. Consciously or unconsciously, philosophers from Augustine to Kant have exalted the gratuitous character of both freedom and the good. The *acte gratuit* has its origin in the conception of divine grace as an entirely gratuitous, arbitrary, and inscrutable gift to undeserving humanity. In Augustinian theology, God's grace and salvation were given to some and not to others, independent of merit. God's *goodness* as well as his *freedom* were linked to the gratuitous character of his grace. In contrast, man was neither good nor free. Man was "in bondage to sin" and was therefore not free to choose the good, except by God's grace. Man's fallen nature was at odds with the good and could take no pleasure in it. As Pelagius pointed out, Augustine's position deprived man of freedom. Later, philosophers reclaimed man's freedom. But many continued to think of the good as both gratuitous and antithetical to pleasure. I believe that both of these ideas are at the root of Kojève's "gratuitous suicide." The latter has the gratuitous character of God's grace as well as the hostility to life that characterizes the self-abnegating asceticism of Augustinian morality. I do not wish to blame Augustine for unleashing the madness implicit in the glorification of the *acte gratuit*, but it is worth noting that existentialism did not create the concept out of whole cloth.[70]

Consciously or unconsciously, what is praiseworthy and free came to be associated with what is ungrounded, capricious, arbitrary, unpredictable, or gratuitous. In André Gide's novels we discover that evil has the potential to be as free, as gratuitous and as disinterested, as good. If it is the case that the good is admired primarily because it is free and gratuitous, then the same admiration is due to evil when it succeeds in being equally unfounded.[71] It may be argued that only the good can have a gratuitous character. But I do not think that this argument is likely to succeed. To my mind, the difference between good and evil does not hang on the gratuitous or arbitrary character of the deed. Nor do I think that good deeds are vitiated because they give pleasure, as Hobbes often argues.[72] Even if Hobbes is right in thinking that we give alms to a beggar only to make ourselves feel good, what of it? After all, what is the difference between a good man and an evil one if it is not their pleasures? The difference between the noble and the ignoble has everything to do with what one is disposed to take pleasure in. The idea that good deeds are disqualified because they give pleasure is rooted in the insistence on the gratuitous, unmotivated, and inscrutable character of the good.

The same assumption is made by gratuitous criminals like Lafcadio. They think that if they can show that their crimes are gratuitous, they will be judged noble and refined. Their crimes are indeed gratuitous in the sense of being arbitrary, capricious, and unpredictable. They do not spring from ordinary motives such as greed, vengeance, or jealousy. The crimes are done for their own sake, or for the simple pleasure they give.[73] Gratuitous criminals like Lafcadio assume that because they are not motivated by the usual material considerations, they are noble. They confuse the distinction between the material and the nonmaterial with the distinction between the noble and the base. Kojève and some of his followers make the same mistake.[74] This explains why they wax ecstatic over the "Fight for Pure Prestige" and why they make every effort to re-create it at the end of history in the form of the *acte gratuit*.

Above all else, Kojève is preoccupied with what is distinctly human, what gives man nobility and raises him above the animals. Instead of thinking that the defining characteristic of man is reason, Kojève emphasizes freedom understood in terms of man's no-thingness. The latter draws attention to man's freedom because, unlike a thing, man is unpredictable. Kojève believes that being free is acting capriciously, irrationally, or gratuitously. Kojève turns his back on reason because he regards it as an ally of the biological, a slave of the desires and instincts, especially the instinct for life. And despite his strident atheism, Kojève exhibits an asceticism that is intensely hostile to life and its pleasures.

Kojève's conception of freedom comes into sharp contrast with Hegel's rationalism. For Hegel, freedom is not arbitrariness and unpredictability. It is the voluntary imposition of rational self-restraint and self-mastery. Nor is this self-mastery intended to be self-flagellating and hostile to life and happiness. On the contrary, Hegel's conception of refinement and development is linked to the capacity for finding pleasure and fulfillment in the rational and the good.

When Kojève realizes that the end-state spells the "death of Man" and the disappearance of manliness, he is disappointed by the cunning of history. But his disappointment is more than assuaged by his discovery of the "gratuitous suicide." The latter bears a strong resemblance to the unprovoked and surprising character of the original "Fight." It is even more exquisite and gratuitous than any negativity that history has contrived, because it lacks any historical purpose.

Kojève expects that the "gratuitous suicide" will rescue the end of history from the boredom of its mechanical and technological predictability by infecting it with the "Negativity" of man (properly so-called). But why a gratuitous suicide? Why not also gratuitous murder? For surely it is the unprovoked, unpredictable, free, and apparently unmotivated quality of the action that attracts him. As Gide's work illustrates, crime can be invested with the same "sacred" quality. There is no doubt that Lafcadio's philosophy would appeal to those who are disenchanted with life among the "automatons" at the end of history. There is no reason why Kojève's *négativité gratuite* must be confined to suicide or snobbery.

CONCLUSION

Kojève's disenchantment with the end of history hardly qualifies as a "turn" in his thinking. Far from being a change in his philosophy, it is the logical conclusion of his earliest premises. Kojève invents a story that glorifies negativity, violence, death, terror, and mastery as the supremely human attributes. Then he asserts that all these great and glorious qualities of man have become the casualties of history and that the historical world of heroic manliness has been irretrievably lost. Next, he wonders how it is possible to live in a world bereft of everything he considered great. Naturally, he waxes nostalgic for the warriors of old. Finally, he stumbles on the Japanization of life as a way of reintroducing into the world the virility of the lost warriors in the form of the *négativité gratuite*. Kojève's "turn" is not a change of heart. History is a tragedy remedied by the discovery of the *acte gratuit* as the solution to the animalization of life at the end of history.

What is objectionable about Kojève's view of history is not just the perversity of his low-brow conception of manhood and virility, but the fallaciousness of his conclusions. Even if we accept his vulgar conception of manhood, there is no reason to conclude that conquest, violence, and the quest for dominion have been banished from the world. There is no evidence for thinking that the world has been depoliticized, emasculated, pacified, and turned into a museum. This picture of the world is characteristic of right-radicals like Carl Schmitt (with whom Kojève corresponded). What is disturbing about this point of view is that it is impervious to the facts. Whatever Kojève or Schmitt may say, history has not eliminated the quest for dominion; it remains a powerful instinct that no civilizing process can erase. And far from being distinctly masculine, it is an *animal* instinct connected to the desire for territory, breeding ground, wealth, and all the things that minister to biological needs. If Kojève is really nostalgic for war, struggle, and dominion, or if he prefers gratuitous violence, then the modern world need not disappoint him.

CHAPTER

■ 5 □

The Lure of Heidegger

Kojève was profoundly influenced by Heidegger. Some scholars even regard Kojève's *Introduction to the Reading of Hegel* as the best commentary on Heidegger's *Sein und Zeit*.[1] Those who listened to Kojève's lectures admit to being simultaneously attracted and disturbed by his existential interpretation of Hegel.[2] By reading Hegel through the lenses of Heidegger as well as Marx, Kojève gave birth to that curious phenomenon known as existential Marxism, which is epitomized by the works of Jean-Paul Sartre. In what follows, I will argue that Kojève's historicization of existential angst accounts not only for the difficulties of his view of history, but for the seductive quality of his thought. I will show that even though Kojève tried to avoid the inconsistencies of Heidegger's historicism, he could not avoid Heidegger's gloom.

Kojève's conception of man, the protagonist of history, is inspired primarily by Heideggerian existentialism. Although Heidegger later repudiated existentialism, his *Being and Time* is the foundation of existential thought. Sartre is often regarded as Heidegger's most original student, but it might be more accurate to describe him as one of Kojève's best students. For Sartre is profoundly indebted to Kojève's innovative approach to Heideggerian themes, and especially to his dynamic mixture of Heideggerian and Marxist elements.[3]

Kojève was attracted to Heidegger's thought partly because of the radical temporality of Heidegger's conception of Being. Kojève thought that Heidegger's conception of Being would lend support to his own temporal interpretation of Hegel.

Heidegger followed Nietzsche in criticizing the excessive transcendentalism of Western thought. For Heidegger, as for Nietzsche, Plato's distinction between Being and Becoming had the effect of radically devaluing the world of existence here and now (Becoming) because it placed all value in an eternal world of unchanging essences (Being).[4] The rest of the tradition aggravated the situation by identifying Plato's Being (the eternal and unchanging ideas and essences) with the biblical God and Plato's world of Becoming with the fallen world of man, history, and wretchedness. Therefore, everything of value was concentrated in the transcendent world, while the world of human existence was divested of all worth. Nietzsche rebelled against this state of affairs and launched a reevaluation of all values in the hope of affirming life in this world. Following Nietzsche, existentialists asserted the primacy of existence as opposed to essence, the here and now as opposed to the transcendent.

Heidegger had a profound awareness of the mere fact of existence. To be so intensely aware of the sheer fact of being *there* is also to be conscious of the inevitability of one's death or of *not* being there.[5] This consciousness of death is a classic theme of existential literature, which abounds with the immanence of death understood as a return to inorganic matter. Existential literature invokes the image of one's own corpse just to bring home the inevitability of one's nonexistence. This is the sort of sensibility which existential dread or *Angst* is all about. And it was Heidegger who made *Angst* the central mood of *Dasein* or the human way of being. Heidegger defines man not by his rationality but by his moods: joy, boredom, excitement, and above all *Angst*. The latter is not fear of this or that but a more general and more disconcerting condition.[6] Its source is our predicament taken as a whole. But far from thinking that such gloomy reflections are a sign of weakness and infirmity, Heidegger believed that *Angst* was the necessary precondition for freedom. Only when driven by *Angst* to face the prospect of one's own dissolution can one awaken to the freedom of one's existence. The reason is that our freedom is hidden from us by our own bad conscience, which is encouraged by the social environment. Society invents countless distractions to conceal from us the truth of our existence and inevitable death. But to be so distracted by the social environment and its oblivion is to live an inauthentic life, to live as others wish and to be what "they" expect, and to do as "they" do. Heidegger describes this inauthentic existence in vivid terms in the first part of *Being and Time* as the life of *Das Mann* or the one who forfeits his freedom to a formless "they." This inauthentic existence mired in "average everydayness" is what Sartre called "bad faith" or *mauvais foi*.[7] Awareness of the imminent possibility of one's death is the bridge from inauthentic oblivion to authenticity and freedom. The prospect of our return to inorganic matter forces us to be conscious of our current free-dom, and prevents us from thinking of ourselves as given, predestined, and preordained. Only in light of our impending death do we become aware of our life as our own free project. Only in the face of our finitude do we become "resolved" to take possession of our life and shape our destiny. It is important to note that Heidegger was not oblivious to the importance of fate, heredity, environment, and the circumstances in which we find ourselves "thrown." Even though man is not responsible *for* his being, he is unique in being responsible *to* his being: his life, his death, and his des-tiny are his project and his responsibility. Man is altogether unlike a rock or a tree—given, static, and identical with itself. Man is sheer possibility. His very nothingness, his no-thingness, is what makes him so extraordinary. Heidegger gives nothingness a creative significance. It becomes a symbol of man's freedom —his singular, exceptional, and remarkable existence.[8]

As we have seen, Kojève also understands man in terms of his noth-ingness, his freedom, and his death. Like Heidegger, Kojève also thinks that man is a self-making project. And like Heidegger, Kojève regards the ever-present possibility of death and finitude as the precondition of man's freedom and creativity. For Kojève as for Heidegger, man's con-sciousness of his own mortality accounts for his privileged place within the order of things. Unless his nothingness is the focal point of his being, man is unfree, inauthentic, and incomplete. But Kojève goes even fur-ther. He claims that man's full humanity requires the conscious risk of life as the precondition of freedom.

By insisting on the conscious risk of life, Kojève dramatized Heidegger's understanding of man in terms of his nothingness. But that's not all. Kojève was not satisfied with existentialism pure and simple. Kojève set out to historicize existentialism. He maintained that the condition of Heideggerian authenticity or the capacity to live consciously in the face of death was the outcome of the historical process. Kojève therefore endeavored to supplement Hegel's philosophy with Heidegger's.

Kojève defines true Being, not as given *sub specie aeternitatis*, but as the *result* of a long process by which man transforms the world by his action. Kojève understood Hegel's concept of *Geist* or Spirit as this anthropo-logical motion. The totality of the creative and dynamic movement of *Geist* is history. The latter is an integral part of Being or reality as a whole. So, to give a complete account of Being, it is absolutely necessary to give an account of history.

Kojève replaces Heidegger's *Dasein* with man as a historical being. It is not an individual at any point in history who takes charge of his life, who faces his nothingness, who becomes his own project, who chooses his destiny. Rather, it is man taken in his historical entirety. It is man as a historical totality who acts, who posits himself, who faces his death, and who is his own self-making project.

Kojève historicizes Heideggerian existentialism by insisting that the authenticity of man as a "Being-toward-death" is an achievement of the historical process.[9] At first, "primitive men" live like animals in the "bosom of nature." In this primordial oneness, man and nature, subject and object, being and discourse, are one. This pristine harmony is suddenly and inexplicably shattered by the appearance of "Negativity incarnate" or man, properly so-called. Conscious of his nothingness, man emerges as a "stranger" in the midst of nature. This extraordinary being sets himself against nature by risking his life needlessly and facing his nothingness. At first, he needs religion to deal with his awareness of his nothingness. But in the course of history, man triumphs over the fear of death. He throws off the yoke of religion and its myths and lives authentically in the face of death. It takes all of history for man to acquire an authentic self-consciousness free of religion, deception, illusion, oblivion, and ideology. Authenticity is the achievement of the historical process.

Kojève does not simply historicize existentialism, he also sets out to supplement Hegel's philosophy with Heidegger's ontology. According to Kojève, Hegel was too caught up in the monism of traditional philosophy and failed to take full cognizance of the "dualistic ontology" discovered by Kant. In Kojève's view, the whole of reality is made up of two mutually exclusive parts—one is *sein*, space, static being, or nature, and the other is *nicht-sein*, non-being, nothingness, negation, history, or man. Whereas nature is eternal and unchanging, man is historical and dialectical. Man comes into being and passes away, but nature "exists before man and after man."[10] Kojève's formula is that the "Totality" consists of "Nature and Man (= History)."[11]

According to Kojève, there are four significant landmarks in the history of Western thought: Plato and Aristotle, Kant, Hegel, and Heidegger. Plato provided the definitive account of nature or static being.[12] But Plato was under the impression that he was describing the whole of reality, when in fact he was describing only one part of the totality. Plato's mistake was in thinking that there is only one kind of being and that man's nature was also given, defined, and forever identical with itself. Between Plato and Aristotle on one hand, and Hegel on the other, Kojève thought that the only significant thinker was Kant. According to Kojève, Kant was the first thinker to grasp the significant difference between man and nature. He therefore represents the earliest attempt to provide a *dualistic ontology*—Kojève found in Kant a radical and extreme dualism between man and nature.[13] Kant is therefore the first thinker to break with Plato's monistic ontology, which has dominated Western philosophy. Hegel capitalized on Kant's discovery and proceeded to give the definitive account of man, action, or history—that part of being that is not static or identical with itself, but dialectical. And even though Kojève regards Hegel as the culmination of human wisdom, he nevertheless thought that Hegel was too much in the grip of the traditional monistic ontology. The latter led Hegel to think that everything that *is* must be in the same way, and this led him to assume that nature is also dialectical.[14] Kojève denies that nature is dialectical on the grounds that it makes nonsense out of science and philosophical discourse. Kojève contends that if *dog* did not mean *dog* today and at the time of Caesar, we could not understand a single philosophical treatise from the past. Kojève also believes that the bodies of men as well as their "animal psychism" belongs to the world of nature.[15] In Kojève's eyes, the greatness of Heidegger has its source in the fact that he returned to the dualistic ontology discovered by Kant. And even if *Sein und Zeit* is not the definitive account of the dualistic ontology, it is in Kojève's view an excellent beginning.[16]

Kojève uses the image of a gold ring to describe his own understanding of the dualistic ontology. He compares nature to the gold and man to the hole in the center. Man is the absence at the heart of being; he is the nothingness in being. The gold would not be a ring were it not for the hole in the middle; but by the same token, were it not for the gold ring there would be no hole, no "presence of an absence."[17] The same relation holds between man and nature. But the image of the ring has its limitations; for it implies that both parts of the whole are equally interesting. But this is not the case. It is the hole, the nothingness or the absence, that is of special interest to Kojève.

Kojève is attracted to the centrality of the nothingness in Heidegger's philosophy. For Kojève, nothingness represents the sudden appearance of man in the midst of the mute reality of the world. Kojève replaces the adventures of *Dasein* with the even more theatrical saga of man. Kojève tells us that man alone gives voice to the mute reality. In the absence of man, the world is meaningless, static, and predictable. Man alone is discourse; man alone is freedom; man alone is history; man alone is finitude. In short, man rescues being from the infinite drabness of existence.

Kojève insists that man's capacity for negation (his negativity) is the clue to his being: "Man is Negativity incarnate."[18] Only a free being can negate the given world, including his own given nature. Man is that "miracle" who negates given being and transforms the world.[19] Man nullifies the animal in himself, he destroys every shred of its familiar, commonplace existence and "renders it sick unto death."[20] Man is a "sickness" in the animal world, but what a delicious sickness is he!

Seduction by flattery is the hallmark of Kojève's discourse. Kojève's historical narrative is a captivating drama in which the listener is invited to identify with the heroic protagonist—man. Kojève tells us that man is the new God who bursts mysteriously and magically upon a primordial and silent world, eternally identical with itself, and remakes it in his own image. He transforms a predictable world with his negativity or his nothingness, which is the sign of his unpredictability, his freedom, and his possibilities. Man pierces the deathless silence with his death and his cries. He dies so that the world can be filled with dynamism and change; he dies so that the world can experience the exhilaration of history; he dies in order to rescue the world from "rigorous determination."[21] In short, he dies so that the world can be reborn and made new.

The intoxicating flatteries have no bounds. Kojève tells us that man is more interesting than God. God, if there is a God, is like nature and the animals; he is constantly identical with himself; he cannot be other than what he is; he cannot change. He is part of given being, "Being-in-itself," which is static. God is therefore not free, and therefore not capable of action. Only man is capable of action; for all action is in history. Man alone is free because he has no given or static nature; he is the result of his own activity; he is the product of an "absolute *power*" that is his own power. Man is that "special" being who is an unrivaled event on the world stage. What is God in comparison to this strange and wondrous creature who bursts upon the scene and rushes valiantly into battle and headlong to his death?

There is no doubt that Heidegger would repudiate Kojève's dramatic appropriation of his ideas, just as he repudiated Sartre's existentialism in his "Letter on Humanism."[22] This work is characteristic of Heidegger's later thinking where he appears to abandon his earlier emphasis on self-assertion and self-positing in favor of a more passive, resigned, and submissive relationship between man and the world. Instead of portraying *Dasein* as shaping and defining Being, Heidegger asserts that *Dasein* is the medium through which Being reveals herself. This "turn" in Heidegger's thought accounts for the more mystical tone of his later writings. Heidegger repudiates all of Western metaphysics as a colossal blunder that he calls "humanism." The latter is generally associated with the Renaissance and is characterized by the rebirth of pagan self-confidence in human abilities and a delight in earthly life. Renaissance humanism was a reaction against the Medieval inclination to belittle man, decry the wretchedness of life, and wait patiently and helplessly for salvation. There is no doubt that humanism was responsible for the flowering of creativity in art, science, philosophy, and other endeavors. But Heidegger regards humanism as the root of the evils of the modern world. He thinks that it is fatally linked to the technological mastery of nature and the accompanying degradation of life. For Heidegger, humanism explains the catastrophe that has befallen humanity as a result of its self-centeredness, self-absorption, and conceit:

> For what indeed is man? Consider the earth within the endless darkness of space in the universe. By way of comparison it is a tiny grain of sand; between it and the next grain of its own size, there extends a mile or more of emptiness; on the surface of this grain of sand there lives a crawling, bewildered swarm of supposedly intelligent animals, who for a moment have discovered knowledge. And what is the temporal extension of a human life amid all the millions of years? Scarcely . . . a breath. . . .[23]

Heidegger believes that Western metaphysics has made the error of giving priority to the human species, with tragic results. Heidegger is not totally insensitive to the charge that his antihumanism may unleash a certain barbarism and inhumanity upon the world.[24] He counters this charge by going on the offensive. The real source of the problem is Western metaphysics—it has taught us to assert, predict, classify, and define. All of these modes of thought have culminated in the rational will to technological mastery, the will to power.[25] Western metaphysics has given rise to a technological society governed by instrumental reasoning. The latter has not only destroyed the world, but has reduced man himself to a commodity or a "standing-reserve."[26] We live in a world in which everything is seen from the instrumental point of view as being there "immediately on hand" to be useful for something.[27] The question of what man is meant to be useful *for* naturally arises. Heidegger suggests that this instrumental reasoning, this view of man as maker and conqueror of the world, ultimately leads to the death camps. Heidegger concludes that Western metaphysics has led to the decline of Europe, the "darkening of the world, the flight of the gods, the destruction of the earth," and much more.[28]

Nietzsche had suspected that truth was probably a woman and that all philosophers, having been so clumsy, awkward, and totally inept where women were concerned, have not succeeded in winning her.[29] Heidegger turned this suspicion into a certainty. He became convinced that the whole tradition of Western metaphysics has been nothing but an estrangement or a falling away from Being (*Verfallen*). The reason for this estrangement is that philosophers have been too busy trying to shape, define, formulate, frame, and rape Being, instead of listening, waiting, and hoping for Being to make herself manifest. Accordingly, Heidegger began to define Being as the enigmatic and elusive possibility of unconcealment. If he is to find his way back to Being, the philosopher will need a "new thinking" about the relation of man to Being. He must abandon the view of man as the maker and shaker of the world, and realize that man is the "shepherd of Being."[30] Heidegger suggests that the philosopher must plough the fields of language, which is "the house of Being."[31] The debasement of language into "chatter" has apparently driven Being away. Besides, how can the philosopher hope to woo Being if he does not have a way with words? In the final analysis, Heidegger turns his philosophy into a romantic escapade with a feminine, coy, mysterious, mystical, and inscrutable Being.

From this Heideggerian point of view, Kojève's reasoning is a microcosm of the tragic history of Western metaphysics. Kojève carries the implications of Western metaphysics to their logical conclusion. The priority of man vis-à-vis Being leads to the technological conquest of the world, which in turn reduces man to an "automaton" or a "standing-reserve"—an entity to be used or disposed of.

It may be objected that Heidegger's criticism of Western metaphysics is simply hypocritical, and that Heidegger's work is hopelessly contradictory. In his early work, Heidegger bids us abandon the oblivion of the world, recognize that we are free, take charge of our lives, and become resolved to define ourselves and live authentically. In his later work, his message seems to be just the opposite. Far from taking charge, asserting our freedom, and defining ourselves, Heidegger bids us surrender to Being. He counsels us to wait and to listen in the event that Being might decide to reveal herself. Far from conferring meaning on Being, *Dasein* is the passive medium of Being's own project of unconcealment. Heidegger denied that there is a break between his early and his later works, and his contemporary disciples continue the denial. But surely, there must be a difference between *resolve* and *surrender,* between taking your destiny into your own hands, and succumbing to whatever fate brings your way. Or is there?

Unravelling this puzzle may shed some light on the hidden merit of Kojève's historicism. The key is to attend to Heidegger's brand of historicism. If there is one thing that Heidegger has been consistent about throughout his writings, it is the fact that Being is historical or temporal.[32] This is a very significant aspect of Heidegger's philosophy in Kojève's view, since it supports his anthropological interpretation of Hegel's *Geist* or Spirit. The very title of *Being and Time* alerts us to the inseparability of the two concepts in his thought. For Heidegger, Being is imbedded in history or "ensnared" in the world.

If we take the temporality of Being seriously, then everything that is real, everything that exists, must belong to Being. However, Being does not just refer to what *is*, but also to what is good and desirable, since falling away from Being is the reason for the decline of the West. So, if Being refers both to all that is immanent in the world *and* all that is good and desirable, then everything that is immanent in the world must also be good and desirable. If we deny all transcendence and insist on radical immanence, as both Heidegger and Kojève do, then we must accept everything that history sends our way, and welcome everything that succeeds. This is precisely what Kojève did, and what Heidegger was unwilling to do.

Even though he insisted that Being is radically temporal, Heidegger refused to accept whatever succeeded historically as a manifestation of Being. Heidegger made no bones about his support and enthusiasm for National Socialism, and the extent of his complicity with the Hitler regime has been fully documented.[33] Heidegger supported the Nazis because he hoped that they would end the technological madness of the world. He thought that they would replace the modern world in which men are rootless cosmopolitan wanderers with a society in which people are rooted in the soil of their birth, living a simple agricultural life sensitive to the "unconcealment" of Being.[34] But when the Nazis were defeated, Heidegger did not accept the triumph of the Allies as the voice of Being. On the contrary, he lamented that the silence of Being was too much to take; the "darkening of the world" was upon us. No one could feel this better than Europe, which was being squeezed by

> great pincers, squeezed between Russia on one side and America on the other. From the metaphysical point of view, Russia and America are the same; the same dreary technological frenzy, the same unrestricted organization of the average man.[35]

For Heidegger, Moscow and Washington were metaphysically the same. The contest between them did not interest him. So despondent was Heidegger in his later years that he thought "only a god can save us."[36]

As we have seen, Kojève shared Heidegger's view that there was no significant difference between Moscow and Washington. But he thought that their triumph was the inevitable result of historical development and must be affirmed as a manifestation of the truth of Being. And even though Kojève also became despondent about the fate of the world, he did not think that such despondency was rationally warranted, or consistent with his historicism, and so did his best not to become melancholic.

If we adopt Kojève's point of view, Heidegger's historicism seems like a sham. Heidegger was not willing to accept the consequences of the radical temporality of Being: he wanted to pick and choose. When the Nazis came to power, Being was speaking, it was in its state of "unconcealment"; when they were defeated, Being fell silent, and this left the world in a terrible darkness. It seems to me that Heidegger's call to surrender to Being is indistinguishable from his earlier existential ethic of "resoluteness" (Sartre's *engagé*), which bids us choose our fate, shape our destiny, and take charge of our existence. Nothing has changed, since Heidegger *chooses* that to which he will surrender. So, despite his claims to the contrary, there is little in his ethic of the spirit of resignation. Far from abandoning the humanism that places man at the center of things, Heidegger reaffirms the "priority of *Dasein*" and the self-assertiveness of his earlier work.[37] The only difference is that now Heidegger is the incarnation of *Dasein;* he alone chooses what is and what is not in accordance with Being; he is the self-appointed mediator between Being and the rest of humanity; he alone hears the call of Being; he is the prophet of Being. But as it turned out, he was a false prophet.[38]

Unlike Heidegger, Kojève repudiates nothing; he even accepts Nazism as a component of history's comprehensive plan. Kojève's historicism is consistent in the sense that he is willing to welcome whatever history has in store. But we cannot say the same for Heidegger.

Despite his historicism, Kojève rejected Heidegger's claim that discourse is temporal. For Heidegger, discourse is always incomplete, partial, exploratory. *Being and Time* is inconclusive. Kojève was not satisfied with this; he longed for wisdom. But he did not think that such wisdom was possible if Being is eternally in flux.

Heraclitus was the first to pose the problem of fluxism, hence Kojève's fascination with the pre-Socratics.[39] How is it possible to know a world that is eternally in flux? Plato liked to mock the Heraclitians by saying that by the time they opened their mouths to speak, the world of flux had moved on, and they were doomed to stating falsehoods. This is the sort of objection to historicism or fluxism that Kojève took very seriously.

Parmenides provided the earliest solution to the dilemma. Led by the Sun Maidens in a chariot that transported him from the realm of darkness to that of light, Parmenides found himself in the company of a goddess who revealed to him "the Way of Truth."[40] She told him that contrary to sense perception, reality is single, indivisible, homogeneous, eternal, and unchanging. Being is all that it is and all that it can be.

In Kojève's view, Plato was Parmenidean to the core. He was able to assert an immediate identity between thought and Being because the latter is complete, static, and unchanging. But this is true only about part of Being. The "dualistic ontology" reveals Being as twofold: *Sein*, nature, or Being-in-itself and man (*Tun*), action, negativity, or Being-for-itself. Whereas the former is given, static, complete, silent, unchanging, and "identical with itself," the latter is dynamic, nonstatic, dialectical, and self-creating (*l'acte-de-se-poser-soi-même*).[41] *Sein* has been the principal object of philosophy since Parmenides.[42] It is now time to turn to that dynamic, dialectical negativity that is man.

Since man is part of Being, and man is a historical project, then Being must also be historical. But if this is the case, then how can we avoid the inconclusive discourse of Heidegger and the fate of the Heraclitians? As we have seen, Kojève thinks that wisdom is possible when the flux of time has come to an end. Being can be grasped only when the historical movement is complete. By insisting that wisdom is possible only at the end of history, because what is in flux cannot be understood, Kojève succumbs to the logic of Parmenides—but not without a fight!

Once man's work is complete, and there is nothing left to do, he rests and reflects upon what he has done. At the end of history, when the dialectic has come to its final culmination, man advances no further and acts no more. He is now "satisfied" to look back on what he has done and is "content to travel again (in philosophical thought) the road already covered (by his active existence)."[43] Complete discourse is possible only at the end of history and the *death of man*. But why must all this excitement come to an end? Why must man (= history) end? Kojève's response is that he is vindicated by the fact that it has already happened. And, if we are skeptical, if we are uncertain that history is indeed over, then Kojève will provide us with the spectacles necessary to see the world around us as the incarnation of the end of history.

It may be objected along Sartrean lines that Kojève's existential premises have the effect of undermining his conclusions about the end of history; and that Kojève would have been more consistent had he followed Sartre in denying that history has any end or that its outcome can be determined in any way. If man is radically free, then he has no given nature. This means that no one can understand history as the process by which man seeks to satisfy his desire for recognition. And if man is defined by negativity, freedom, death, and struggle, he cannot be expected to settle for anything or any situation in which his distinctively human characteristics are not exercised. Man will continue to negate the given; a being defined by negativity will not cease to negate, to change the world, to fight and to struggle, simply because Kojève states that we have arrived at the end of history and that he should be satisfied.

Sartre chose to become a Marxist for the sake of the revolutionary struggle itself. He had absolutely no hope that the revolution would suc-ceed in attaining its goals. If he thought that the goals of Marxism were attainable, he would not have embraced them. Sartre thought that the best goals to fight for are those that are impossible. Nothing can insure the perpetuation of "negativity" like aiming for the unattainable. For it is the fight or struggle itself that makes us human. Like Kojève, Sartre believed that the master-slave dialectic was the key to understanding the human condition. But unlike Kojève, he did not think that this dialec-tic would ever be resolved. Nor did he think that such a resolution would be desirable. The master-slave dialectic is a permanent feature of human existence, both individually and globally. Every human encounter is an attempt by one party to reduce the other to an object or thing and the one who is so reduced must struggle to be *other* than what he is defined to be. The same struggle takes place at the global level—espe-cially between the Europeans and their colonies. Even though Sartre joined Frantz Fanon in recommending a united socialist revolution throughout the Third World, he did not think that such unity was gen-uinely attainable or that such a revolution would liberate the colonies and inaugurate a new golden age for Africa; he merely believed that a total and uncompromising struggle against the colonial oppressors would be rewarding in itself because it would give the colonized a taste of their lost humanity.[44] This is consistent with Sartre's claim that the French were truly free only during their resistance to Nazi occupation.[45] It is also consistent with his claim that the only project worthy of man is to be God—the impossible project par excellence.

Kojève's *dualistic ontology*, which Sartre fully endorsed, is more com-patible with the permanence of the dialectic than with its completion. If we take the dualistic ontology seriously, as a complete and permanent description of Being, and if we acknowledge that man is essentially and truly a nothingness that necessarily introduces strife, discord, and negativity into the world, then we would have to follow Sartre in thinking that struggle and negativity are permanent features of the human condition.

While acknowledging the cogency of this Sartrean argument, I believe that a Kojèvean response to this objection can take one of two forms. First, Kojève could concede that the end of history implies that the dualistic ontology is but a temporary description of reality. In this case, the death of man would signal the eclipse of the dualistic ontology itself. In this case, the dualistic ontology would not be a permanent account of Being, but a description of a strange and exotic eruption in the deathless stillness of the world.

Second, Kojève could use a different strategy in responding to the Sartrean objection. He could argue that even though the end of history spells the dissolution of historical or purposeful negativity, a post-historical, purposeless, gratuitous negativity may flourish. And after all, this is precisely the sort of negativity that appeals to existential tastes. This position brings Kojève closer to Sartre.

Kojève's philosophy of history is no doubt seductive, but if we can escape the seduction long enough, we may recognize some of the difficulties it poses. First, who is this abstraction called man who makes history? Is he merely the ghost of the banished God? Or does *man* refer to historical individuals? If historical individuals make history according to an idea, then they must all agree on the same plan. If they disagree, then history will be nothing more than a struggle between competing visions. And if champions of these alternate visions are not satisfied with small local manifestations, each insisting that theirs is the truth that must be globally realized, then a grand struggle will ensue. The triumphant one will rule the world. On the other hand, *man* could refer to a given human nature with universal needs and desires that operates mysteriously behind the activities of individuals who, in pursuing different ends, eventually converge on a single outcome. In this way, Hegel's "cunning of Reason" is replaced by Engels's "cunning of History." Kojève certainly writes as if the latter is the case. He writes as if there is a single set of human needs, desires, hopes, and aspirations that are eventually realized in the course of the historical process. And if this is the case, then the final outcome will be acceptable to all the different parties. This means that divergent actions in history must be understood merely as conflicts about means rather than ends. As we have seen, this is Kojève's view. I do not believe that it is so easy to separate means from ends, but no matter. But what if all the parties are not satisfied with the final outcome? What if the end-state is too cold and formal to qualify as everyone's idea of the good society? In this case, disputes among individuals, nations, and groups will be disputes about ends and not simply about means. In the absence of common goals and purposes, history remains a conflict between individuals who are bent on different and sometimes mutually exclusive ends. Kojève avoids the difficulty by denouncing his opponents as "sick" and suggesting that they be "locked up." This is hardly the way to deal with one's intellectual opponents. But it reveals that if history comes to an end in a universal and homogeneous state, that state must be a tyranny, achieved by force. In this way, the abstraction *man* necessarily becomes the basis of a tyranny of some men over others—a tyranny justified in the name of truth, reason, and a common humanity.

Second, is it reasonable for the listener to Kojève's discourse to identify with the abstraction called man? Has Kojève not made the blunder of endowing man with all the attributes that existentialism usually associates with individuals? Kojève tells us that man is a finite, self-creating project. Kojève attributes to man (= history) the same finitude that rightly belongs to individuals. Kojève confuses the finitude of individual men with the finitude of man. This confusion leads him to believe that since man is history and man is finite, then history must also be finite. But just because individual human beings are mortal and have finite projects, it does not follow that man (= history) is also a finite project.

In conclusion, Kojève's historicization of existential *Angst* explains the seductively exotic quality of his philosophy of history. His extravagant vision of man in history makes the unmitigated gloom of his final reflections inevitable. Starting with a wildly rapturous picture of man, delighting in his nothingness, romanticizing his negativity, and gazing in wonder at this "sickness" in nature, it is only natural for Kojève to lament the death of man. In comparison to the arid rationality of the end-state, the wild frenzy of the slaughter bench of history is irresistible. And since Kojève does not insist on historical determinism, since he believes that history ends because men are satisfied and no longer have any desire to act, then there is nothing to prevent his listeners from reinventing history and keeping alive the dialectical excitement that he taught them to relish. On the other hand, they may decide to celebrate the post-historical or gratuitous negativity that Georges Bataille aptly labeled "unemployed negativity." In either case, Kojève's historicization, dramatization, and romanticization of existential *Angst* leads to a fascistic reading of Hegel that valorizes struggle, war, terror, and death as the human preoccupations par excellence.

CHAPTER

▪ 6 ▫

The Triumph of the Last Man

It is my contention that Kojève's transfiguration of Marx's "realm of
freedom" into the abysmal apocalypse of Nietzsche's "last man" was
the result of his inversion of the Hegelian dialectic—and when
inverted, the latter is indistinguishable from Nietzsche's genealogy of the
slave morality. It is not surprising that Kojève's end of history bears a
striking resemblance to Nietzsche's grim prognostications. But unlike
Nietzsche, Kojève did not look forward to a new rebirth. Despite his
rejection of determinism, Kojève was prone to a fashionable fatalism that
led him to paint the last man as the final and insurmountable result of
a historical drama with a tragic finale. Kojève's view of history was so
captivating that it managed to provide the spectacles by which his
admirers could see the world in terms of the tyranny of reason, the victory of the slave morality, and the triumph of the last man. This vision
of the world accounts for the disenchantment with modernity that is one
of the defining characteristics of postmodernism. Kojève bequeathed the
same vision to the Left Nietzscheans in France as to the Right Nietzscheans
in America. And, in my view, postmodernism is primarily a dispute
between the right- and the left-wing disciples of Nietzsche.

For Nietzsche as for Hegel, Socrates was the pivotal figure in the history of Western civilization. However, Nietzsche's account of Socrates
was an inversion of Hegel's. As we have seen, Hegel saw the Greek world
as animated by a collective "we" that personified a spontaneous harmony
of ideas and feelings. Those who were part of this collectivity were at
home in the world because their personal feelings and inclinations were
in complete concord with the social order. But alas, not everyone who
lived in the Greek world was enveloped by this collective "we." And so,

for all their coziness and comfort, the Greeks were morally infantile. Their ethos was little more than a thoughtless conformity to conventional morality. According to Hegel, Socrates discovered an "I" deep in his soul that was the voice of a universal conscience higher than the collective concord of the Athenian "we." And thanks to Socrates, the West got its first glimpse of the "universal Idea" or the "true good."[1]

Nietzsche inverts Hegel's account of Socrates, and this inversion is the key to the Kojèvean interpretation of Hegel and the Kojèvean view of history. Abandoning the subtlety of Hegel's analysis, Nietzsche sees Socrates as an unforgivable scoundrel. According to Nietzsche, Socrates intentionally destroyed an aristocratic world of mastery, beauty, nobility, and instinct—a world epitomized by the "shining fantasy of the Olympians."[2] He deliberately ruined a civilization in which physical beauty, high birth, strength, prowess, virtuosity, and display were held in high esteem. He slyly infected a healthy culture that celebrated life in this world with the sickliness of the otherworldly. Consciously, methodically, and cunningly, the wily Socrates shattered the confidence of a civilization that understood the distinction between the noble and the base—simply, clearly, naturally, instinctively, and without self-doubt or inner torment.

Nietzsche treated Socrates like a common criminal. He set out to discover the motives of his crime. He thought that Socrates lacked everything that the noble race of men esteemed—he had neither physical beauty nor high birth.[3] Motivated by envy and resentment, the crafty plebeian intentionally destroyed the noble and heroic with his dialectic. He proclaimed that every code of conduct worthy of being esteemed must be the product of reason. Accordingly, he demanded a rational justification of the Greek way of life. But the noble Athenians could provide no such account. Nietzsche thought that "like all noble men, they were men of instinct, and never could give sufficient information about the reasons for their actions."[4] Socrates laughed at them as they floundered and became confused. He fooled them into thinking that he possessed a higher ethic, an ethic grounded in reason—an ethic of which he could give a rational account. But Nietzsche is sure that he was just bluffing, because no such ethic exists.

Nietzsche thought that Socrates must have known that what he demanded was impossible, since every ethic is but a product of the will, which alone has the capacity to value and esteem. Socrates had a wisdom full of tricks and therein lies "the real falseness of that great ironic, so rich in secrets."[5] Plato, the "sphinx," kept his secret and died with a copy of Aristophanes under his pillow—which is to say, he died laughing.[6]

According to Nietzsche, Socrates was the "Pied Piper of Athens," who cast a spell on the whole of Western civilization.[7] It was not just Alcibiades who was bitten by this "viper's tooth;" countless generations have followed him with reckless abandon. The wily Socrates inaugurated a new world, a new horizon, a new culture—Nietzsche called it "Socratic culture."[8] The new ethos set a premium on reason (instead of instinct), knowledge (instead of belief), purity of soul (instead of physical beauty), good intentions (instead of achievement and success).

In Nietzsche's view, the mesmeric effect of the Socratic vision has had a most "corrosive" effect on the development of the West, and has ultimately led to the specter of the last man. But how? According to Nietzsche, the deadly elements of the Socratic sensibility were effectively mobilized by Christianity in the development of a secular, scientific, technological, and democratic world. Christianity may seem at odds with the modern world of science and technology, but Nietzsche thinks, as Kojève does, that they are kindred spirits.[9] Two aspects of Christianity explain why it is ranked by Kojève as by Nietzsche as the supreme architect of modernity: first, its belief in the equality of all souls before God, and second, its love of truth and veracity.

According to Nietzsche, Christianity is "plebeian" at heart because it sets a premium on the inner psychic life of man. This may have had the effect of deepening the soul, but it is also responsible for the leveling tendencies of the modern world. Because its conception of virtue was tied to the inner life, Christianity blessed the low, the weak, the sick, the deformed, the diseased, the ill-born, and treated them as equal to the strong, beautiful, healthy, talented, and well-born. For who knows what nobility of soul the sick and deformed may harbor, or what depravities lie hidden in the souls of the beautiful and well-born? God alone can judge. Nietzsche concludes that it was only natural that such a religion would give birth to a democratic age.[10] Equality before God gave way to equality before the law. The outcome was an "autonomous herd" opposed to "every special claim, every special right and privilege." So, by means of the principle "equal before God," Christianity has bred a "most ridiculous type, a herd animal."[11] And that is partly how the "animalization" of man was accomplished.[12]

By connecting the process of "animalization" to equality before the law, Kojève follows Nietzsche in inviting an abhorrence to the most elemental forms of social justice. And as we shall see, this attitude is particularly pronounced among Kojève's right-wing devotees in America.

The second part of Nietzsche's story is about reason, truth, and science. According to Nietzsche, the Socratic devotion to reason and truth is destructive of culture because all culture is "entirely composed of beguilements"—science, religion, art, music, and tragedy are among them. By venerating reason and truth, Socratic culture gives birth to science, which in turn uses reason to destroy Christianity, art, and all the other beguilements of culture. Nietzsche's objection to science is that it insists on being sovereign. In the name of truth, it conquers the entire culture and destroys art, myth, illusion, and religion in its wake. In so doing, it threatens life; for "all living things need an atmosphere" or a "mysterious mist" in which to thrive. Life needs a "veil of illusion" or a "protecting cloud," without which it cannot flourish, become ripe, creative, overabundant, and overflowing. Insofar as science robs life of its protecting illusions, it invites impotence, decadence, and decline.[13] In the end, science gives birth to a totally disenchanted and dehumanized world—a world characterized by the tyranny of reason, the victory of the slave morality, and the triumph of the last man.

Nietzsche imagined a nauseating generation of self-satisfied brutes who were well-fed, well-clothed, well-sheltered, and well-medicated. Their biological needs satisfied, they were like contented cows. It is difficult to describe them as happy, even though they thought they had "invented happiness."[14] They strove for nothing beyond their animal pleasures and their "creature comforts." They were altogether without longing; so impoverished were their spirits that they could not possibly "give birth to a dancing star."[15] Such a race of men could not dream up something like Pythagoras's "golden hips."[16] Last men have no dreams, hopes, or aspirations. Zarathustra anticipates this ghastly future, saying:

> Alas, the time of the most despicable man is coming, he that is no longer able to despise himself. Behold, I show you the last man.[17]

Like the men who inhabit Kojève's *dernier monde*, the last men are completely satisfied; they are contented with what they are: they are well adjusted and like themselves.

All of the elements of Kojève's *dernier monde* are borrowed from the world of Nietzsche's last man. In both worlds, there are no myths, religions, or ideologies. Men live only by the naked light of truth. Theirs is a totally disenchanted world—a world stripped of everything splendid and sublime. They have nothing to worship and nothing to fight and die

for. Their world has neither gods nor battles. They are supremely peaceful; they do not quarrel, and if they do, they become quickly reconciled,
because quarreling is "bad for the digestion." They are hedonists: they
have their "little pleasures for the day" and their "little pleasures for the
night." If they display any self-restraint, that is out of concern for their
health. They are prosperous; they still work, but not too much. For
them, work is entertainment, as long as it does not get "too harrowing."[18]

In Kojève's end-state as in Nietzsche's fictive world of last men, men
are know-it-alls. They are the self-styled pinnacle of the historical
process. They regard history as a tragic comedy intended for their
amusement. They believe that "formerly, all the world was mad."[19] They
consider themselves a haven of sanity in a history of madness. But like
Zarathustra, Kojève longs for a little madness.

At the end of history man becomes a herd animal; no one rules and no
one is ruled, not just because they "both require too much exertion," but
because the world of the last man is spontaneously organized into a herd:

> No shepherd and one herd! Everybody wants the same: who-
> ever feels different goes voluntarily into a madhouse.[20]

And if they don't go voluntarily, then Kojève's universal tyrant is ready,
able, and willing to compel them, since the herd man is the "only per-
missible kind of man."[21] He is tame, easy to get along with, benevolent,
sympathetic, and has an abundance of pity for the weak, the infirm, and
the unfit. He gives everyone equal recognition regardless of merit.

The last man is the symbol of the decline of the West. He is the reason that Nietzsche laughed at the philosophy of historical progress.[22]
And insofar as Kojève's historical drama ends with the last man, his view
of history is a story of decline.

Unlike Kojève's fashionable melancholy, Nietzsche did not believe that
the last man was the last word. Zarathustra came out of his mountain
retreat to save the world from the last man, and offer it the *Übermensch* instead. For when the herd animal or last man has triumphed, the
strong type of man, the *Übermensch*, a man who knows how to com-
mand, a man with powerful instincts, strong passions, and an abundance of spirit, the man who is "lightning" and "frenzy," is eclipsed.[23] But
Zarathustra longs for a little lightning and frenzy.

Enemies of Enlightenment like to think that Kojève's work contains
a struggle between Hegel and Nietzsche in which the latter emerges victorious. In other words, the more Kojève explores the end of history the

more the realm of freedom gives way to the cold indifference of
Nietzsche's well-fed and well-medicated androids. In this view, the logic
of Enlightenment necessarily leads to the morbidity of the last man.[24] A
Nietzschean need not quibble with Marx's view of history as the victorious march of reason, freedom, equality, and prosperity, but he does not
relish it. He regards reason as the ploy of the rabble (instinct alone is
noble); he thinks that freedom is something for which only the few are
fit; he fears that prosperity may put an end to suffering, which is the
wellspring of creative genius; and as for equality, it is anathema to one
who waxes ecstatic over the ingenuity of the caste system. If history
keeps marching in its current direction, then the eclipse of civilization,
the twilight of humanity, and the death of man are at hand. Kojève is the
one who discovered this truth. Kojève was the thinker who enthusias-
tically embraced the hopes of Enlightenment rationalism and carried
them valiantly and unflinchingly to their logical conclusion. Moreover,
Kojève is the only modern sage with the courage and the insight to
declare that Nietzsche's bleak predictions have become a reality.

This is the source of the right-wing enchantment with Kojève. But as I
have shown, this interpretation of Kojève is based on a sleight of hand. As
I have argued, Kojève's premises are neither Hegelian nor rationalist—and
his conclusions follow logically from *his* premises. The immoderate character of Kojève's thought has nothing to do with an excess of rationalism.

Kojève's admirers on the left are equally disenchanted with
Enlightenment rationalism. They share Nietzsche's view that all claims
to truth are merely disguised manifestations of the will to power. And
they agree with Kojève that the modern world is the realization of the
historical victory of reason, which rules in the name of a universal truth
equally applicable and equally satisfying to all. Kojève confirms their
worst fears by insisting that this rational tyranny is the end of history,
which cannot be surpassed. This gives their disenchantment with modernity a more tragic temper. It allows them to historicize their predicament
and give themselves the aura of those who must endure a hitherto unrivaled catastrophe. They are convinced that of all the powers that have
ever ruled the earth, there has never been a power more formidable,
more ubiquitous, or more totalitarian than that of reason ruling in the
name of truth, health, and humanity. Never has a power had such a
stranglehold on the human imagination. So overpowered are these postmoderns by the specter of this ingenious tyranny that they have no positive political plan. For thanks to Kojève, they seriously doubt that the
tyranny of reason can be subverted. Their *modus operandi* is to devise

ways by which to subvert the ruling powers—but since they doubt that anything will come of their revolt, they romanticize the act of sabotage itself. Since they believe that this formidable tyranny operates primarily on the mind, their tactics tend to be theoretical in nature. And no less than Kojève's right-wing admirers, the admirers on the left long for a little madness, lightning, and frenzy.

It is my contention that the single most important effect of Kojève's work is to furnish the spectacles with which his admirers can see the world in terms of the triumph of the last man. The trouble with Kojève's spectacles is that they provide a distorted and utterly simplistic vision of the ills of modern society.

First, it is difficult to see the modern world as an egalitarian nightmare of uniformity and homogeneity. There is a profound conflict between science and capitalism on one hand and the egalitarian spirit of the modern world on the other. There is nothing particularly egalitarian about either science or capitalism. Kojève's optimism regarding the latter seems to have been totally unwarranted. Even within the developed world, capitalism continues to augment the gulf between the very rich and the very poor.

Second, Kojève had an altogether naïve faith in science as the servant of humanity. Kojève is quite mistaken in thinking that a scientific and technological society would be either peaceful or democratic. There is nothing democratic about science. Far from promoting equality, it gives the few immense powers over the rest. Nietzsche's analysis, while seriously flawed, was richer, more complex, and more prescient. Nietzsche was not oblivious to the barbaric potentialities of the scientific spirit. He realized that once science destroys Christianity, once God is dead, the mist that sanctified and dignified man will evaporate; the atmosphere in which man could make special claims will vanish. Man will emerge naked, unadorned and unsanctified. Science may well devote itself to the brutish satisfactions of the last man, but there is another and more likely scenario. Once man is a herd animal, he will be a thing to be manipulated by science. And this is probably the reason Nietzsche suspected that a purely scientific culture could easily give way to "wholesale slaughter."[25] He suspected that science may be used "for the practical egotistical ends of individuals and nations," and that the result may be "universal wars of extermination" and an age of barbarism.[26] It seems to me that this scenario is a more plausible explanation of the Holocaust than Kojève's claim that it was a nonevent, or history's way of democratizing Germany.

Third, Kojève fell into the same trap as Nietzsche. In order to avoid the placid animality of the last man, Nietzsche felt compelled to opt for the raucous inhumanity of the superman. Kojève's *acte gratuit* is grounded in the same spurious dualism. Nietzsche thought that when the herd instinct triumphs so completely, the appearance of the *Übermensch* is experienced with great relief, as if an "intolerable pressure" were being lifted. He regarded the enthusiastic reception of Napoleon as a case in point.[27] He tried to camouflage the ignobility of his preference by describing his superman as a "Caesar with the heart of Christ." Kojève thought of Stalin as that secular Christ. But in truth, there is no dialectic so mighty that it would not choke at the enormity of this contradiction.

What both Kojève and Nietzsche failed to realize is that in a mass age in which men feel subject to impersonal forces beyond their control or comprehension, they will be so hungry for the superman that they will succumb to any *superbrute* who may come along.[28]

In the twentieth century, those who have tried to come to grips with the Nazi Holocaust have understood it through Nietzsche's categories. Either it was the triumph of the superbrute or it was the revolt of the masses and the victory of the last man. The Left Nietzscheans are wedded to one side of the story, the Right Nietzscheans to the other. But far from being mutually exclusive, these two scenarios are intimately linked. The dehumanization of man into a herd animal invites the appearance of the superbrute. Kojève's universal tyrant is a case in point, even though Kojève insists that he is only a "cog in the machine."

In conclusion, Kojève's transfiguration of the Hegelian dialectic into Nietzsche's genealogy of the slave morality provides the spectacles with which his postmodern admirers can see the world as the tyranny of reason and the triumph of the last man. Kojève is often criticized for giving a totally anthropocentric version of Hegel's dialectic. But it is more accurate to say that Kojève abandons the dialectic altogether in favor of a stark dualism: being and nothingness, truth and ideology, reason and madness, feminine and masculine, master and slave. Moreover, the struggle between these opposites does not end in a reconciliation. In Kojève's interpretation, the outcome of the struggle is the complete annihilation of one and the triumph of the other. The end of history spells the absolute and unmitigated victory of being as opposed to nothingness, of truth as opposed to ideology, of reason as opposed to madness, of the feminine as opposed to the masculine, and of slavery as opposed to mastery. Banished from the world are any hint of negativity, mastery, inequality, ideology, madness, or virility. The result is a profound disenchantment with the world born of the belief that everything great and glorious, strong and masterful, delirious and delightful, has been irretrievably lost. This Kojèvean sensibility accounts for the melancholy, the nostalgia, the political extremism, the monumental impotence, and the dark romanticism of those who have succumbed to his spell.

Part II

KOJÈVE'S INFLUENCE IN FRANCE

■ 7 □

Queneau's Heroics

Raymond Queneau was among the most devoted admirers of Kojève. He was a regular member of Kojève's Hegel seminar and was responsible for collecting, editing, and publishing Kojève's lectures as the *Introduction to the Reading of Hegel*. Kojève's influence on Queneau was remarkable.

In a review essay on Queneau's novels, Kojève observed that Queneau has succeeded in expressing Kojève's philosophy in the language of the streets.[1] Kojève praised Queneau for having brilliantly portrayed Hegelian sages living in the "sabbath of man."[2] This assertion has invariably been dismissed as eccentric or bizarre. Commentators are puzzled by Kojève's essay. They don't see what Queneau's novels have to do with Hegel. The insipid, mindless, and zany characters that populate Queneau's work seem to them like the furthest things from Absolute Mind. Of course, Kojève is referring to his own Hegel, which is not what commentators generally have in mind—and this may explain why they find Kojève's remarks bewildering. But to my mind, Kojève's interpretation of Queneau—even though it is neither well expressed nor supported, is absolutely accurate. It is my contention that Queneau's novels cannot be fully appreciated without knowledge of the philosophical outlook he inherited from Kojève. By the same token, Queneau's work sheds light on the original inspiration of Kojève's historical vision—the vision that he had difficulty sustaining once he realized that the owl of Minerva takes flight only upon "le *soir* de la journée historique" and that her flight foreshadows the coming of the night.[3]

According to Kojève's original inspiration, man makes history according to an *idea* he has of what human life ought to be like. After years of fighting, working, and struggling, he succeeds. The result is a carefree world of ease and gaiety, laughter and frolicking—a world without scarcity, war, religion, hatred, or nationalism. Queneau's novels give us a glimpse of that original inspiration.

Queneau is often associated with André Breton and the surrealists. But the difference between Queneau and the surrealists is considerable. A comparison of Queneau with Breton, leader of the surrealists, will explain what I mean. Queneau was a Kojèvean who accepted the end of history thesis, and as we shall see, depicted it vividly in his novels. In contrast, Breton, who attended Kojève's Hegel seminar occasionally, regarded the Hegelian (i.e., Kojèvean) thesis about the end of history to be a reactionary betrayal of the revolutionary possibilities inherent in the dialectic.

Breton was thoroughly versed in Freud before turning to Hegel. He was inspired by the Freudian awareness of the irrational and the unconscious, which he interpreted as the result of the repressions of bourgeois civilization.[4] But he thought that Freud was himself a product of the repressive civilization he helped uncover. Freud was resigned to the necessity of repression, but Breton thought that buried deep in the subconscious of man and in dreams is the secret to redemption. Breton's insistence on total freedom and his abhorrence of all discipline is reminiscent of postmodern writers like Gilles Deleuze and Félix Guattari, who are also influenced by Freud and who also reject his repressive inclinations. Freud was resigned to the eternal opposition between desire and reality, but Breton demanded a reconciliation. Hegel seemed to offer hope. Breton thought that Hegel held out the prospect of reconciling the subjective and objective, but his expectations were dashed. Still, he clung to the idea and defined surrealism as the attempt to

> present interior reality and exterior reality as two elements in process of unification, of finally becoming *one*. This final unification is the supreme aim of surrealism: interior reality and exterior reality being, in the present form of society, in contradiction (and in this contradiction we see the very cause of man's unhappiness, but also the source of his movement).[5]

In literature as in art, surrealism is famous for its stark juxtaposition of the two realities. Yet Breton never gave up hope that the two could be reconciled. This is precisely why communism appealed to him. But the discipline required to belong to a political party proved to be more than surrealism could endure.[6] In his *Surrealist Manifesto*, Breton renounced the claims of society on the individual. He hated the state and he regarded religion as its repressive instrument. He celebrated chance, dreams, the marvelous and the irrational, and was therefore opposed to the incarceration of the insane.

Breton's famous semi-autobiographical work *Nadja* is in many ways paradigmatic. The novel is based on Breton's encounter with the young woman whose name is the beginning of the word *hope* in Russian. Nadja is marvelous and free; she can hardly be said to belong to the world of reality, yet she is real.[7] For Breton, she represents those rare and wondrous moments when the world of dreams and the world of reality come together; and she testifies to the fact that the world of dreams is not so much unreal as surreal, which is to say that it is an integral, but elusive, component of reality. Breton thought that love alone can weld together the two realities. He cast Woman in the role of mediator who possesses rejuvenating and redemptive powers. Since man's thought has brought him trouble, he must look to Woman for guidance.[8] Unlike man, she seems to have escaped the debilitating effects of civilization; she does not know the repression or "opacity" from which man suffers but exists in a state of total "transparency" and obeys entirely different laws from those of "masculine despotism."[9] This deification of Woman was also shared by Jacques Lacan, a regular member of Kojève's seminar who has had a significant impact on modern feminism.[10]

Breton was influenced by Hegel as well as Freud, and though he rejected the latter's irresoluble conflict between the "pleasure principle" and the "reality principle," he did not embrace the reconciliation implicit in Kojève's end of history.

In contrast to Breton, Queneau was the quintessential Kojèvean. Unlike Breton, Queneau did not experience the anguished conflict of the inner and outer worlds. Nor did he live in revolutionary anticipation of such a reconciliation. He began with the Kojèvean assumption that whatever reconciliation is possible has already been accomplished. Queneau poked fun at surrealist themes like the preoccupation with the unconscious and the interest in dreams. His novel *Odile* was partly an autobiographical account of his break with Breton and the surrealists in 1929.[11] In the novel, a young man becomes entangled with a group of pseudo-intellectuals whiling away their lives in cafés consorting with prostitutes. Like the surrealists around Breton, the pseudo-intellectuals in the novel have an absolute and utter contempt for reason, and believe that it is a hindrance to knowing anything that transcends the totally mundane. They believe that reason must be silenced if we are to reach knowledge of a deeper world. They glorify the unconscious, even madness.

Like the surrealists, they are forever in search of "inspiration," they experiment with "automatic writing,"[12] they drown themselves in metaphors, flirt with communism, and even join the Communist Party. And like the surrealists, they do not know how to reconcile their belief in the irrational and the unconscious with the rationalism, determinism, and materialism of the communists. They want to save the people, but they also despise those they so dearly wish to rescue—the people harbor so many "reactionary ideas," they love their parents and their country! The group splits over membership in the Communist Party—some believe that they cannot reconcile the ideas of the communists with their own, but others believe that they must make the revolution first and solve the theoretical problems later. This is the story of the conflict between Breton and his surrealists on one hand, and the communists on the other—a conflict that ultimately led Breton to sever his ties with the Communist Party.[13]

Queneau's early autobiographical novel has a certain seriousness that sets it apart from the antics of the novels that made Queneau famous. His best-known novels are consciously set at the end of history. There is a lack of expectation in these novels that is understandable in light of the fact that history is over. The characters live from day to day in what seems like an eternal present in which nothing serious or significant ever happens. Nor do they have much to do. Their world is filled with laughter, cavorting, and frolicking. People still have to make a living, but they don't work too hard. They are carefree and gay, even though they have their worries—but these are of such a trivial nature that they serve only to add to the general atmosphere of hilarity.

In what follows I will examine three post-historical themes that recur in Queneau's novels: history, manliness, and fine feelings or lofty sentiments.

First, Queneau often deals with history itself. In his first novel, *Le Chiendent* he depicts a war between the French and the Etruscans that leaves the story exactly where it began.[14] This has given some commentators the impression that Queneau has a cyclical view of history.[15] There is a sense in which the Kojèvean view of history is cyclical; but it is not cyclical in the same sense as it was for Polybius or Machiavelli—always repeating itself in different guises. The Kojèvean view is cyclical in the sense that the world begins with given being or nature and returns to it after the historical journey is completed. Queneau notes the similarity between history and story-telling: both rely on human misfortune. As a result, happiness has no history. Once man reaches happiness, history ends and there is no story to tell. So, if many of Queneau's novels lack a plot, it is precisely because they are often an account of the happiness of man at the end of history.

In *The Blue Flowers*, history is also a central theme.[16] Queneau contrasts the Duke of Auge, who is enmeshed in the historical past, with Cidrolin, who belongs to the eternal present of the post-historical. Each one dreams of being the other. The duke dreams of a carefree life without Crusades, infidels, knighthood, chivalry and war, while Cidrolin dreams of the glories of history, the ideals of knighthood, and the world of chivalry. By making history a dream of a post-historical character, Queneau casts doubt on its authenticity. History is the invention of bored modern men who project their fantasies into the past. In this way, Queneau captures the postmodern view of history as being on a par with fiction. He also undermines the Kojèvean inclination to romanticize history, a tendency that makes the end of history difficult to bear. The blue flowers represent our lofty ideals and sentiments, especially about the past. But this rosy picture of the past is altogether unwarranted if the Duke of Auge is any indication—he is as faithless and as hypocritical as they come. In the novel, Queneau suggests that history may not be so lofty or glorious to those who must live it. Queneau backs up this conviction by depicting just how fun-filled the end of history can be.

Queneau's novels are peppered with wildly enthusiastic tourists for whom history is a finished work of art. Like everything in the post-historical world, history is entertainment and big business.[17] Queneau's characters have a passion for sight-seeing: Notre-Dame, the Sainte-Chapelle, Le Havre, and the site of the battle of Jena are frequently cited.

In *Zazie dans le métro*, Queneau's most famous novel, tourism and sight-seeing are the central activities. The novel is set in the hustle, bustle, and mayhem of Paris.[18] Hordes of tourists—mindless, gullible, jabbering nincompoops—make their way through the traffic jams of Paris to see the Sainte-Chapelle, a gem of Gothic art. But this proves so difficult that they kidnap Gabriel (Zazie's hefty uncle) as their "archguide" through the museum of history. Zazie is not one of these idiotic tourists, gaping at a past that is entirely beyond their comprehension, consuming history like the "slop" they mistook for French cuisine. She does not dote over the Sainte-Chapelle. She is interested in the *métro*. Nor is Gothic her idea of art. She is awaiting the real artistic treat of the evening: her uncle Gabriel—with his professionally epilated thighs, his tutu, his lipstick, and his meticulously manicured nails, dancing the part of the "dying swan" at a gay bar. Welcome to the post-historical world.

Le Dimanche de la vie, more than any other novel, explores the end of history theme. In the novel, history and tourism play a significant part.[19] Valentin Brû, the main character, wishes for nothing more than to visit the site of the battle of Jena. This is the battle where Napoleon, called Nappy in the novel, gains a decisive victory over the Prussian forces. This is the battle that had such an impact on Hegel, and that Kojève regarded as the beginning of the end of history. The tour takes Valentin to the house of the "German Philosopher" who thought that Nappy was the "Soul of the World." He also visits the home of Goethe, another Francophile, who advised the Germans to cooperate with the French because they were the cleverest and strongest—Nappy gave him the Legion of Honor. The tour guide points out that Franco-German rapprochement is a *fait accompli,* but the old men on the tour snicker and would have no part of it. They dream of the glory of war, and denounce the German philosophers for not being "real men."[20] But Valentin knows they are fools, living in the past, not able to see or face reality. The defeat of the Prussians is decisive. The battle of Jena is the battle to end all battles. There will be other battles, like the one of 1939, but the battle of Jena has already determined their outcome. What makes Valentin "heroic" is that he does not live in the shadow of the past or its illusions. He is completely satisfied with the present.[21] He does not glorify war. Nevertheless, he thinks of life as nothingness punctuated by war. And although he is very stoical in his deportment, he becomes very excited at the mention of rifle butts.

The second end of history theme that Queneau explores is manliness or its absence. Unlike the old men on the tour, Valentin has no dreams of glory and manliness. These are things of the past that lead only to war and conquest. Valentin has transcended manliness and the desire for mastery that supposedly goes with it. But Valentin is not just unmanly in the perverse Kojèvean sense of having no appetite for conquest and death, he is also spineless and unspirited. Queneau takes the basest aspect of the "historical" relation between the sexes and reverses it. In his novels, it is quite common to find women of means marrying young men with neither brains nor prospects for no reason except that they are pretty to look at. In *Le Dimanche de la vie,* Julia Segovia, a woman of about forty or forty-five who owns her own haberdashery, resolves to marry Valentin Brû, a handsome young man of about twenty or twenty-five who happens to walk past her shop. She has never spoken to him and does not even know his name. She asks her sister to seek him out, discover his name, and inform him of her plan. Having no prospects and no plans of his own, Brû does not object.

Once married, Valentin becomes Julia's possession. And even though she cherishes him—she warns all the women in the neighborhood to keep their hands off him and fires every maid who so much as asks if Monsieur would prefer chicken or pork this evening—Julia does not regard Valentin with respect. She invariably refers to him as "my Valentin," "my poppett," "my treasure," "my pompon," "my little husband," and "good-looking boy." Nor does he have any objections to the condescending way she treats him. He does not rise up in protest against these public humiliations, not even in his private thoughts. It is not just Julia's insults that he puts up with, but the insults of others as well. Against the latter, Julia is disposed to come to his defense.

When Valentin's boredom with retailing (selling lace, buttons, and other odds and ends) reaches its limit, he hits on a bright idea—maybe he should get his baccalaureate. When he tells Julia, she dismisses him with "but darling, you haven't the mind for it." He never gives it another thought. Valentin is always agreeable, never contrary, and on the whole, a good little husband. Only once does he speak to Julia with an "irritated, authoritarian nuance in his voice which was very 'husbandlike.'"[22] Needless to say, he was very ashamed of himself.

The third aspect of the "sabbath of man" that these novels portray is the absence of the sort of sentimentality and refined feelings that are supposedly the contrivances of civilization. Queneau portrays a totally disenchanted world where men live happily in the naked light of truth. This is the reason that Kojève says (without irony) that Queneau's new and final world is *brave*.[23] For example, it is easy to regard the crudity of Zazie's language and her proclivity for gratuitous cruelty as a sign of a lost generation and a harbinger of a decaying civilization. But Zazie is a genuine post-historical heroine. Her vulgarity is integral to her unabashed and even ruthless veracity. It is clear that the grown-ups cannot withstand so much truth. Zazie's vulgarity is iconoclastic—she sweeps away long-standing traditions regarded with incomprehensible sentimentality by the grown-ups. But even the grown-ups have difficulty sustaining the old illusions. When Mado, a shopkeeper, gets engaged to Charles, a taxi driver, she romantically comments that "it might as well be him as anyone else." If nothing more, the marriage will allow them to "mount each other legally." Still, the grown-ups try to cling to their illusions: they tell the shopkeeper that virginal white with a touch of silver is a must for engagements, and Gabriel thinks he should throw rice. But in the end, Mado decides to omit the virginal part and forgets about white altogether in favor of a gaudy combination of neon colors. Zazie observes with equanimity that in the near future, people will simply not get married. Zazie cannot comprehend why the grown-ups allow themselves to be strangled by these meaningless traditions. And of course she is right—there is no sense in clinging to traditions that have lost their meaning. Traditions can live only in people's hearts and minds, otherwise they die.

Zazie has no hopes or dreams, but neither is she inclined to be despondent. She is incapable of love, but she is also not capable of hatred. Her cruelty is altogether gratuitous. She has no illusions about her choice of career—she's going to be a teacher—but not because she likes children or wishes to educate them. She thinks she'll enjoy "bitching up the kids." And when her uncle Gabriel informs her that the current trend in teaching is in the direction of kindness, gentleness, and understanding, she decides to become an astronaut instead—so she can "bitch up the martians." That's her version of Kojève's *négativité gratuite.*

In *We Always Treat Women Too Well*, Queneau contrasts the sentimental, traditional Irish revolutionaries with the modern Girdie Girdle—shameless and bereft of illusions either about herself or the men who hold her captive.[24] Overtly sexual and totally lascivious, Girdie manages to seduce the Irish men one by one, all the while making them believe that they have violated her pure innocent self. In this way, she destroys their own lofty conceptions of themselves as heroic fighters for their beloved Ireland. Even when she ridicules them and laughs in their face, they continue to harbor illusions about her purity, innocence, and suffering. They blame their lecherous selves for her lost innocence. They preoccupy themselves with the "proper" rules of conduct in their dealings with her. Each one secretly confesses his chaste, eternal, and undying love for her. But all their delusions about the fair sex (probably the result of so many prayers to the Virgin Mary) prove to be their undoing. In the end they die in disgrace before a British firing squad while Girdie sticks out her tongue at them. Given a few more years and a few more curves, Zazie could easily be cast as Girdie.

The complete absence of sentimentality is also apparent in the character of Valentin Brû. For example, he regards a sexual encounter with his sister-in-law as part of the attractions of a day at the Expo: certainly nothing that could inspire shame or regret, only fear of being found out by the possessive Julia. By the same token, Valentin describes a funeral as "shovelling a lousy carcass into the ground."[25] Likewise, the sight of his beloved at the dinner table is little more than an organism shoveling food down her "digestive tube."[26] But none of these things plunge him into despair. Hope for love does not inspire him. And he is quite ready to bury the age of "fine feelings" with his mother-in-law.[27] He is completely "satisfied" with the present and enjoys his pedicures.

Kojève recognized in Queneau's novels not only his own portrait of the end of history, but also his own heroic quest to affirm the inescapable outcome of the historical process. For example, in *The Flight of Icarus,* Queneau makes it clear that there is no escaping one's fate. In his naïveté, Icarus thinks that he has escaped from his fate as a character in a novel.[28] But once he is out in the big world, he becomes attracted to flying and plunges to his death just as he is supposed to. By contrast, the heroic characters are the ones who embrace their fate with gusto, and, in so doing, display the Nietzschean virtue of *amor fati.* If life at the end of history is meaningless and trivial, then the heroic thing to do is not to bemoan one's fate, but affirm it and make it one's own.

There is no doubt that Queneau means to portray his post-historical heroes and heroines as brave. But does he succeed?

All his efforts notwithstanding, Queneau's post-historical sages are so flat, colorless, insipid, and insensitive that they are not interesting enough to be contemptible. To the uninitiated reader, ignorant of the human condition in the sabbath of man, the novels are often drab, lifeless, and even bleak. Valentin hardly strikes the unsuspecting reader as a Nietzschean *Übermensch* living in the face of the abyss, even though he enjoys staring at the clock until his mind goes blank. Not surprisingly, critics are bewildered by Kojève's claim that Valentin Brû is a Hegelian sage. He strikes them more as a "vehicle for satire than a representative of Absolute Mind."[29] Even the most intimate familiarity with the intriguing philosophical assumptions behind Queneau's characters does not succeed in giving them more depth.

The great appeal of novels in general is their ability to allow the reader to observe the characters from the inside. As readers, we are able to enter their world, and vicariously live their lives. We discover their innermost thoughts, their best-kept secrets, and their feelings about their most intimate experiences. In this way, we discover the motives of the characters; we gain insight into why they do what they do, and whether they are proud or ashamed of their conduct. This great appeal of novels is altogether missing in Queneau's work. His prose does not afford us a glimpse of his characters from within. Whatever we find out about Queneau's characters is information imparted from the outside. Sometimes they seem so dull and superficial that one is happy not to know more about them. It often seems as if Queneau is in the same

predicament as the writers in *The Flight of Icarus* who have no characters to write with. In short, his characters are so devoid of *character* that
it is difficult to regard them as heroic.

For example, prior to meeting Julia, Paul (Julia's brother-in-law) warns
Valentin against the marriage. He urges, entreats, and begs Brû not to
marry his sister-in-law. Paul even collapses into a puddle of tears before
Brû; but he does not give any reason why the thought of this marriage
drives him to distraction. Valentin is unmoved. And the reader is left to
wonder if there could be some sinister trap awaiting the simple, trust-
ing Valentin? Alas, the plot reveals nothing so intriguing.

In the next chapter we encounter the couple—Julia and Valentin—
already married and settled down to a humdrum existence. Unable to
afford a honeymoon, they agree that Valentin should go on the honeymoon by himself. The only reason given for this curious arrangement is
that "one gets tired of too much intimacy."[30] And true to form, the novel
does not contain the smallest shred of intimacy.

There is certainly no intimacy between the characters and the reader.
We never find out why Valentin agreed to the marriage, other than
because of the haberdashery. He never tells us how Julia treats him in
private or how he feels about her or if he feels anything at all. We surmise that love is out of the question since it is never mentioned, and
apparently its absence is not missed. We never find out why Julia
Segovia, committed spinster who once loved a soldier who was killed in
the First World War, decides to marry after so many years, or why she
chooses Valentin, other than that he is handsome and has "chaste lips."[31]
Nor do we find out how she intends to keep him loyal, for she intends
it since she is wildly jealous and possessive. This is difficult to reconcile
with sending him off alone on the honeymoon.

I venture the following explanation. In the twilight of time, there are
no reasons or motives for action. Life is little more than a parody of
everything that used to be serious, noble, lofty, or "historical." For example,
both Valentin and Jacques (in *Loin de Rueil*) are fascinated with saintliness and decide to try their hand at it.[32] Valentin discovers that hiding
his self-sacrifice is the most difficult part of the exercise. Jacques spends
his time following strange funerals, caressing beards, knitting woolen
stockings, giving his money to the poor, and rushing to assist overbur-
dened deliverymen. But he too finds it a tricky business because he is so
proud of his saintliness. Sexual abstinence is the part of saintliness that
Queneau's characters ignore—they admit that it is the part they neither
understand nor fancy.

Queneau's novels are a heroic attempt to face the end of history with humor, courage, and even joy. In a world with nothing left to do, nothing to fight or strive for and no one to love, Queneau does not despair. His heroes and sages are those who live in full consciousness of their post-historical situation, without nostalgia for the past or despondency in the present. They enjoy the lighter side of life that the sabbath brings. Accordingly, their lives are filled with capers, antics, fun, and frolicking. There is not a hint of unhappiness in these novels. So, why is it that some critics cannot help noticing a "throbbing note of sadness"?[33]

It seems to me that there is a time in every civilization's history when the weight of the past becomes intolerable. At these moments, people feel paralyzed by the burden of the old monuments. They feel that their lives are meaningless and drab in comparison to the significant intensity of the lives of their predecessors. In comparison to the magnificence of the heroes of old, they feel worthless. This sense of worthlessness has the effect of sapping life of whatever meaning it might have. If a civilization does not periodically tear down its monuments, it will surely become strangled by them. As the legends around the old heroes grow larger than life, life itself becomes diminutive. Even Nietzsche, who was predisposed to romanticizing the past, realized that this "monumental view of history" poses serious dangers to life itself. He counseled us to feast our eyes on Plutarch and dare to believe in his heroes, yet at the same time he realized that the legends can grow too large and begin to threaten life—and Nietzsche always liked to think of himself as being on the side of life and what is life-giving. He never failed to champion the "life-giving illusions" as opposed to the "deadly truth." But when the illusions themselves become deadly, what then? What could possibly be gained from contemplating Pythagoras's golden hips?

At times of such colossal impotence in the face of the old monuments, there seems to be two possible courses of action—either to live in the twilight of history or to make a clean break. Those who are daring and strong refuse to live in the shadows. They resolve to make a fresh start. They start by pulling down the monuments that hang like a dead albatross around their necks. This is the only way that they can give meaning and significance to their lives. It is the only way that they can begin to live with joy, purpose, or resolve. In our own time, the assault on the "dead white males" that make up the canonical texts of Western civilization is a case in point.

I am totally sympathetic to Queneau's efforts to disenchant the past— I have no doubt that many a Crusader was motivated by the prospect of bitching up the infidels!

Queneau was insightful enough to realize that it is impossible to live bravely or to live at all if the past is exalted into a monument of grandiose proportions. Queneau must have recognized that the Kojèvean proclivity to romanticize history has the effect of reducing the present to "la tombée de la nuit."

Queneau disenchants the past and tears down the monuments—maybe the past was not as glorious and lofty as men who deplore the meaninglessness of their lives like to think; maybe it is only us moderns who have invested the past with so much significance. Queneau has no intention of investing the present with depth and significance. He does not regard the present to be any more significant than the past. We must accept our fate in the twilight of history with courage and laughter. Therein lies our heroic modernity. That is Queneau's uplifting message.

Yet despite his heroic efforts, Queneau fails to invest the end of history with joy. There is a an unmistakable joylessness in all his laughter. The reason is that Queneau has fully accepted Kojève's vision of modernity as totally disenchanted—no ideologies, gods, myths, illusions, or fine feelings. Like Kojève, Queneau assumes that everything lofty is a concoction of "history" that authentic men must transcend once they are able to look death in the face without concealing it with dreams of sugarplums. That is what Heideggerian authenticity requires. But what if all enchantments are not the fabrications of culture or history? Is nature not filled with enchantments? If we assume that all beauty and enchantments and fine feelings belong to history, to ideology, to false consciousness, then we will strip ourselves of everything great and glorious and we will be reduced to the impoverished condition of Valentin Brû, who can only see his beloved as an organism shoveling food down her digestive tube. If we assume that everything magnificent and majestic is a concoction of culture meant to veil our eyes from the truth, then we will become insensitive to the beauty of the world. Then, the *death of man* will undoubtedly be at hand.

■ 8 □

Bataille's Revolt

Georges Bataille (1897–1962) was a sociologist, anthropologist, philosopher, and pornographer. He was one of the regulars at Kojève's seminar and his friendship with Kojève and Queneau lasted long after the Hegel seminar.[1] Bataille accepted Kojève's interpretation of Hegel according to which history was a tragedy that ends in the *death of man*.[2] Bataille saw the world with Kojève's spectacles. He thought that the triumph of reason has robbed the world of life and vitality and left it homogenized, routinized, and utterly disenchanted. But unlike Kojève, Bataille had no intention of resigning himself to the aesthetic and emotional barrenness of the world. And unlike Queneau, he was not ready to cavort and laugh about the matter. He was determined to fight against the twilight of man. He resolved to liberate everything that reason has vanquished—madness, frenzy, anguish, heterogeneity, duality, and contradiction.

In what follows, I will show that by taking Kojève's assumptions and values to their logical conclusion, Bataille becomes the father of postmodernism. I believe that Bataille is the key to understanding the most enigmatic aspects of postmodernism—its self-refuting character, its Dionysian frenzy, and its dark romanticism.

Like Kojève, Bataille did not hold an academic position; he was a librarian. And like Kojève, he was an extremely prolific writer. He was the founder of the famous French review *Critique*, and journals such as *Documents* and *Acéphale*; he was the central player in "The College of Sociology" along with Roger Caillois, Pierre Klossowski, Michel Leiris, and others.[3] Twelve volumes of his work have been published and most of them have recently appeared in English translations. The over-

whelming interest in Bataille's work has a great deal to do with the interest in postmodernism as a whole and the growing recognition of his monumental impact on that movement. Leading postmoderns like Michel
Foucault and Jacques Derrida have acknowledged their profound debt
to him and Heidegger has hailed him as "one of France's best minds."[4]

THE FIRST MAN

As a sociologist, Bataille sets out to comprehend the nature and origin
of human society. In my view, the simplest way to understand Bataille's
sociology is to begin with his reflections on a riddle borrowed from
Claude Lévi-Strauss. Bataille solves the riddle by supplementing Lévi-
Strauss's theories with elements of Kojève's Hegelianism. The results are
utterly astounding.

In *The Elementary Structures of Kinship*, Lévi-Strauss is struck by the
universal character of the prohibition of incest. He surmises that this
prohibition is the "fundamental step" that marks the "transition from
nature to culture."[5] Lévi-Strauss rejects the thesis that the prohibition
indicates a natural or instinctive repugnance on the grounds that psychoanalysis has shown this to be false; besides, if there is such a natural
repugnance, why bother with the prohibition? Instead, Lévi-Strauss
proposes his famous theory of "the gift." He surmises that marriage was
part of an economic system of exchange since a wife was the most
important and precious article of wealth. It was necessary that the dis-
tribution of women be governed by rules that would avoid hoarding.
Women were therefore pledged to "communication," they became
part of the social show of generosity. The man who would keep his
daughter for himself is like the owner of champagne who would drink
up his stock by himself and never invite any friends.[6] The prohibition
on incest was therefore an affirmation of the importance of generosity
in a world where every generous act contributed to the circuit of generosity in the community. And because the sexual act is a form of communication, it requires an "outward movement" as opposed to a
"withdrawal into self."[7]

Bataille regards Lévi-Strauss's theory of the gift as a "brilliant, captivating hypothesis."[8] He agrees with Lévi-Strauss that there is no natural
repugnance against incest and that exogamy requires the renunciation
of a coveted object. He also agrees with Lévi-Strauss that the prohibition of incest is critical in understanding the transition from nature to
culture. However, Bataille thinks it is implausible for a prohibition to be

imposed so strongly if its sole purpose is to enhance the circuit of exchange. In Bataille's view, Lévi-Strauss makes the mistake of wondering what the prohibition is *for*. He makes the mistake of trying to figure out why in some tribes the cousins whose mothers are two sisters or whose fathers are two brothers are prohibited from marrying, but in other tribes, they are encouraged to marry. Bataille surmises that Lévi-Strauss's theory is too pragmatic and unerotic.

Bataille thinks that it is useless to try, as Lévi-Strauss does, to find the reasons for these prohibitions. The search assumes that the prohibitions serve a *useful purpose*. In contrast, Bataille considers prohibitions to be totally *arbitrary*.[9] He believes that they have no rationale beyond themselves—prohibitions are "sovereign," which is Bataille's way of saying that they are an end and not a means.[10] Sovereign activities are always "gratuitous," needless or unnecessary. In Bataille's view, man's capacity for "sovereign" activities distinguishes him from the animals.[11]

Like Kojève, Bataille is totally preoccupied with the question of what is distinctively human—what distinguishes man from the animals? What sets man apart from nature? How does culture, the distinctively human world, come into being? Bataille's response is vintage Kojève: what sets man apart is his capacity for living sovereignly—acting in a surprising, gratuitous, and unfounded manner. The earliest manifestation of man's sovereignty is his *negation of nature*. By negating the *given*, which in the first instance is nature, man transcends necessity and displays his freedom, autonomy or sovereignty; he proves that he is not a *thing* that is fixed or determined from the start. Sovereignty therefore affirms the Heideggerian conception of man as a *no-thing* or a self-determining being.

In classic Kojèvean fashion, Bataille suggests that the prohibition of incest is just one aspect of man's *negation of nature*, including his own animal nature. By renouncing the sexual objects at hand, by rejecting the immediacy of animal gratification, and by spontaneously and voluntarily setting a limit on his own sexual satisfaction, man negates the order of nature and its instincts and sets himself apart. He becomes a happening or an "event" that disrupts the "calm regularity" of nature.[12]

Bataille's fictive history is a variation on familiar Kojèvean themes. In the beginning, man lived like a stupid animal in the bosom of nature. Then suddenly, and without explanation, man decides to do something totally unnatural, extraordinary, and unprecedented. He refuses to give in to the demands of his own animal instincts—this refusal marks a break with his animality. Work, war, and sexual prohibitions are all examples of man's negation of nature.[13] Willingly, freely, without compulsion, need, or reason, man adopts a way of life that is hard, arduous, and unnatural. There is absolutely no rationale for man's surprising behavior.[14] Man's "abhorrence of nature" leads him to create an artificial world—a clean house, polished floors, and furniture.[15] Human culture is a sanctuary from the disorder, dirt, and violence of nature. Culture invents an abode fit to be inhabited by "venerable persons" who are "naïve and inviolable, tender and inaccessible."[16] Culture fashions a pristine world by obliterating every trace of nature. Culture is man's way of creating a world in which "respect, difficulty and restraint prevail over violence."[17] Nature is the thesis and man is the antithesis.

Bataille believes that the effect of man's initial negation of nature is to *heighten* and *intensify* man's experience of life. For example, the voluntary relinquishing of the coveted sexual object as a "gift" underscores the value of the object. The sexual prohibitions invented by human society have the effect of transfiguring mere animal sexuality into human eroticism. Prohibitions turn a "fleeting impulse, destitute of meaning" into something infinitely more interesting.[18] Delaying gratification has the effect of intensifying the sexual experience. Prohibition and restraint are absolutely vital in understanding the eroticism of man as opposed to the sexuality of animals. Sexuality belongs to nature, but eroticism belongs to man. Sexuality has a purpose—namely, reproduction, but eroticism is like war, it is a "sovereign" activity—a manifestation of man's being, an exploration of his possibilities.[19]

Like Kojève, Bataille romanticizes the "dawn" of history when the "first man" crosses the threshold from animality to humanity. History begins with the first man's "refusal of the given condition."[20] Bataille believes that never has humanity had a "more astounding, more glorious moment."[21] The first man's "creative revolt" is proof that man is an "event," a "dance," a "drama," and a "leap." Bataille is dazzled by the daring and boldness of the "first man," who has launched us on a historical journey that Bataille, like Kojève, finds absolutely exhilarating.

For all his emphasis on man's negation of nature, Bataille does not think that man's antipathy to nature is his defining quality. Man is *not* defined by his capacity to replace the violence of nature with order and restraint. As we shall see, it is the *negation* that is critical. What is negated is arbitrary; but this arbitrariness is regarded by Bataille as the supreme manifestation of human freedom and autonomy. It is important to note at this point that for Bataille, freedom is a "dangerous breaking-loose" that recognizes no limits, including justice.[22]

THE HISTORICAL TRAGEDY

In examining the history of civilizations, Bataille finds that every civilization has its own unique way of displaying man's autonomy from the world of things. Every civilization subordinates production to something "sovereign," which is then understood in terms of free, wasteful, and purposeless expenditures or "consumptions." Every civilization lavishes resources on that which it holds in the highest esteem. Bataille examines the Aztec civilization in Mexico, the Islamic civilization in Arabia, Lamaism in Tibet, and Roman Catholicism in the Middle Ages. In every case, he finds something "sovereign." In Aztec civilization, war is an end in itself. In Islam, conquest of territories in a holy war against the infidels is the sovereign end.[23] In the Lamaism of Tibet, the proliferation of monasteries and idle monks are the sovereign ends of that civilization.[24] In the Roman Catholicism of the Middle Ages, Gothic spires, cathedrals, abbeys, idle priests and monks are sovereign. In each case, the civilization devotes itself to something altogether useless and wasteful, *especially from a biological point of view*. And insofar as wastefulness is the criterion of sovereignty, Bataille admires the Aztecs most of all because they regarded the utter wastefulness of war and killing as ends in themselves (and not just a means to expanding the empire as is generally the case). In Bataille's view, the "pure, uncalculated violence" of the Aztecs was the supreme manifestation of sovereignty.[25]

In contrast to all the splendor of the past, Bataille finds modernity altogether bereft of sovereignty. Everything sovereign, purposeless, or gratuitous—everything worthy of the glory that is man—has given way to cold, rational calculation. Here is a world dedicated wholeheartedly to scientism, utility, and productivity—a world that shuns consumption, display, ornamentation, splendor, luxury, and all forms of lavish extravagance. Here is a world that has been mechanized, homogenized, and Sovietized. For the first time, man seems to have lost the secret of living sovereignly—which is to say that he has lost himself. Bourgeois civilization, if it can be called a civilization, has created a world in which nothing is sovereign. It has created a world of things or commodities in which man himself has been reduced to a *thing* or a commodity—a "standing reserve" to be deployed for some end or other.[26]

Science has turned our civilization into a "sanitary installation" that is so "meticulous" that Bataille considers it "sick." Insofar as technological society has minimized the *struggle* against nature, it has dwarfed our humanity. Ironically, the more we triumph over nature the closer we get to animality. Tragically, the long history of labor and struggle against nature has brought us back full circle to the ease and unconcern of animal life.[27] We are now as far away from struggle as we are from sovereignty—the essential ingredients of civilization. Like Kojève, Bataille understands history as a tragedy. But he has every hope that man will rise out of the ashes. For despite the demise of man, the historical process has bequeathed to him a summit of consciousness. Even if he has "lost the world," man has "nonetheless become that *consciousness* of having lost it."[28] This irony of history gives Bataille hope in an apocalyptic rebirth of sovereignty.

Initially, Bataille was attracted to the fascists because he thought that they were the new reincarnation of sovereignty; but later, he rejected them because their violence was not wasteful and purposeless enough— apparently it was a mere means to power.[29] Nevertheless, he did not lose hope, and this explains his rejection of the finality of Kojève's end of history and death of man.

KOJÈVE'S END OF HISTORY

For Bataille, the abominable condition of modern civilization has, not surprisingly, led sages like Alexandre Kojève to declare that the end of history is at hand, and the death of man is imminent. In a published letter to Kojève, Bataille admits that the idea that history is over "except for the wrap-up" is a "likely assumption." However, Bataille denies that the end of history could be construed as a "summit" because "no one would 'recognize' a summit that would be night."[30] Bataille drew the correct conclusion from Kojève's historical dialectic—as we have seen, it is not possible to construe the Kojèvean dialectic as a progressive movement toward a climax. As Bataille insists, following Kojève's own logic, to remain without change, to be totally satisfied, to live in the absence of any "*révolte créatrice*" is to be an animal.[31] And if this end of history comes to be, then we will not even be able to say that it is the end of history, because it would be like death. But since we can still speak of it, then there must be some hope. Bataille surmises that man is not yet dead, even though he has been *castrated*. What is needed is to devise some means by which man could regain his virility.

Bataille thinks that wherever there is man, there will always be a possibility of negation. Bataille objects to the circularity of Kojève's Hegelianism. In other words, he rejects the idea that history must return to the primal unity or oneness from which it began; he repudiates the conception of history as a brief interregnum preceded by nature and animality and culminating in a return to nature; he denies that history must bring man full circle back to animality without any hope of escape. He tells Kojève that he regards his own life, or "the open wound" that is his life, as "constituting a refutation of Hegel's closed system."[32] Bataille is determined to preserve the dialectic by magnifying its dualism until it is experienced as a *"laceration* that exposes the whole of divided being."[33] He revels in the fervor, struggle, and dualism that epitomize the dialectic. He has no intention of seeking a reconciliation, a closure or an end. And while he agrees that we have returned to animality, the very fact that we are conscious of our demise is reason for optimism.

Bataille's letter to Kojève reveals that his objections to Kojève's Hegelianism are a result of his ardent adherence to the assumptions and the premises at the heart of Kojève's thought. If negativity is the key to man's humanity, as Kojève maintained, then making sure that the negativity of man is not extinguished, is all that matters. As long as the possibility of negation has not been extinguished, then man is not dead, regardless of history. Writing to Kojève, Bataille claimed that even the man who has "nothing left to do" retains the negativity peculiar to his humanity. If history is not over, then negativity will have historical manifestations—like the conquest of nature; but if history is over, then the "unemployed negativity" will have to find other outlets.[34] As we have seen, Kojève himself arrived at the same conclusion in his conception of the *négativité gratuite*. The question is: What is man to do with his unemployed negativity?

Bataille's answer is as follows. At the "end of history" or at a point in time where man's triumph over nature has become decisive, negativity needs to be revitalized; it needs new outlets; it can no longer be directed at nature. In the dawn of humanity, nature had to be negated because it was the *given*. But today, situated as we are in a rational, sanitized fortress, in a civilization where nature has been all but banished, human negativity must be directed toward the new *given*—toward civilization itself.

LEARNING FROM THE PRIMITIVES

Bataille was repelled by a world where the triumph over nature was complete, where the excitement of the dialectic was extinguished, where negativity and transgression were unthinkable, where reason had triumphed over life, and where ecstasy had given way to calculation.[35] But he was determined not to succumb to cynicism, resignation, and despair. He thought that it was possible to revitalize and reenchant the world, and he was surrounded by intellectual friends and associates in "The College of Sociology" who shared the same sentiments. Bataille played a decisive role in the College. The participants in the College studied shamanism, gnosticism, knights, primitive societies, religions, rituals, brotherhoods, festivals, and myths, all in an effort to reenchant the world. Along with others in the College, Bataille was eager for the participation and support of Kojève, but the latter declined. Kojève did not deny that the triumph of reason and science have disenchanted the world. However, in Kojève's view, the College had embarked on a hopeless task. Kojève argued that to regress from science back to magic is as impossible as finding a magician who falls prey to his own tricks. No amount of theorizing about magic will return the world to its prescientific stage. Kojève compared Bataille to the "sorcerer's apprentice" who marvels at his own sleight of hand.[36]

In response to Kojève, Bataille gave a lecture entitled "The Sorcerer's Apprentice," which set the tone of the College.[37] In this lecture, Bataille compared the human condition in the modern world to that of a man who has lost his manhood. Even though such a man feels no pain, Bataille maintained that he is nevertheless stricken. The "absence of virility" makes him less of a man, and in Bataille's view, there can be no "calamity" that is to be more dreaded—especially because there is no "alarming pain to be connected with this half-dead state."[38] Modern men are castrated men who are not even conscious of their afflictions. Bataille made it clear that he was not willing to resign himself to this state of affairs.

In Bataille's view, our broken world is made up of three disconnected parts and three corresponding types of men. Bataille rejects all three. He heaps abuse on the scientist because he epitomizes the "slavishness to function" characteristic of our world. Science and reason are at the root of our afflictions; they are responsible for our lifeless, castrated existence.

The artist does not fare as badly as the scientist, but he does not fare a great deal better.[39] And if Bataille does not think him a castrated man, he certainly does not believe that he is virile. According to Bataille, the artist withdraws into a world of ghosts, phantoms, and fictions of his own making. Surrounded by these shameless falsehoods, he lives a "shadowy and fugitive existence" and leaves the world as "rigorously split" as it was before.[40]

The man of action seems to be the most virile—Bataille describes him as one who fulfills the "need to be a man." He combines fiction and truth.

He forces the world to conform to "dream's caprice."[41] He bends reality to his will. He is more manly than either the scientist who studies the world passively or the artist who withdraws from reality into a world of fantasy. The trouble with men of action is that they are often tempted by the desire for success to betray their dreams. They end up serving what already exists. Bataille must have had Kojève in mind here—he started out as a man of action, a man with a dream, and ended up as an apologist for the status quo or the end of history. Such men delude themselves into thinking that they have succeeded, that the world corresponds to their ideals; but Bataille thinks that they have betrayed their dreams.

For Bataille, only the lover can experience the fullness of life. But love has the effect of increasing "lucidity and suffering" in the face of a "broken-down society." So, Bataille suggests that we make our world whole again by taking a clue from primitive societies.

According to Bataille, the myths of primitive societies are not fiction; they are a living truth that "enters the bodies of those it binds together" and makes them a people sharing the same expectations, the same rhythms, the same dance. Myth is a "vital human reality" that reveals a real accord whose "festival excitement" brings existence "to its boiling point."[42]

Bataille thinks that long ago, men recognized the inevitable failure of the initial movement. At the dawn of history, the first movement negates nature and creates an artificial world that Bataille calls the "profane world"—supposedly because there is no profanity in nature. The profane world is a negation of nature through work and prohibitions. Primitive men knew that we cannot deny sexuality, filth, and death; because the carnal origin is our origin and because we are all destined to rot and cannot escape the "fatal appointment."[43] In their prescience, the primitives incorporated into their existence a ritual return to nature in the form of the festival. The festival was an opportunity for transgression. It was an occasion in which the animal forces were liberated in a ritual license. The death of a king was often an excuse for a festival. During festivals everything that was generally prohibited was permitted—sexual license, killing, and mayhem.

All this seems puzzling in view of Bataille's insistence on man's "abhorrence of nature." If man is horrified by nature, then why should he affirm the natural animality that he has struggled so hard to escape? How can he direct his negativity at civilization and its prohibitions? Is Bataille suggesting that we return to animality? Does he intend to return us to the filth from whence we have made such a valiant effort to escape?

Bataille argues that it is not the original nature to which he bids us return. He insists that he is not suggesting that "man return to his vomit."[44] Bataille claims that the original nature from which we have emerged has been permanently "transfigured by the curse" of the original prohibition.[45] Bataille's point is that the nature which is desired *after* being prohibited is not desired in "submission to the given," and hence the desire for it is not strictly speaking animalistic, but distinctly human. Bataille assures us that this is a "new movement of refusal, of insubordination, of revolt."[46] It is intended to recapture the fervor and delirium of the original movement—the glorious leap of the first man. If we are to return to the vitality of the first man, we must return to nature *and* to the abhorrence of nature. The festival accomplishes this through its excesses, which lead to the reinstatement of the taboos. Bataille thought that the festival was the secret of the vitality of primitive society because it insures a never-ending cycle of taboo and transgression in which the drama of the first man is perpetually reenacted.

For all his emphasis on our abhorrence of nature, Bataille does not think that it is the defining quality of man. On the contrary, Bataille maintains that early man's aversions are "ambiguous" and therefore allow "reversals."[47] It seems that the rules and prohibitions that man adopts as a way of negating his animality are merely "provisional." This is the significance of Bataille's insistence against Lévi-Strauss that the prohibitions against incest are arbitrary or have absolutely no rationale. Even though the abhorrence of nature is built into man's "essence," Bataille denies that it is *natural* on the ground that children do not experience it. We are therefore led to conclude that man is not distinguished from the animal by his prohibitions and restraint, and that man's triumph over nature and violence is only part of the story. It seems that the human characteristic par excellence is negativity, or the capacity to negate the given, *whatever it may be.*

But how can we return to the festive rituals of the primitives? Bataille suggests a "secret society" with an artistic capacity for "mythological invention."[48] But he is quick to add that it must *not* be understood in the "vulgar" sense of a "conspiratorial society." It must not become a cynical elite fabricating mere fictions for the masses. Bataille insists on a secret society that is seduced by its own myths—just like the sorcerer's apprentice.

Alas, the College was very short-lived (1937–1939) and contained too many disparate voices to constitute a conspiratorial elite of any sort. Nevertheless, Bataille did not abandon the project of reinvesting the world with intensity and vigor.

TRANSGRESSION

In Bataille's view, the deathlike state of modern life has its source in the undisputed triumph of God and his prohibitions, reason and its calculations, science and its utilitarianism. In an effort to reinvigorate the world and restore the exhilaration of life at the dawn of history, Bataille resolves to rediscover the original dualism. Accordingly, he sets out to restore what has been banished, liberate what has been subjugated, uncover what has been hidden, reveal what has been repressed, applaud what has been marginalized, and affirm what has been negated. Only by reawakening the original dualism can the vitality of life be restored.

The first task at hand is to kill God and replace him with the vanquished Satan, since God represents the prohibitions of civilization. To reject God is to reject transcendence in favor of the "immanence" achieved through intoxication, eroticism, human sacrifice, and poetic effusions. Replacing God with Satan also means replacing prohibition with transgression, order with disorder, and reason with madness.

Insofar as the prohibitions of civilization are directed at sexuality, eroticism is the form which transgression assumes. Bataille's literary enterprise is a monument to the inventiveness of unemployed negativity. His *Story of the Eye* and *My Mother* are classic illustrations of his transgressive project. Published in 1928 under a pseudonym, *Story of the Eye* is the chronicle of the orgiastic debaucheries of the heroine, Simone. With the cooperation of her male partner, Simone manages to drive a young friend into an asylum. After helping this girl escape from the asylum, Simone and her lover lure her into more of the orgies that had driven her to distraction in the first place. The girl soon hangs herself, which is an occasion for a sexual escapade between Simone, her lover, and the corpse. After escaping to Spain, Simone and her lover enjoy the bullfights where they dine on the raw sexual organs of the bull. Later, Simone seduces, rapes, and murders a priest in the "holy sepulchre." And in the "high summits" of her lust, she has his eyes cut out to use for further obscenities.

Even though the novel is classified as pornographic, it does not fit the usual definition of pornography. The latter is supposed to titillate, yet there is little that is titillating in the *Story of the Eye*.[49] Bataille does not simply wish to titillate, but to bring what has been subverted or prohibited into full view; he aims to liberate the hidden, dark, subterranean, and violent passions. Bataille inverts the order of things. He portrays the evil and iniquity of Simone as sweet, natural, and pure. The narrator, who is Simone's lover and accomplice, portrays her as a "girl" and describes her as "innocent" and even "virginal." The white dress she wears in Spain symbolizes her innocence, though it must be added that undergarments are foreign to her—such formidable obstacles would no doubt interfere with the pace of her adventures. Even after she fornicates with the priest whom she has strangled and mutilated, the narrator describes her as "more angelic than ever." She seems unaware of the prohibitions she transgresses; and her crimes do not keep her awake at night. Only her lover and Sir Edmund, the wealthy Englishman who finances her debaucheries, are conscious that her actions are *transgressions*. By portraying her as innocent, Bataille implies that she is not human, that she is the incarnation of nature and of life—feverish, delirious, ecstatic, orgiastic, tumultuous, free, uninhibited, and sovereign— there is not a shred of utility or profit in her crimes, they are completely gratuitous. In the eyes of her lover and Sir Edmund, Simone is fit to be adored. The inversion of the world is now complete—at least in fiction, if not in life: Simone has replaced God.

The same inversion of the world takes place in Bataille's *My Mother.* This is the story of a young boy on the verge of manhood. He adores his mother and hates his father. His mother is beautiful, pure, quiet, and eloquent. In contrast, his father is a boorish drunkard who abuses the mother. When the father dies, the boy feels a sense of peace and relief— but that is not to be. His mother decides to tell him the truth about herself. She tells him how she made his father's life a living hell, which drove him to drink; she tells him that she went out each night in search of lascivious pleasures with strange men and women. It seems that the death of the father is like the death of God—now the boy must live in the face of the sordid truth; all the illusions that sustained him have disappeared. After shattering his illusions, his mother makes a strange request. She asks her son to have the same veneration and respect for her as he had when he idolized her saintliness. The story is about Pierre's descent into his mother's world of infamy. He is sexually seduced by his mother and her female lover. He discovers beneath the surface of bourgeois respectability a world of unspeakable anguish, horror, and ecstasy. In time, he exchanges his own ardent religiosity for a new religion. By descending into the dregs of pleasure, Pierre discovers the hidden God.

Using an inversion of the Gnostic motif, Bataille emancipates the darkness held captive in the midst of light; he unmasks the respectability of human existence to reveal the filth concealed beneath the surface. Evil is the hidden God who has been conquered and suppressed so successfully by the triumph of reason and goodness. Yet, the dark forces have not been completely destroyed; they linger deep in the human psyche. The task at hand is to liberate these elemental forces. It may be disturbing at first, but in the end, the process of unmasking is wild, rapturous, and liberating.

Bataille admired the Gnostics because they emphasized the dualism of the world—the dualism that he regards as the betrayed heart of Hegelianism.[50] But he reverses the Gnostic imagery of light trapped in darkness—the soul trapped in the carnal body and separated from the God of light for whom she longs. Instead, Bataille seeks to liberate the darkness.

PERPETUAL NEGATION

Once the world has been turned upside down, once God has been replaced by Satan, transcendence by immanence, prohibition by transgression, order by disorder, reason by madness, discourse by the unspeakable, restraint by excess, sobriety by intoxication, puritanism by eroticism, utility by sovereign expenditure, what is man to do?

Bataille's answer is that the new disorder will become the next *given*, and it will be necessary to negate *it*. At that point in time, it will be necessary to affirm God, order, reason, prohibition, restraint, puritanism, and even utility (although this latter is likely to stick in Bataille's throat). But this time has not yet come. For now, Bataille resolves to celebrate the Dionysian. But *in principle*, Bataille regards the Apollonian god of light as equal to the Dionysian god of darkness.[51] Even though Bataille understood history in Nietzsche's categories as the triumph of the Apollonian (reason, order, and self-restraint) over the Dionysian (madness, lawlessness, and self-abandon), it is not altogether accurate to say that Bataille was a champion of Dionysus.[52] Insofar as Dionysus has been vanquished, Bataille presents himself as his champion. But theoretically speaking, Bataille insists on a tension between opposite forces as the secret to the "poetic dynamism" of existence.

The point is not to affirm anything in particular, except *negativity*. Only the latter can insure the continued vitality of the dialectic. Bataille's project is one of *perpetual negation* or "ceaseless overturning."[53] Such an endeavor requires irreconcilable dualism—it requires a thesis and an antithesis held together in a permanent tension that underscores their duality.

Bataille's transgressions are not simply intended to overturn the puritanical order and reveal the dark passions; they are also intended to reawaken the "archaic horror" of nature. This latter is bound to send us scurrying back to civilization to repeat the process all over again, in an eternal recurrence of the same. In other words, Bataille's transgressions simultaneously subvert *and* reinforce the order of civilization. This accounts for the self-refuting character of postmodern critique. The goal is to preserve the duality, contradiction and conflict, which is the spice of the dialectic. The point is to avert the stagnation of the end of history and recapture the intensity and vitality of the dawn of humanity. To this end, Bataille resolves to keep us on a treadmill of ceaseless overturning, trembling with horror and rapture at the same time.

THE TRANSGRESSIONS OF GILLES DE RAIS

Nothing illustrates the contradiction and duality of existence better than the phenomenon of the holy sinner with which Bataille was so fascinated. The holy sinner embodies the extremes of debauchery and puritanism in an irreconcilable and impossible tension. Bataille did not share the anticlericalism of Nietzsche or the Enlightenment. He did not believe that the Church's unnatural repression of sexuality had the effect of deforming a healthy and natural instinct.[54] The endless abominations attributed to priests in our own time would have delighted him. Bataille is attracted to these holy sinners. He needs God, the Church, and their prohibitions to underscore the enormity of transgression. The "holy sepulchre" is the necessary backdrop to the erotic abominations and sadistic horrors perpetrated by his protagonists. There is nothing that Bataille's fornicating characters love more than a celibate priest for an audience.[55] Their pleasure is derived not so much from their own sexuality but from witnessing his anguish and ecstasy, his terror and delight.

Bataille's fascination with the holy sinner is particularly manifest in his study of Gilles de Rais, a notorious criminal of the late Middle Ages. Bataille has collected all of the documents of this trial, organized them chronologically, and commented extensively on them in *The Trial of Gilles de Rais.*[56] Gilles de Rais was a sadistic nobleman who lured innumerable little children of both sexes to his castles, and offered them up as sacrifices to the Devil. He tortured them, sexually violated them, and slit their throats in orgiastic exaltation. Drenched in blood, he would sleep while his servants and accomplices cleaned the castle and burned the cadavers.

Bataille believes Gilles de Rais is the legendary Bluebeard whose castles still stand as monuments to the enormity of his transgressions. Bataille regards Gilles de Rais as a holy sinner; he describes him as a "sacred monster" and claims that he was a "good and devout" Christian to the end.[57] The secular courts condemned Gilles de Rais to be tortured, hanged, and burned. The ecclesiastical courts also found him guilty and regarded his crimes as "inexpiable" and so ordered him excommunicated. Throughout the trial, Gilles de Rais was insolent and unrepentant. Before the torture was to take place, he asked for a postponement, saying that he needed more time for reflection. His request was granted. Then he decided to confess his crimes, and went to great lengths to expose his depravities—he described how his accomplices chose the prettiest among the decapitated heads for him to kiss; and he confessed his laughter at the "grimaces of the dying."[58] Falling to his knees, he begged for the forgiveness of his judges and beseeched them to save him from the torments of eternal damnation by repealing his sentence of excommunication—and they forgave him! Then he had a few more requests: he wanted the Bishop of Nantes, the Inquisitor of the Faith who presided over the ecclesiastical tribunal, to lead a procession of the people to his place of execution and pray to God for the salvation of his immortal soul. He also wanted his body removed from the flames before it was consumed, placed in a coffin, and given a proper burial. And, amazing as it may seem, all his wishes were granted. A huge procession followed him to the place of his execution, and prayed for the salvation of his soul. These were the very same people he had treated with contempt all his life, and whose children he mercilessly tortured and killed. And after he was hung and his body committed to the flames, "women of noble lineage" pulled him out as soon as possible, placed him in a coffin, and gave him a proper funeral service *in the Church*.

Having examined the evidence, Bataille does not interpret the matter simply. He does not see it as the case of a heinous criminal, an accomplished fraud, and gullible judges. Nor does Bataille dismiss the confessions of Gilles de Rais as a sham intended to avert the torture and delay his execution. Bataille does not condemn the Church's treatment of Gilles de Rais, especially when compared to its treatment of Joan of Arc only ten years earlier. Instead, Bataille claims that Gilles de Rais is integral to Christianity: because the latter is grounded in forgiveness, it contains a "pressing demand for crime."[59] This is precisely what Bataille understands by Augustine's "felix culpa!" that fortunate sin of Adam and Eve without which the sweet redemption of Jesus Christ would have been unnecessary. Christianity needs Gilles de Rais.

Bataille's work on Gilles de Rais casts light on Bataille's own concept of transgression. But it also tells us something about his concept of history. Bataille believes that Gilles de Rais represents the death-throes of a glorious age. In the Middle Ages, noble warriors like him used to live "sovereignly" or beyond the law—slaughtering, burning, and pillaging. They had a "hunger for carnage" and butchery and were unfamiliar with reason and its calculations, since "intelligence or calculation are not noble."[60] Bataille thinks that Gilles de Rais was a casualty of the march of reason in history. Gone were the days when war was a sovereign activity, a game of lords, with no purpose beyond itself—an *acte gratuit*. Bataille is full of sympathy for Gilles de Rais, whose "tragedy" consists in the misfortune of belonging to a "worn-out feudal world" that "put him on the shelf" and deprived the noble warrior of his exalted revelries.[61]

In Bataille's eyes, the genius of Gilles de Rais was his ability to turn his death into a grand spectacle. Since he could not live gloriously, he resolved to stage a sensational death. Such a death was possible because the public execution was still a "spectacle intended for the entertainment and anguish of the crowd."[62] And what is absolutely ingenious is that he managed to win the sympathy of the crowd, while Joan of Arc did not.

Bataille is sure that the paradoxical spectacle of the "repentant great lord" confessing his infamies must have dazzled those who witnessed it.[63] He is convinced that Gilles de Rais moved the crowd by his atrocities as much as by his nobility and grandeur—Bataille thinks that the two are intimately linked. Gilles de Rais combines the high and the low, the noble and base, the sacred and profane, the puritanical and erotic, pleasure and anguish, sex and death. By turning him into the legend of Bluebeard, the monster, Bataille suggests that we moderns deny the truth which the crowd that witnessed his death acknowledged—namely, that the infamous criminal is "like everyone in the crowd."[64] Everyone? What could he mean?

For Bataille, Gilles de Rais is like everyone in the crowd because he is the personification of the paradox, duality and contradiction—the "open wound" that is man. Man is subject and object, autonomy and unity, discontinuity and continuity, sin and atonement, sex and death. In short, man is *The Impossible!*[65] It is easy to see in this conception of man the Hegelian idea of alienation, diremption, insufficiency and incompleteness as well as the Hegelian longing for unity, oneness, and completion. But in Bataille's view, man's longing for oneness, completion, wholeness, and unity is possible only through death. History itself is testimony to the paradox. The historical project to eliminate duality and attain oneness has nearly led to the death of man.

What is true of history is also true of the individual, who is the microcosm of history. Only by putting an end to our existence as autonomous or "discontinuous" selves is it possible to become one with the totality of "continuous existence." And that, according to Bataille, is the reason we have both a horror and a fascination with death.[66] It is also the reason that causing death and witnessing death (as in the public execution) is pleasing: it allows one to identify with the victim and to experience the loss of self without actually dying. Bataille thinks that orgasm has the same appeal and that is why it is called *le petit mort*.[67] All this leads Bataille to the misguided conclusion that sexuality reaches unspeakable heights of ecstasy when it is combined with violence to the point of death. It also leads him to identify erotic criminality with religious mysticism. In the end, he is unable to distinguish between Gilles de Rais and Saint Theresa, who graces the cover of his book on *Eroticism, Death and Sensuality*.[68]

Instead of denouncing him as a monster, instead of ridiculing the Church for believing that his repentance was genuine, instead of pitying the gullible and ignorant crowd who prayed for him, Bataille valorizes Gilles de Rais. He regards him as a noble warrior who belonged to a golden age where war was a sovereign activity and an end in itself. He portrays him as the casualty of the ruthless march of reason in history. He celebrates his lust for carnage and brutality as the supreme characteristics of nobility. At the same time, Bataille paints Gilles de Rais as the personification of the paradox of humanity—the holy sinner who embodies the impossible tension that defines humanity, and that Bataille's perpetual negation is intended to preserve.[69]

Although Bataille was nostalgic for the Middle Ages, he did not think that a return to faith was possible. Nevertheless he thought that he could recapture the mysticism (now without God), the sacrilege (now without faith), the depth (now without meaning), and the ecstasy (now without joy) that gave religious life its intensity.

CONCLUSION AND CRITICISM

In summary, Bataille's philosophical saga is from beginning to end a response to Kojève. Starting from Kojève's assumptions regarding the nature of man and the course of history, Bataille drew the logical conclusions. In the dawn of history, man manifests his superiority to animals by his sovereign and altogether purposeless *negation*. But ironically and tragically, the triumph over nature has been so colossal that the *struggle* that defined man is no longer necessary. Nevertheless, Bataille denies that man is dead, he thinks that man has been castrated. The problem is to find a way to give man back his lost virility. If manhood is rooted in negativity, then a new movement of negation, refusal, or revolt is necessary to insure the vitality of man. However, the new negativity cannot be directed at nature, since the latter has been totally subjugated. Negativity must now be directed at civilization itself. Bataille therefore portrays everything prohibited by modern civilization (even excrement)[70] as a natural flower that has been ruthlessly crushed, vanquished, subjugated, and repressed—then he sets out to rescue the beleaguered. There is a certain romanticism in this motif. Like the romantics, Bataille abhors reason and its cold detachment; he believes that modern industrial civilization has invented everything drab, humdrum, and tedious; he fears the loss of fervor and intensity; and he hungers for a hidden nature that is passionate and rich. However, the nature that Bataille reveals is full of horrors. Bataille's is a dark romanticism and an inverted gnosticism. Revealing the darkness hidden in the midst of light is not enough to invest life with passion, significance, and intensity; Bataille thinks that only *perpetual negation* and ceaseless overturning can preserve the vitality of life. Only conflict, contradiction, and duality can preserve the spice of the dialectic. Only an endless cycle of prohibition and licentiousness, saintliness and sin, taboo and transgression, sobriety and intoxication can express the impossible paradox of humanity and save the world from stagnation.

It is not difficult to sympathize with Bataille's disenchantment with the mechanization and routinization of life in modern society. Nor is it difficult to share Bataille's love of life's exuberance and vitality. But despite its imaginative energy and its beguilements, Bataille's thinking is seriously flawed. I will argue that Bataille's philosophy has the effect of undermining precisely that which he holds in the highest esteem. I will make four criticisms as follows.

First, instead of jettisoning the instrumentalism of modernity, Bataille succumbs to a crude form of means/ends rationality. Bataille's celebration of everything useless, wasteful, and sovereign is itself dependent on the utilitarian distinction between means and ends. I think that Bataille is right in thinking that we cannot understand a civilization unless we focus on that which it values above all else. However, this understanding is not best served by relying on the utilitarian categories of means and ends or associating production with the means and consumption with the ends. What a civilization holds in high esteem is usually *a way of life*, which cannot be understood as a thing intended to be consumed. Understood as that which is wasted or consumed, an end is reduced to a static or given thing to which all life, action and energy are mere means. Contrary to what Bataille thinks, the ends of a civilization are not cathedrals, ornaments, and idle monks. If the end is understood as a way of life, then it cannot be absolutely distinguished from the means necessary to achieve it. In other words, *means* are often constitutive of the ends that they supposedly serve. Bataille's preoccupation with the means/end distinction reveals the extent to which he is subject to the very modes of thought that he dearly wishes to escape. Besides, his conception of sovereignty is absolutely arbitrary. He pronounces whatever he likes to be sovereign, and when it loses favor, he decides that it had a purpose after all, and denounces it. So, even though he declared that war was one of the supremely sovereign activities of man, he surmised that the violence of the fascists was not sovereign enough, and that the wars of bourgeois civilization were intended only to avoid stockpiling.

Second, instead of promoting man's freedom and autonomy, Bataille's philosophy celebrates the total servility of man to the impersonal forces of nature. The key to Bataille's way of thinking rests in his conception of life and its vitality; for it is in light of the latter that he judges modernity to be stagnant, castrated, and deathlike. For all his "abhorrence of nature," Bataille uses nature as the model of *human* life and vitality. For Bataille, life is a "tumultuous movement that bursts forth and consumes itself," an "effusion" that is "completely contrary to equilibrium, to stability."[71] Life is exuberant, lavish, magnificent, and completely "untouched by the defilement of merit or intention."[72] Life is a "perpetual explosion" that requires that the "spent organisms give way to new ones, which enter the dance with new forces." Life is a "costly process" exemplified by "expenditures that are finally excessive."[73] Death illustrates the ruinous extravagance of life. Life is a fantastic expenditure of energy toward a summit that is not. Life has no purpose other than death or nothingness. In the context of the "general economy," which has absolutely nothing to do with producing at the least expense, death is the ultimate "luxury." It is a testimony to the sovereignty of life—an expenditure without purpose or utility. Besides, death makes room for new life, and in so doing, accounts for "the youth of the world."[74] It is the secret to the ceaseless prodigality and splendor of nature. And far from lamenting this world of nature as our "accursed share," Bataille bids us embrace and emulate it.

Bataille's vision of life is the model he uses to understand sexuality, civilization, history, and his own inner psychic torments. All these phenomena are subject to the same laws of nature, the laws of the "general economy." Sexual eroticism is a microcosmic enactment of nature—it is an outlandish expenditure of energy toward a summit that is nothing. By the same token, every civilization (except modern industrial civilization) is defined by ruinously wasteful expenditures—human sacrifices, conquests, monks, monasteries, and Gothic cathedrals. The human psyche itself mirrors the paradoxical nature of life: man longs for a Dionysian loss of individuation and a oneness of being that is possible only in death. History follows the same laws of the "general economy"—it is nothing more than a costly effort to reach a summit that is the death of man.

Despite his efforts to establish a distance between man and nature, a distance intended to underscore man's freedom from the impersonal and instinctive forces of nature, Bataille ends up using nature as the model of human life and freedom. Bataille's work on eroticism, history, and civilization succeeds merely in illustrating that the laws of the "general economy" to which nature is subject are also the laws to which human life and history are equally subservient. Far from understanding man (properly so-called) as distinct from nature and animality, Bataille reduces him to a manifestation of the same tumultuous laws of the "general economy."

Third, Bataille intended to celebrate life, but he ends up glorifying death instead. Bataille's longing for self-abnegation and mortification as well as his thirst for death and annihilation is radically contrary to a joyful and exuberant celebration of life. Bataille's atheistic mysticism, if it makes any sense, must be deemed the worst of all possible worlds because it combines the nihilism and meaninglessness of atheism with the self-abnegation and mortification to which theism is inclined.[75]

Fourth, Bataille was determined to replace the cold indifference of modernity with a profound, even violent intensification of life. He experienced the modern world as a living death from which he needed to be rescued. He thought that only a cycle of extremes could dispel the spiritual and emotional vacuum from which he suffered. He believed that he could give life a renewed vitality by embarking on a program of perpetual negation and ceaseless overturning. However, Bataille's means frustrate his ends. Instead of magnifying the vitality and intensity of life, Bataille's strategy of perpetual negation incites a cold nihilism and a profound indifference. Bataille's literary work is a case in point. His novels often read like scripts for grade B horror films. The latter try to terrify their audience, but elicit laughter instead. By the same token, Bataille's efforts fail to arouse our archaic horror, provoke a feverish delirium, or simulate a sense of sacrilege. Instead of driving us to distraction, Bataille's literary work deadens the senses. For it is difficult be morally horrified by characters whose conduct is as arbitrary or as "sovereign" as bolts of lightning.

In conclusion, it is my contention that Bataille is the father of postmodernism. First, he has bequeathed to postmodernism a Dionysian madness rooted in the abhorrence of reason. Following Bataille, postmodern writers like Foucault believe that all the drabness and homogeneity of modern life has its source in an excess of rationality, order, and restraint. Accordingly, they follow Bataille in urging man to "escape from his head" like a condemned man from a prison.[76] Second, postmodernism owes a great deal to Bataille's use of gnostic as well as romantic motifs. The alluring power of postmodernism lies in its capacity to pose as the liberator of what has been hidden, repressed, vanquished, and downtrodden. Third, Bataille has bequeathed to postmodernism an appetite for endless negation and "ceaseless overturning." Starting from Kojève's assumption that negativity is the distinctive and glorious quality of man, Bataille reached the logical conclusion that negativity must be celebrated. What are postmodernism and its projects of genealogy and deconstruction if not a perpetual negation and unmasking of *the given*— the "hegemonic" or "logocentric" discourse, *whatever it may be.* In politics as in thought, the postmodern ethos consists of negation for the sake of negation and revolt for the sake of revolt. This explains the self-contradictory and self-refuting character of the postmodern enterprise. Like Bataille, postmodernism affirms only the exhilaration of unmasking and overturning, and it assumes that perpetual negation will empower and revitalize a drab and homogeneous world. But in the end, postmodernism is bound to succumb to the same fate as Bataille's literary efforts: instead of a heightened sense of vitality, intensity, and exhilaration, it will engender only indifference, numbness, and nihilism.

9

Foucault's *Folie*

Postmodernity is the latest chapter in the history of Western civilization. It is born out of a profound disenchantment with modernity. Foucault is the leading figure of this new epoch because he articulates this disenchantment while offering a small glimmer of hope in the possibility of a new dawn. But despite the widespread dissemination of his work and the enormity of the secondary literature devoted to its study, the heart of Foucault's philosophy remains obscure, enigmatic, and self-refuting. It is my contention that recognizing the debt Foucault owes to Kojève and Bataille will shed new light on his philosophical enterprise and on postmodernism in general.

In what follows, I will show that Foucault's conception of modernity as the grim and guileful tyranny of reason is vintage Kojève. Foucault's disturbing account of the rise of disciplinary power bears a remarkable similarity to Kojève's universal and homogeneous state, the death of man, and the onslaught of animality. Foucault shares Kojève's view of reason as cold, arid, homogenizing, and normalizing. He also shares Kojève's view that reason is an ally of the animalistic, the biological, and the necessary as opposed to the human, surprising, spontaneous, and free. But like Bataille, Foucault is not willing to accept the victory of reason as definitive or irreversible. He is determined to fight against this global tyranny even though he is pessimistic about the chances of success. He wages a war not in the name of truth and justice, but in the name of freedom. However, Foucault does not think of freedom as absence of external restraints or internal repressions. I will argue that Foucault shares Kojève and Bataille's conception of freedom as negativity or transgression. I believe that Foucault has no positive recommendations because he shared

Bataille's assumption that only a program of perpetual negation and ceaseless overturning can revitalize the world and give life the intensity and significance it once had. And far from being the liberator he is believed to be, Foucault longs for the forms of power that make transgression glorious.

THE HOMOGENEOUS WORLD OF DISCIPLINARY POWER

Since the dawn of the Age of Reason, or the "classical age" as Foucault likes to call the Enlightenment, a type of power, hitherto unknown, has been steadily gaining strength. Foucault refers to the new power as *disciplinary power* and contrasts it with *sovereign power,* which is the form that power has generally assumed before the "classical age." Sovereign power was overt, conspicuous, pompous, and grand. Moreover, it did not shy away from displaying itself in all its lavish and extravagant grandeur. It had all the qualities of Bataille's concept of the "sovereign." Foucault portrays sovereign power dramatically in his *Discipline and Punish.* He argues that the public execution was one of the occasions for the display of sovereignty.[1] According to Foucault, public executions were not intended primarily to serve justice, but to display the power of the sovereign. The punishment was not intended to expiate the crime, but to reinforce sovereign power and underscore its total freedom—its arbitrary and gratuitous character. Since the crime was an affront to the sovereign, the sovereign was free to suspend both the law and vengeance with a *pardon* delivered dramatically at the eleventh hour. These pardons were often received with cries of "God save the King!" In this way, sovereign power sought renewal in the very act of displaying itself as a superpower.

Sovereign power inspired awe and terror precisely because it allied itself with *death.* The "spectacle of the scaffold" and its terror were its distinguishing marks.[2] Knowing that the sovereign did not shrink from atrocities struck fear into the hearts of the subjects. Foucault's harrowing description of the public execution of the would-be regicide, Damiens, is meant to show that sovereign power did not shrink from gratuitous and altogether unnecessary cruelty.

Despite its horrors, sovereign power was limited in scope. First, it could act only on the body of the accused and not on the mind, the passions, and the desires. Second, sovereign power was dependent on the consent or support of its subjects. The public execution gave people the opportunity to give their support to the sovereign power or to withhold that support and revolt.[3] In the context of sovereign power, transgression was possible. Third, the people still had the power to determine what would pass for truth. They could transform a criminal into a hero and a crime into a great deed. They could delay the executioner, pretend a pardon was on the way, and eventually compel the sovereign to grant a pardon. In this way, they could turn the guilty into the innocent. And so, they remained makers of truth and therefore the proprietors of power, and not just its victims.

Although it has not disappeared, sovereign power has lost its monopoly of power in modern society. Side by side with sovereign power, a new form of power, *disciplinary power*, has emerged. Unlike sovereign power, disciplinary power is not pompous or grand, overt or conspicuous, terrible or terrifying. The new power is silent, unobtrusive, covert, and clandestine. It may *look* less awesome, but appearances are deceptive. It may *seem* less terrible, but it is more vigilant. For it is "possessed of highly specific procedural techniques, completely novel instruments, quite different apparatuses."[4] The success of the new power lies in the fact that its locus of operation is not centralized or concentrated (like sovereign power), but diffused. Unlike sovereign power, the new power is widely dispersed and operates on many different fronts. Its "polymorphous techniques of subjugation" are located in a great variety of "micro-powers."[5]

Like any other power, disciplinary power has generated its own "discourse of truth," which gives it legitimacy and support. Just as sovereign power had generated its own "discourse of right" based on law, so disciplinary power has generated its own "discourse of normalization," based on the idea of a *norm*. The discourse of normalization is the discourse of science. This is the secret of the success and authority of the new power. Science is the handmaid of disciplinary power and accounts for its ability to homogenize, medicalize, and routinize our lives with our consent. It tells us what is normal and abnormal, healthy and unhealthy, sane and insane. The new power has therefore staked out new "territories," which were inaccessible to sovereign power—like madness, punishment, and sexuality. Disciplinary power has medicalized these aspects of life and turned them into objects of science. What is so dreadful about disciplinary power is that it is totalitarian, which is to say that it regards every aspect of life—social, cultural, economic, and biological—as its rightful domain of control and surveillance.[6] This extensive control over the populace and the territory requires a detailed knowledge of citizens, their productivity, their incomes, their employment, their skills, their marriages, their divorces, their birth rates, their diseases, their delinquencies, their accidents, their gerontology, and their deaths. The new "savoir" is the basis of a new tyranny—a tyranny of reason and science.[7]

The secret to the success of the new power is its "positivity." While sovereign power operates by prohibiting and punishing, disciplinary power induces pleasures and incites desires. Instead of saying no, it says yes. Instead of relying on terror and the fear of death, disciplinary power resorts to psychology. And, instead of allying itself with death and terror, it has allied itself with *life* and *productivity*. This new power is not "sovereign" in Bataille's sense of the word because it has abandoned its "murderous splendor" in favor of the values of life and utility.[8] Its objective is "life" understood as the "basic" biological needs of man.[9] This is a familiar refrain that echoes Kojève and Bataille's portrayal of modernity as a return to the biological and animalistic.

Foucault paints the new bio-power in the most sinister terms. Bio-power seeks to manipulate and control life understood as populations, demographics, diseases, diets, and gerontology This power must "deploy" sexuality for its ends. Foucault points to a racist element in this preoccupation with biology. He comments that it is ironic that the Nazis who were so interested in bio-power never discovered the importance of "deploying sexuality" as a mechanism of power. Instead, they transformed the "blood myth" into a "bloodbath."[10] In other words, disciplinary power succeeds where the Nazis failed.[11]

Dedicated as it is to the control of the biological stuff within its jurisdiction, bio-power must gain access to the sexual lives of its population. But sex cannot be drawn into the sphere of power if it remains hidden. Bio-power therefore resolves to seek it out, track it down, and rob it of all its secrets, mysteries, and hiding places. Medicine and psychoanalysis lend themselves to the task. Together they make sex into a question of hygiene, medicine, and mental health. They initiate a plethora of discourses about sex. They study its every detail and leave it no "respite." And as if that were not sufficient, they force it to speak. Secularizing the methods of the Catholic confessional, the psychoanalyst replaces the priest and forces sex to confess, on the pretext that the truth will cure. Foucault explains that this is why we live in a society that never stops talking about sex while exploiting it as the "secret" that it once was.

HOW SEX WAS RUINED

The case of the hermaphrodite Hurculine Barbin is an excellent illustration of the effects and the tactics of bio-power on the erotic life of man. Foucault claims to have discovered the memoirs as well as the medical reports of a hermaphrodite of the "classical age."[12] The memoirs are written in a style that is so gripping, polished, and accomplished that there has been some suspicion that Foucault has written them himself. But no matter. The story is quite plausible. It is about a girl whose whole life is spent among girls in a convent school, later as a lady's maid, then as a school mistress. She grew up among women in a world where the sexes were radically segregated. Upon puberty, when her companions were starting to blossom into womanhood, Hurculine remained flat-chested, did not menstruate, and became noticeably hairier than her schoolmates. Medications were to no avail. Later, as headmistress of a girl's school, Hurculine's friendship and affection for her colleague Sara turns into a great passion. Hurculine and Sara have a secret sexual affair for two years in which Sara begins to refer to Hurculine as *"mon cher."* But the secrecy is intolerable, besides which Hurculine has bad pains in the groin. Forced to see a doctor, Hurculine's secret is discovered. A scandal ensues and Sara's reputation as well as the school's is ruined. Hurculine must now acquire a new legal identity as a man. She would have loved to marry Sara and be her husband, but she is perceived as someone who has betrayed everyone's trust and has taken advantage of her position. Hurculine is thrown into a new life among men in a man's world. Unable to gain employment, ridiculed and treated harshly, Hurculine finds life intolerable and commits suicide. The memoirs have a lusty flavor and read like a Gothic novel filled with a forbidden sexuality that is intensified by the convent setting. The effect would no doubt have pleased Bataille.

The story is significant for Foucault as an illustration of the effects of scientism on the world. Foucault believes that in the Middle Ages, it was the responsibility of the father or godfather who named the child upon baptism to determine its sex in those cases where the two sexes are juxtaposed in some proportion or other. But later, when it was time to marry, hermaphrodites were free to choose if they wished to remain as the sex designated to them upon baptism or to change. But, whatever they chose, they had to stick with it on pain of being declared sodomites. Foucault is certain that hermaphrodites were not persecuted in the Middle Ages, unless they were suspected of sodomy. But with the ascendancy of disciplinary power, the freedom of the Middle Ages disappeared. Scientists and medics took over. They decided that there is no such thing as hermaphroditism—no doubt because it was antithetical to their lust for defining, classifying, and formulating. They declared that there is always a "true sex" that they, the medical experts, alone can determine. To Foucault, this is a classic example of the domination of the scientific instinct, and reveals the extent to which the "will to knowledge" is an unsurpassed will to power. Nothing escapes the gaze of this new *savoir* that refuses to leave anything undefined, "indeterminate," and free.[13]

According to Foucault, sex was a sphere that was shrouded in darkness, and this very fact lent it a degree of freedom that disappeared under the relentless gaze of disciplinary society. Sex was not a domain accessible to sovereign power. Foucault's *History of Sexuality* is meant to give us a glimpse of how disciplinary power has brought its new techniques of control to bear on sexuality and how it has ruined it in the process.

Foucault's *History of Sexuality* mirrors Bataille's *History of Eroticism* in several important ways. Like Bataille, Foucault believes that sex is an eternal domain of prohibitions. And like Bataille, he thinks that the erotic, secretive, and exciting aspect of sex is the invention of society. This is what he means by asserting that sex is not some natural force that exists prior to law, but is "constituted" by the law. In other words, sex is a "historical construct" or the invention of society.[14] Bataille put it more clearly when he distinguished between sex and eroticism, saying that while the former belongs to nature and animality, the latter belongs to man and is constituted by society, its prohibitions, and the transgressions it invites. The medicalization of sex exposes it to the light of day and undermines its secretive and transgressive quality. In complete agreement with Bataille, Foucault asserts that sexuality knew its "greatest felicity of expression" in the Christian world of sin.[15]

Foucault's popularity is intimately connected to the fact that he poses as a liberator and is understood as such by his admirers. His work has a sense of mission and urgency. Nothing short of our salvation seems to be at stake. And even though Foucault wishes to break the spell of disciplinary power, he denies that freedom from power is possible. I will argue that contrary to what his admirers believe, Foucault has no program of liberation in any of the usual senses of the term. Nor was his life inspired by a Nietzschean quest for self-discovery, as his recent biographer James Miller has claimed.[16]

If Foucault is interested in freedom, it is freedom understood as transgression, or the capacity to negate the given. The trouble with disciplinary power is that its dominion is not overt enough to leave room for transgression. Foucault's discovery of the "positivity of power" is not glad tidings. On the contrary, the positivity of disciplinary power is what makes it so difficult to overturn. The triumph of reason and science has managed to silence opposition. Foucault therefore sets out to liberate the "subjugated knowledges" and restore the dualism necessary for transgression and negativity.

THE CELEBRATION OF MADNESS

Foucault portrays the triumph of disciplinary power as the ineluctable outcome of the absolute and uncompromising victory of reason—cold, technical, and glum. The cost is our humanity—we are destitute of spirit, divested of madness, and robbed of desire. Everything glorious, resplendent, mysterious, splendid, satanic, and sublime has been banished or silenced. Foucault's analysis of modernity in terms of disciplinary power is one more Bosch-like image to add to a now famous collection. Modern men are "last men," trapped in an "iron cage," suffering from a "mechanized petrifaction," normalized, homogenized, and animalized, deaf to the "call of Being," and lost in the "night of the world." All this is the result of a deadly devotion to reason, knowledge, and truth.[17] There is in this demonization of reason a subtle glorification of madness.

Foucault is a case in point. His demonization of reason brings him dangerously close to the celebration of madness and even crime. Madness is one of the "subjugated knowledges" that he aims to liberate. In *Madness and Civilization* Foucault laments the eclipse of madness by reason. He maintains that the Renaissance gave madness its rightful place as a manifestation of that part of the human soul that, after Freud, came to be called the unconscious. As the representatives of that dark, mysterious, hidden, and inscrutable part of the soul, the mad were regarded with fear and reverence as representatives of a world that beckons all of us. The paintings of Hieronymus Bosch, Mathias Grünewald, Stephan Lochner, Albrecht Dürer, and others served to dignify madness and give it legitimacy.[18] In contrast, the age of reason seeks out the mad, confines them to hospitals, and entrusts them to physicians. There are no madmen anymore—only the mentally ill. Foucault paints the classical age as a monologue of reason about madness—a monologue called psychiatry. True to its character, the classical age banishes from the world everything mysterious and sublime—it outlaws both God and the Devil. Religious men who are dismayed with the spiritual wasteland of secular society regard Foucault as an ally. But those who embrace him fail to understand that Foucault is on the side of all subjugated knowledges and does not prefer God to the Devil. Like Bataille, he likes both.

Despite his claims to the contrary, Foucault's philosophy has an activist side, even though it cannot be called an ethic. Nevertheless, it tells us subtly what we *must* do if we hope to break out of the spell of disciplinary power and its rationalism. The subtle message is that we must exalt the wild, mad, violent, dark, deranged, distraught, and demented. It behooves us to unleash our wildest passions, become unbridled, unruly, and unhinged. The romantic excesses of postmodernism is one of the sources of its appeal.

THE TRANSGRESSIONS OF PIERRE RIVIÈRE

Foucault's attraction to madness, even madness that ends in crime, is particularly evident in his study of Pierre Rivière, a nineteenth-century parricide, whose memoir was published by Foucault, along with detailed reports of the trial.[19] This is a story of a young man who slaughtered his pregnant mother, his sister, and his brother, in cold blood—with an axe. The trial was of particular interest to Foucault because it came at a time when psychologists and psychiatrists were beginning to exert a significant influence on the law and the courts. The defense maintained that Pierre Rivière was mad, at least when he committed the crime, and therefore could not be held responsible for his crimes. The jury condemned him to death, but his sentence was later commuted. Rivière committed suicide in jail. What is peculiar about the case is the fact that Rivière wrote a very long, detailed, and articulate memoir in which he gave details of his life and the reasons for his crime. The memoir reveals that Rivière's crime was not a function of passion or madness and that he knew exactly what he was doing and was willing to accept his own death as the consequence of his crime. The memoir does not read like the incoherent ravings of a madman, even though it contains a gruesome logic.

Rivière explains that his crime was intended to liberate his father from the countless humiliations and incessant torments to which his willful and capricious wife (Rivière's mother) had subjected him for years. Even more interesting is the fact that Rivière considered his mother to be the representative of a new world order in which Woman ruled supreme, and in which men were the helpless victims of endless caprices, persecutions, and torments. So, in liberating his father from the tyranny of his mother, Rivière imagined that he was liberating the world from the tyranny of Woman. And he was willing to die in order to accomplish his self-appointed mission of world salvation.

Foucault objects to those psychiatrists who declared Rivière mad in their testimonies before the court. He argues convincingly that the manuscript left behind could not have been written by a mere imbecile. The memoir clearly reveals that Rivière knew what he was doing, and was willing to accept the consequences of his actions—his own death. I agree with Foucault that Rivière was entitled to be treated as one who was worthy of being held responsible for his actions. I think that Foucault is right in thinking that the defense of madness belittles a man. But, Foucault goes much further.

On behalf of Rivière, Foucault protests that in declaring Rivière to be mad, the court has silenced an act of protest against the regime of reason. By dismissing him as a madman, the court divested all his actions of their significance. By placing his actions outside the domain of sanity, the regime of reason makes Rivière's actions null and void. In this way, the regime emasculates, disempowers, and disarms all its critics. No doubt, Foucault regards this as a ruse of reason. Rivière's view of the world is remarkably similar to Foucault's. For Rivière as for Foucault, the "post-revolutionary order" may appear soft, feminine, and compassionate, but its despotic tyranny is more cunning than anything man has ever encountered before.

Foucault does not focus on the event as a *murder*, but as a *protest*—not an act of killing, but an act of dying and sacrificing. Foucault asserts that Rivière was deprived of the "glory" he sought by "risking his life"—the glory to which he was entitled. Foucault argues that Rivière risked his life and that such a risk is a route to glory from which modernity deprives men like Rivière.

There is no doubt that there are circumstances under which risking one's life is glorious. But risking one's life (i.e., accepting the inevitable punishment of the law) by killing one's mother in cold blood is not one of them—not even if a memoir identifies the mother with the new and wildly tyrannical regime of Woman. Such identification is madness, even if it is not the madness of one who cannot be responsible for his deeds.

Foucault's study of Pierre Rivière mirrors Bataille's study of Gilles de Rais. Both writers are impressed with the enormity of the transgressions involved. Both writers regard their criminals as representing a noble world that has been crushed by the juggernaut of reason. Both writers see the crimes as legitimate protests against a world that deprives men of their sovereignty and their manhood. These works are part of a genre that includes Jean-Paul Sartre's veneration of Jean Genet.[20] They are all intended as protests against the effeminization of the world, or the triumph of the feminine principle in Kojève's historical drama.

THERE IS NO TRUTH

The central philosophical unfoundation of Foucault's theoretical edifice is the insistence that there is no truth, only fictions, no text, only interpretations, no reality, no good or evil, only constructions of power. The objections to this Nietzschean epistemology are familiar. If there is no truth, then how can Foucault pretend to tell us so much about the world? If there is no truth, then what is the status of Foucault's famous "histories"? If all claims to truth are products of power, then Foucault's own philosophy must be a manifestation of the will to power.

It is my contention that all these objections miss the mark when they are directed at Foucault, just as they did when they were directed at Nietzsche. These criticisms disqualify and silence the speakers. But the tactic is a failure as is evidenced by the enormous popularity of Nietzsche and Foucault.[21]

The claim that there is no such thing as a truth independent of our constructions is not necessarily a denial of the existence of an independent world. Rather, the point is that whatever this reality is, it is inconsequential, uninteresting, or animalistic. In contrast, the human world, the world in which we live, is always a world of our own making, an arbitrary construction of the imagination, and a testimony to our own will to power. The truth about man is that he is a creature without a truth, without a fixed or given identity—he is a no-thing. Man is his own project; he makes himself by his prohibitions and his transgressions.

Traditional philosophy as it has been practiced in the West has wrongly assumed that there is an Archimedean point from which the philosopher can examine the world and give us an impartial account; it has wrongly assumed that the philosopher has a privileged perspective. But on the Nietzschean epistemology, philosophy is itself a manifestation of the will to power. This discovery means that philosophy as we have known it in the West must come to an end. It can no longer ask the simple question: what is truth? It must ask: what is the relation between power and the production of truth? Philosophy must turn its analytical powers against itself, it must dissect itself. There is nothing contradictory in this view. It does not exempt itself from the fate it inflicts on all other philosophies. It is quite willing to consider any picture of the world it may offer as a fiction, a fabrication or a construction and not a given or objective reality. It is quite willing to consider any recommendations it makes about how we should live and what we ought to do as its own aesthetic preferences and not inviolable moral truths. And it is quite willing to dissect itself and its own relation to the powers that be. There is no doubt that Foucault has made a significant contribution to this Nietzschean mode of philosophizing.

POWER AND TRUTH

Foucault is often misunderstood as a latter-day Thrasymachus who claims that those in power decide what will count for truth and justice. But his position is far more sophisticated. I would describe it as follows. Power generates truth or a "discourse of truth," which in turn lends support to the power that has generated it: it gives it legitimacy. But this generated truth is not a *mere* product of power or a slave of power. A discourse of truth, once it comes into being, has a vitality of its own that allows it to attain a distance from the very power that engendered it. Divesting itself of the servility of its birth, the new discourse can launch an attack on the existing order. Confronted with this unmistakable "power of truth," power retreats and devises new "strategies" compatible with the new discourse of truth. Finally, a new power or a new form of power emerges—a form of power legitimized by the new discourse. In this way, power creates truth *and* truth in turn creates power. The relation between power and truth is not a one-way street but a dialectical relation in which one engenders the other and the other in turn transfigures that which engendered it. This is what I think Foucault means by saying that the relation between power and truth is "spiral."[22]

Here is an example. In the sixteenth and seventeenth centuries, sovereign power generated a "discourse of right" intended to lend it support and give it legitimacy. This discourse of right was preoccupied with questions of legitimacy, jurisdiction, obligation, powers, rights, and laws.[23] Its effect was to legitimize sovereign power by providing reasons for obedience or inventing theories of obligation. Foucault has in mind the writings of James I, Jean Bodin, Robert Filmer, Thomas Hobbes, and John Locke. Even though the discourse of right was a product of sovereign power, it did not continue to be its slave. It has managed to acquire a power of its own, and in so doing, has launched an assault against absolute and unbridled sovereignty. But sovereign power did not simply collapse when it was confronted by its own discourse of right. It withdrew, but only to regroup its energies and reemerge in a new form compatible with the new discourse of right. The discourse of right succeeded in forcing sovereign power to submit to the laws it imposed on its subjects. In this way, absolute monarchy gave way to constitutional monarchy.

The discourse of right was therefore responsible for generating a new and more limited form of sovereign power. The relationship between power and truth (or reality and philosophy) is a "spiral" relationship, similar to the relationship between desire and prohibition, taboo and transgression.

GENEALOGY AS PERPETUAL NEGATION

Genealogy is a new discourse that lends itself to the project of perpetual negation by unmasking the constructions of power. Genealogy breaks with the methods and assumptions of traditional historiography in a way that is required by the Nietzschean epistemology. Nietzsche's *Genealogy of Morals* is the paradigm of this new type of history, and his *Use and Abuse of History* informs its theoretical underpinnings. It is easier to characterize genealogy negatively—by what it avoids or rejects rather than what it aspires to. Genealogy is not a simple search for origins. It does not seek the origin of present phenomena and practices in a pure and pristine past; it rejects the "distant ideality of the origin."[24] Genealogy does not try to explain phenomena in terms of a teleological beginning that unfolds and is realized in the course of its development. Nor does genealogy seek out the unifying thread that links different historical periods and events into a single narrative. What then is genealogy and to what does it aspire? Can it be characterized positively?

I think that one can safely say that genealogy, like traditional history, also seeks out origins. But it aspires to reveal something left unsaid by the old histories. It aspires to show that the origins are not natural embryonic beginnings that flower and take shape in the course of their development. Instead, it aspires to show that far from being natural, the origins are constructions; far from having embryonic beginnings, they appear on the scene full-blown; and far from being natural developments, they are surprising and totally unanticipated eruptions.

The effect of genealogy is to break with both the teleological or organic approach to history as well as the historicist or Hegelian approach. In contrast to the teleological approach, it rejects the idea of history as an organic development from a natural, pure, and pristine beginning toward fulfillment and completion ending in decline and death. Moreover, it rejects the Hegelian, historicist, or rationalist approach according to which history is the progressive triumph of reason in the world. The effect of genealogy is to underscore the surprising, arbitrary, free, or gratuitous quality of human history.

In "Nietzsche, Genealogy, History," Foucault shows how Nietzsche's three kinds of history—*monumental, antiquarian,* and *critical,* are meta-morphosed into three aspects of genealogy. *Monumental* history erects monuments to the great ones of the past; it is history done in the style of Polybius and Machiavelli. Nietzsche approves of this kind of history insofar as it celebrates greatness, and in so doing, inspires life in the present. Nietzsche counsels those who would be great: "feast your eyes on Plutarch and dare to believe in yourself when you believe in his heroes," he bids us.[25] By the same token, Nietzsche worries that monumental history can become debilitating or paralyze action in the present by painting the past so gloriously that nothing in the present can possibly compare—like the golden hips of Pythagoras. We have seen that this is precisely the problem of Kojève's legacy—he has turned history into a monument relative to which life in the present is meaningless. When this happens, then the spell of the past can only be broken by transfiguring monumental history into *parody.* This is precisely what Foucault accomplishes. Foucault's genealogies parody the past, unmask it, and laugh at its self-proclaimed greatness and at its monuments. However, genealogy does not set out to reveal the truth behind the mask, since it denies that there is a truth, at least one that is worth knowing. History is nothing more, and nothing less, than a world of masks. The object of the genealogist enterprise is to study the masks, their beauty, their ugliness, their effects, and their purposes.

The second type of history identified by Nietzsche is *antiquarian* history. The latter seeks to preserve the past by endowing everything ancient with a special worth and inviolability. The antiquarian reveres the past and looks upon it with love and trust. The advantage of this type of history is that it provides comfort in the "daily round of toil" and it makes it easier to bear the drab and painful conditions of life because the venerable ancestors also lived on the same "bare mountainside." Antiquarian history is conservative since it serves as an antidote to "restless cosmopolitanism" and the "unceasing desire for novelty."[26] The danger of this approach to history is that it might come to regard everything old and moldy as "equally venerable" and every "new spirit" as a foe. In so doing, "it hinders the mighty impulse to a new deed and paralyses the doer."[27] The undisputed triumph of disciplinary power results in an equally stagnant and eternally fossilized world that shuns every new spirit as an enemy. Given this state of affairs, genealogy must undo the damage by metamorphosing antiquarian history into what Foucault calls dissociation. This means that instead of seeking continuity, sameness, or a link between the present and the past, genealogy must uncover discontinuity, differences, new eruptions, and surprising beginnings. And by unmasking the dominant order, it also *invites* new beginnings. The third type of history identified by Nietzsche is *critical*. The latter judges and condemns the past. Nietzsche thinks that every past deserves condemning because "life and injustice are one." But he also thinks that a certain "forgetfulness" is necessary for life. He intimates that if we dwell upon the injustices of the past, we will become bitter and forfeit all the opportunities and the good fortune of life in the present. Foucault rejects critical history insofar as it assumes that it is possible to have access to a truth independent of history. Accordingly, he transfigures critical history into a relentless examination of the knowing subject. Critique turns on itself. The will to knowledge ends in the destruction of the knowing subject. It ends in self-destruction. We can say that the fate of man in the history of the West mirrors the fate of Oedipus. Having solved the riddle of the Sphinx, Oedipus brings destruction on himself and his city.

Foucault regards his histories of medicine, punishment, madness, and sexuality as "genealogies." They seek out discontinuities and uncover strange, new, and surprising beginnings.[28] They illustrate that the Enlightenment is a watershed, a break with everything that went before. They unmask the triumph of reason and reveal it as an arbitrary construction and a manifestation of the will to power. But unlike any other "eruption" in history, this particular one will be difficult if not impossible to expose, to unseat, and to make way for a new beginning. The reason for the difficulty lies not only in the insidious nature of the new power, but in the crippled condition of the knowing subject. The latter can no longer criticize in the name of truth, goodness, justice, or freedom.

Genealogy spells the death of philosophy as we know it. Now that the philosophical subject has been shattered, philosophy has reached its limit and has reduced itself to silence. One cannot help thinking of the silence of a self-proclaimed sage like Kojève. But postmodernism is not satisfied with this silence. On the contrary, it is determined to break the silence by reinventing philosophy in a new form and giving it a new language and a new voice. Even though he acknowledges that philosophy is a "multiple desert," Foucault denies that it is dead. On the contrary, he believes that the "freshness of its experience" has not been lost even though it has been "divested" of the language that was "natural" to it and rendered speechless. In his eulogy to Bataille, Foucault looks to him as "exemplary" of the new voice that will break the silence of post-history.[29]

CONCLUSION

My thesis is that Foucault's disciplinary society is a version of Kojève's end of history and the animalization of man. Disciplinary power homogenizes, routinizes, and normalizes the world. Its devotion to biological life instead of death marks the triumph of the feminine principle that Rivière rightly identified as the rule of Woman. This new order threatens to bring about the death of man. Foucault shares Kojève and Bataille's conception of man as a being who negates the given, risks life, flirts with death, and acts in a way that is altogether surprising, unpredictable, and exhilarating. Foucault's genealogical unmasking of disciplinary power is intended to destroy the latter and invite a new beginning. However, this is no reason to think of Foucault as a liberator. Freedom from power is not possible, since man is always constituted by power understood as the limits arbitrarily imposed on his conduct. In the absence of such limits, transgression or negation is impossible. And far from abolishing the "limit" that it transgresses, transgression affirms it. In the past, God provided that limit. But now that God is dead, man must create his own limits and his own mortifications of the flesh.

Foucault is not the liberator his admirers take him to be. The only freedom that Foucault aspired to was the exhilaration of transgression, perpetual negation, and ceaseless overturning. These latter require overt, obtrusive, and repressive forms of power that set severe limits. What is needed is a form of power that allies itself with death and terror. The transgression of such a deadly power is heroic and glorious because it involves the *risk of life*. But alas, disciplinary power turns transgression into an illness to be pitied. It therefore robs us of the glory of transgression—as the case of Pierre Rivière illustrates. Moreover, the medicalization of sexuality robs us of the raptures of the forbidden; and the devotion to biological life robs us of the terror and anguish of death. Foucault is not an enemy of power. On the contrary, he longs for the forms of power that make transgression perilous and glorious—the forms of power that intensify life and experience. Foucault longs for a world of taboos and prohibitions without which man lives like an animal in the bosom of nature.[30]

Kojève's picture of the modern world is the foundation of Foucault's postmodernism. Foucault begins with Kojève's assumptions about man and the world. He begins with the assumption that man's freedom rests in his negativity and that the modern world gives him nothing to negate. The reason for this belief is that man's negativity originally stemmed from the fact that the world fell short of what reason demanded. But modernity is the incarnation of reason. The march of reason in history has ended in a universal tyranny that is soft, feminine, and unobtrusive, yet totalitarian and complete. This is the ultimate tyranny—a global tyranny, a tyranny without a tyrant and without the overt signs of masculine power, which have been associated with tyranny in the past. This new tyranny controls the mind and robs man of his appetite for negation. Man was accustomed to negating in the name of reason, its truth, and its justice; but modernity is the incarnation of reason, truth, and justice. Robbed of his negativity, man is castrated.

For Foucault as for Bataille, the task at hand is to restore man's virility. This can be done only by a program of perpetual negation and ceaseless overturning. Genealogy is meant to serve that task. Genealogy is not the death of philosophy, but its new incarnation. Philosophy was the motor of history and its negativity. But in the past, it negated only in the name of reason, its truth, and its justice. Now, it must negate the rational world order in the name of madness, crime, and everything that has been subjugated and crushed by the march of reason in history.

Part III

KOJÈVE'S INFLUENCE IN AMERICA

■ 10 □

Debate with Leo Strauss

Were it not for his nearly lifelong friendship with Leo Strauss, Kojève would have been unknown in North America. Strauss's students have been, and continue to be, instrumental in publishing Kojève's work in English translation.[1] Nowhere is Kojève's influence in America more apparent than in the work of disciples of Leo Strauss, such as Allan Bloom and Francis Fukuyama.

Kojève met Strauss in Berlin in the 1920's when both of them were engaged in the study of religious thought.[2] In 1929, Kojève moved to Paris, and in 1932 Strauss went to Paris on a Rockefeller Fellowship. In that year, Strauss and Kojève attended a seminar on Hegel's early religious writings offered by Alexandre Koyré at the École Pratique des Hautes Études.[3] Kojève and Strauss saw a great deal of each other in Paris until Strauss moved to England in 1934. They kept up their friendship through a long correspondence, which has recently been published.[4]

At first blush, the interest that Strauss took in Kojève's thought seems peculiar. The two men seemed to have hardly anything in common. Kojève was a Hegelian, Heideggerian, and Marxist—to Strauss, he was the personification of modernity. In contrast, Strauss was a self-proclaimed champion of ancient wisdom. A dialogue between Strauss and Kojève is therefore expected to be the quintessential model of the dialogue between ancients and moderns. This is precisely how Strauss's students have regarded it.[5]

In what follows, I will argue that the debate between Kojève and Strauss is much more interesting than the caricature above would allow. I believe that the debate can best be understood as a disagreement between a commissar and a superman in which the latter forces the former to accept the superior logic of his position. I will show that the disagreement between Kojève and Strauss has been highly exaggerated since the commissar and the superman are the same human type. I will divide the debate into two parts. The first part revolves on the connection between philosophy and tyranny. The second part focuses on the end of history. In the first part, Kojève scores some spectacular points against Strauss. But in the second and decisive part, Strauss emerges triumphant.

PHILOSOPHY AND TYRANNY

The occasion of the debate between Strauss and Kojève is Strauss's *On Tyranny*, which is a translation and commentary on Xenophon's *Hiero*. The latter is a dialogue between a tyrant, Hiero, and a wise man, Simonides. In the dialogue, Hiero confides in Simonides that even though he is all-powerful, he is unhappy. He tells Simonides that he is not even privy to the simplest pleasures of ordinary folk. He cannot enjoy the pleasures of eating and drinking without fear of being poisoned. He cannot enjoy the pleasures of traveling and sight-seeing without fear of being assassinated. And he cannot enjoy the pleasures of sexual love, even though he can have any boy or woman he fancies. It seems that the pleasures of love are not a matter of having whomever one desires, but of being desired in return. But the tyrant cannot know if his lovers admire him, or are just going along out of fear. The upshot of the matter is that the tyrant's pleasures are considerably less than those of ordinary citizens. The dialogue mirrors Plato's more eloquent account of the psychic torments of the tyrant in the *Republic*.

The *Hiero* is vintage Xenophon—which is to say that it is not particularly profound or philosophically sophisticated. However, Strauss believes that the dialogue contains the most explicit account of the Socratic teaching on tyranny—the "tyrannical teaching," as Strauss calls it.[6] This is a very dangerous doctrine that wise men ought not to state without the utmost caution and reserve. And in Strauss's estimation, Xenophon displays that "quiet grandeur" and "noble reserve" that makes him a genuine spokesman for ancient wisdom.[7] But in his commentary, Strauss, for all his reserve, brings the tyrannical teaching into full view. Strauss regards that teaching as the cornerstone of ancient wisdom. It is the view that tyranny, or rule independent of law, is the best form of government when exercised by the wise. It comes closest to being realized when those in power listen to the advice of wise men like Simonides.

As Strauss notes, Simonides's advice to the tyrant is much like Machiavelli's.[8] He advises Hiero to take bold steps and use "criminal" measures (at least in the short term) to achieve something grand and durable that would benefit his city and crown him with glory. Hiero soon realizes that Simonides is not what he appears to be—he is not a silly poet with his head in the clouds. He is a "hardboiled" man who could be dangerous. Hiero therefore proceeds to exaggerate the miseries of the tyrannical life.[9]

For Strauss, the key to understanding the dialogue, as well as the key to understanding ancient wisdom, is to grasp the "hierarchy of beings" at its core.[10] According to Strauss, the dispute between Hiero and Simonides is about their relative standing in this hierarchy. Hiero thinks that he, the man of action, is the "real man." But Simonides thinks that he is the most "divine" human type.[11] Needless to say, Strauss agrees with Simonides against Hiero. But Strauss does not simply dismiss Hiero's claim to greatness. He believes that Hiero is a "real man" when compared either to "gentlemen" or to the ordinary folk who seek wealth and pleasure. Strauss admires the tyrant's quest for glory as a manifestation of the "aristocratic virtues" that have disappeared from the modern world.

The man of thought and the man of action and glory are the two contenders to the highest rank in the hierarchy of beings. In Strauss's understanding of the dialogue, the issue between Simonides and Hiero is: which type of life is to be preferred as the life worthy of a "real man"?

Simonides makes the claim for the life of contemplation on the ground that the man of thought has the most pleasant and the most self-sufficient life. Unlike the tyrant, he does not have to depend for his glory on what others think. So, there is no reason for him to be servile and spend his time serving his fellow men. He can devote himself to his own pleasures.

The philosopher's pleasure lies in the pursuit of eternal and unchanging truth. But the truths of philosophy are not intended for the masses. On the contrary, they are quite dangerous to society as well as to the philosopher himself. The truth is that there is no moral truth independent of the constructions of power. There is no moral order and no God who could lend support to the human attachment to justice. And as to nature, it is radically hierarchical or contains a rank order of beings. And the philosophers cannot afford to reveal *that* truth, in view of the fact that the multitude always rules. The masses are the greatest enemy of philosophy, because their convictions are so contrary to nature, which is the subject of the truth of philosophy. So, if the truths of philosophy were found out, the philosophers would surely be torn limb from limb.

The death of Socrates at the hands of democratic Athens is a case in point. The philosophers must therefore withdraw and consort only with one another. Strauss explains that the philosopher is too grand for human things. The philosopher's general proximity to the divine, eternal, and imperishable makes him as "unconcerned as possible with individual and perishable human beings."[12] His detachment from the paltry things of this world—his city, his family, and the like—is just the necessary counterpart to his attachment to "eternal beings."[13] Indeed, his "sole business" is to "transcend humanity" and be "dead to all human things."[14] We cannot therefore expect such a man to seek the adulation of the "incompetent many" or to have any "recourse to utterly incompetent people."[15] His "self-admiration" is sufficient. Besides, he is naturally "repelled" by the "ill-ordered souls" of the nonphilosophic.[16] What could he possibly want with these "mutilated" human beings and their "mutilated" virtues?[17] The philosopher prefers a life of "splendid isolation" in the company of like-minded souls. He needs to consort with philosophical "friends" whose "well-ordered souls" he cannot help loving.[18] It is only natural for him to be attracted to the young "potential philosophers."[19] These kindred spirits are his "friends" and his attachment to them is "deeper than his attachment to other human beings, even to his nearest and dearest."[20]

Strauss is quick to point out that the philosopher's love for his kindred spirits is no sign of weakness. Strauss insists that the philosopher is not himself in need of love. He is too self-sufficient for that. Men who need love are servile; they must serve others to gain their love. Hiero needs love, but Simonides does not. Although Hiero and Simonides are among the highest types, Simonides is superior to Hiero because he is more self-sufficient. Love interferes with self-sufficiency.

Strauss does not deny that philosophers should and do influence tyrants when the opportunity presents itself. However, the influence they exert in the world, at least if they are true philosophers, is not intended to bring about the realization of the universal and homogeneous state. Such a state is antithetical to the truth of philosophy, which is to say, the hierarchy of beings. Philosophy will always be at odds with the world, because its truth cannot be actualized unless the wise rule. But this is highly unlikely, because of the aversion that the world has to the truth as well as the aversion that philosophers have to the world. So, in influencing tyrants, the best that philosophers can do is to make sure that the world is safe for philosophy. And, to do this, they must use all the sophistry at their disposal to convince society (contrary to the truth) that philosophers are not dangerous and "irresponsible adventurers." Strauss calls this serious business "philosophic politics."[21]

The exchange between Strauss and Kojève begins from substantial agreement. Both men reject the radical historicism of Heidegger and Max Weber that relegates philosophy to partial and complete discourse, rather than to the discovery of truth. Kojève does not like historicism any more than Strauss. He prefers to call his position "Hegelian absolutism." As we have seen, Kojève thinks of time or *completed history* as providing a privileged perspective that makes knowledge possible.[22] Both men are preoccupied with the role of the philosopher or the wise man in the world. They agree that there is a special affinity between philosophy and tyranny. Kojève praises Strauss for having correctly grasped the connection and he congratulates him for recognizing, contrary to commonly accepted opinion, that the philosopher is a "hardboiled man" who understands politics and is more capable of wielding power than anyone else.[23] As Kojève explains, philosophers are less restrained by conventions and more capable of resorting to terror, and other measures that may be deemed "criminal," whenever such measures are effective in accomplishing the end in view.[24] Philosophers have always been "drawn to tyranny" because they cannot be bothered with democratic politics: witness Socrates and Alcibiades, Plato and Dionysius, Aristotle and Alexander, Spinoza and DeWitt.[25]

Having established the philosopher's special talent for tyranny, it remains to inquire into its practical ramifications. Kojève's view is clear and straightforward. Philosophy needs tyranny if it is to succeed in actualizing its truths. The philosopher knows that only a universal and homogeneous state could satisfy man. But he also knows that such a state needs to be brought into being by courage, daring, and ruthless measures—and he knows exactly how to wield them. Once man is satisfied and history is completed, the philosopher will be a god.[26] Sitting back, he will contemplate the completed world he has created.[27] At the French ministry, Kojève tried to practice what he preached.[28]

Even though Kojève shared Strauss's conception of the divinity of the philosopher, he balked at Strauss's claim that the philosopher does not seek recognition and that his own "self-admiration" suffices him.[29] Kojève argued that this self-satisfied philosopher is like a lunatic who thinks he is Napoleon, or God the Father, or that he is made out of glass. Strauss's philosopher cannot possibly know if he has "attained Wisdom or sunk into lunacy."[30] If the philosopher were really satisfied with self-admiration, he would not write anything or communicate with anyone; so we would not even know that he exists.

Kojève also ridiculed the recognition that the philosopher received from his friends as hardly any more respectable than the lunacy of self-admiration. Kojève compared Strauss's philosophers to the Epicureans who withdrew into their gardens and academies and cultivated an elite altogether separate from the world of the uninitiated. Kojève rightly argued that to endure, these cloistered societies must recruit new members, and since they are persuaded that their truths are radically at odds with those of the mob beyond their walls, they are compelled to resort to esoteric forms of instruction. Consequently, those capable of decoding the "dissimulated allusions and tacit implications" are instantly deemed the best and the brightest; this results in what Kojève rightly calls the "cloistered mind."[31] Any society that is closed upon itself is bound to perpetuate and consolidate prejudice. Regardless of one's conception of truth, one has to admit that the sectarian or cloistered mind that is cultivated and perpetuated in these gardens is antithetical to the philosophical life. The true philosopher is one who, like Socrates, shuns prejudice, and uses philosophy to question and expose it. A real philosopher will therefore flee the wretched servility of the sect and head for the marketplace. Otherwise, he "runs the risk of considering worthy all those, and only those, who admire and agree with him."[32] So, even if Strauss's philosopher escapes lunacy, he cannot avoid the servile stupidity of the sect.

In Kojève's view, Strauss has betrayed the philosophical quest for an independent standard of judgment, since this standard cannot be sustained in the cloistered atmosphere of the sect. A sectarian standard cannot make any claims to objectivity. Indeed, it betrays philosophy by turning its truth into a form of collective lunacy. In contrast, Kojève thinks that his own claim to divinity rests on more solid ground.

For Kojève, the apotheosis of the philosopher into a god is the outcome of the end of history. And even when he began to see the end-state as abominable, Kojève could not conceive of abandoning it without also abandoning absolute knowledge and making his own divinity a sham. In contrast, he thinks that Strauss has simply asserted the divinity of the philosopher a priori, independent from history.[33]

Kojève's claim to divinity rests on his claim to absolute knowledge, which in turn rests on his judgment that history is completed and all that could ever be realized has already been realized, which leads to the assertion that nothing significant is possible. However, anyone who challenges this string of dubious assertions and suspicious claims is by definition unwise—a mere mortal, not a god. Anyone who suspects that some post-Napoleonic event, achievement, or thought is significant must be disqualified from the divine circle of sages. Kojève's view is not wisdom, but dogma. Wisdom can give an account of itself. In contrast, Kojève's claims can only be upheld dogmatically in the face of a plethora of examples to the contrary.

Kojève can sustain the claim that history has ended only by systematically belittling every event, achievement, or thought, no matter how colossal. This is the defensive tactic that leads Kojève to regard Hitlerism as nothing more than history's way of democratizing Germany, and to dismiss the First and Second World Wars as nonevents. The folly of this post-historical babble is plain for all to see. It is impossible to distinguish this post-historical nonsense from the ravings of madmen. How can we know if Kojève has attained wisdom or sunk into lunacy? How can we know that he is a sage? Perhaps his own self-admiration suffices him.

Such philosophical dogmatism has a dangerous affinity to tyranny. There are no horrors that a tyrant armed with the truth would not inflict in the interest of the perfect satisfaction of man. Anyone not satisfied must be "sick" and fit to be "locked up."[34] Having none of the inhibitions or compunctions of ordinary men, Kojève's tyrant will not shrink from the "necessary" atrocities regardless of their magnitude. Like the religious fanatic who thinks that he is the instrument of God's will, the tyrant intoxicated with history tramples over everything and everyone in the single-minded pursuit of history's true end or goal.

Strauss's philosopher-tyrant is hardly more appetizing. He is as mean-spirited as he is narrow-minded. Strauss paints a portrait of a man who is a "stranger" to the sentiments of ordinary mortals. He shuns love, or the "unqualified attachments" to other human beings.[35] He is indifferent to human things, and repelled by the nonphilosophic multitude. Such a man might indeed delight in wielding despotic power. But who would trust him? The gravest iniquities might not weigh heavily on the conscience of one who is "dead to all human things." Strauss assures us that the philosopher "will not hurt anyone," but his words sound hollow. How could anyone so contemptuous of ordinary citizens and their "mutilated virtues," and so intoxicated with self-admiration not hurt anyone? Such a man is unfit for power, let alone absolute power unlimited by law. The appeal of the Platonic conception of the rule of the wise in the absence of law rested on the demonstrable wisdom and goodness of the philosopher. But Strauss fails to convince us that his philosopher is either wise or good. Strauss's philosopher has such a cloistered, sectarian mind that it is difficult to take his wisdom seriously. Sectarianism replaces wonder with a crust of dogmatism. Strauss's philosopher is free of all the doubts and devils that plague a truly wise man. As Kojève deftly illustrates, Strauss's sectarianism has the effect of emasculating philosophy. Strauss transforms the dialectical contest of ideas into the collective concord of the cloister, and the intelligent freedom of the philosopher into the slavish servility of the sectarian.

Kojève's critique of Strauss's sectarianism is one of the most devastating critiques ever delivered. And Strauss's response serves only to confirm the truth of Kojève's insights. However, the same criticism could just as well be made of Kojève's claim to divine omniscience. At the end of history, philosophy, understood as the love of wisdom or the quest for it, is replaced by wisdom itself. History replaces the murky disputations of philosophers with the limpid truths of sages. Once wisdom is achieved, all the debates, disputes, and disagreements characteristic of the philosophical life come to an end. Among the wise, there can only be agreement. We are therefore back to the concord of the cloister. And despite the brilliance of his castigation of Strauss, Kojève cannot escape the perils of the cloistered mind.

In conclusion, Strauss and Kojève share a great deal in common.[36] They have the same conception of the philosopher as someone who transcends the moral scruples of ordinary humanity, and is therefore fit to advise tyrants and to shape history. But Strauss laments that it has been the wrong philosophers—philosophers enchanted by the prospect of a universal and homogeneous state—who have shaped the destiny of the West. In the second part of the debate, Strauss will try to turn Kojève in his direction. Strauss's followers like to think that Kojève's "turn" was the result of his exchange with Strauss. And while I think that Strauss was not without influence, his triumph over Kojève does not exactly amount to conquering the tycoon of modernity.

THE END OF HISTORY

What Kojève and Strauss share in common is the view that ideas, and hence philosophers, make history, or are the moving force of history.[37] Kojève believes that history would have been a lifeless affair had philosophers not actively negated what is in the name of what will be. In a limited sense, he agrees with Strauss that human history has been characterized by a conflict between philosophy and the world. This conflict accounts for the progressive transformation of the world in the direction of philosophical truth. But once this process is completed, the conflict between philosophy and the world is resolved.

According to Kojève, the resolution of this conflict will require tyrannical power. This is why it would be incompetent for philosophers to condemn tyranny "on principle."[38] Tyranny is a necessary means to the historical actualization of philosophy. Tyranny and wisdom collaborate in bringing about the end of history, which is the philosophically best political order. The latter is the universal and homogeneous state of free, equal, and prosperous men and women.

There are numerous objections that could be made to Kojève's vision of the end of history. For example, it may be objected that what parades as the truth of history is but naked will. It may be objected that the historical process does not aim at the satisfaction of man: frustration and dissatisfaction are man's permanent lot. It may be objected that history is not necessarily linear and progressive, and that civilizations will always rise and fall. It may be objected that the truth is not singular but plural, and that there is no such thing as a single best political order like the universal and homogeneous state. Moreover, even if there is only one best order and one right way, it is unlikely that mankind will unanimously embrace it. It may also be objected that the conquest of nature leads only to augmenting the power of the few over the many, and hence to the most terrible tyrannies imaginable.[39] It may be objected that humanity's collective triumph over nature is bought at the expense of individual liberty; and that technological society is characterized by impersonal yet autocratic forms of domination.[40] But Strauss makes none of these objections.

Strauss's fundamental objection to the universal and homogeneous state is that it is too egalitarian. Strauss abhors the egalitarian principles of universal recognition of human dignity, the equality of opportunity, and the devotion to material prosperity. First, the recognition of everyone's human dignity is an assault on excellence because everyone can have recognition of his human dignity but not everyone can achieve excellence. This is an example of how modernity "lowers the standard" of politics to make it attainable to all. But how could what is attainable to all be of much value? Recognition loses its luster as it "gains in universality."[41] Strauss reasons that a classless society can make people equal only by eliminating the higher types, which is contrary to nature. Second, Strauss is not impressed with equality of opportunity—that is a thrill only for the "humble citizen" who gets to enjoy all the "opportunities that correspond to his humble capacities."[42] Third, Strauss balks at prosperity: what is the prosperity generated by the conquest of nature but the modern preoccupation with creature comforts? It is clear that Strauss is hostile to the most modest forms of equality.

Strauss's most impassioned complaint against the universal and homogeneous state is that it has the power to deal philosophy its deadliest blow. The universal tyrant will

> forbid every teaching, every suggestion, that there are politically relevant natural differences among men which cannot be abolished or neutralized by progressive scientific technology. He must command his biologists to prove that every human being has, or will acquire, the capacity of becoming a philosopher or a tyrant.[43]

Philosophers who express the truth about the "hierarchy of beings"—about "real men"—are bound to be persecuted.

For Strauss, the universal and homogeneous state is a global tyranny of the "incompetent many" over the exceptional few. Strauss argues that the idea of a global tyranny is a concoction of modernity that was unimaginable in ancient times, because it presupposes the technological mastery of nature. The universal tyrant rules in the name of the rabble. Modern tyranny differs from ancient tyranny by being global, technological, and egalitarian.

For all his praise of Jane Austen[44] as opposed to Dostoevsky, Strauss's final objection to the universal and homogeneous state is vintage Dostoevsky. Strauss contends that *even if* everyone had good reason to be satisfied with the universal and homogeneous state, it does not follow that no one would rebel against it. To think otherwise is to overestimate the power of reason and underestimate the power of the passions.[45] In fact, Strauss thinks that men *will* have good reason to revolt. And, in Strauss's estimation, they would not be real men (*andres*) if they did not.

His objections notwithstanding, Strauss agrees with Kojève that ideas make history and that history has been marching inexorably toward the universal and homogeneous state. The latter is modernity's ignoble delusion—the delusion that has governed the destiny of Western civilization and brought it to its sorry state. The universal and homogeneous state is the symbol of modernity's revolt against ancient wisdom and its "hierarchy of beings." The universal and homogeneous state is the result of modernity's progressive elimination of the highest types. Machiavelli set the foundations for the modern project by exalting action at the expense of contemplation; and in so doing, eliminated the highest type (the philosopher). Hobbes built the modern edifice on the foundations set by his predecessor. He denounced the love of honor and glory as the source of all evil; and in so doing, eliminated the second-highest type (the aristocratic warrior in pursuit of glory). Hobbes completed the Christian assault on aristocratic values; and despite his atheism, he was the most powerful instrument of Christian ideology (i.e., the slave morality).[46] Now that the higher types have been exorcised, preoccupations of Simonides and Hiero have disappeared; and all that is left is the preoccupations of the lowest types—safety, security, profit, and animal pleasures. For Strauss, as for Kojève, the end of history is the placid animality in which *we are already living.*

Strauss does not think it a great exaggeration to say with Kojève that "the universal and homogeneous state is fated to come;" but he understands this fact to be "absolutely tragic" because he thinks that the universal and homogeneous state is indistinguishable from the state of Nietzsche's "last man."[47] Strauss regards the latter as a compelling reality and not simply the product of an overactive imagination. For Strauss, the universal and homogeneous state, the state of Nietzsche's last man, is the brainchild of modernity. To understand it is to understand our predicament. Therein lies the significance of Kojève.

NIHILISTIC REVOLT AND ETERNAL RECURRENCE

The most significant difference between Kojève and Strauss has to do with whether the end-state is here to stay. Kojève believes that there is no escaping the end of history. In contrast, Strauss conceives of history in terms of the eternal recurrence of the same. Strauss is confident that "real men" will put an end to the universal and homogeneous state and plunge us back into history.

In the face of history's inexorable march toward the universal and homogeneous state, Strauss does not despair. According to Strauss, the end of history may be "fated" to come, but it is not destined to stay. Strauss does not pretend to know how or when the universal and homogeneous state will perish, he knows only that it will "perish sooner or later," and that it will perish at the hands of the *andres* of this world.[48]

Strauss explains that "there will always be men (*andres*) who will revolt against a state which is destructive of humanity."[49] In a world where "there is no longer a possibility of noble action and great deeds," the rebels against the universal and homogeneous state may be "forced" into a "nihilistic revolution" that is not "enlightened by any positive goal."[50] This "nihilistic negation" is the "only great and noble deed that is possible once the universal and homogeneous state has become inevitable."[51] Strauss links his use of the term *andres* to Kojève's use of the term *masters* as distinct from the slaves, whom he refers to by the Greek *anthropoi*.[52] Strauss lives in hopeful anticipation of the return of pagan mastery.

For all his "noble reserve," Strauss ends his reply to Kojève with what can only be described as a revolutionary call to action:

> Warriors and workers of all countries, unite, while there is still time, to prevent the "coming of the realm of freedom." Defend with might and main, if it needs to be defended, the "realm of necessity."[53]

Strauss's right-radical rhetoric has reached new heights. The "realm of freedom" is modernity—liberal, egalitarian, democratic, and herdlike. It is up to the *andres* of this world to dismantle it or prevent it from taking root. Under the abominable conditions bequeathed to us by modernity, where there is nothing to conserve, the only "noble deed" is "nihilistic revolt," which is to say, destruction without any "positive goal."

It may be objected that no matter how abominable the conditions of modernity may be, nihilistic revolt cannot possibly accomplish anything. Strauss anticipates this objection and responds as follows. It may well be that the nihilistic dismantling of the universal and homogeneous state would serve only to drive back the historical process to its beginnings in the primitive horde. Strauss asserts that there is nothing wrong with repeating the historical process from its primitive beginnings, even *if,* in repeating it, we end up once again at the same final abomination—the universal and homogeneous state in which we live. On the contrary, "such a repetition of the process" would be a "new lease of life for man's humanity."[54] And this would be infinitely preferable to the "continuation of the inhuman end."[55] As Strauss remarks, "do we not enjoy every spring although we know the cycle of the seasons, although we know that winter will come again?"[56] Strauss's response is a clear expression of Nietzsche's "eternal recurrence" of the same.

The actions of the "real men" who will destroy the universal and homogeneous state are not possible without the efforts of philosophers. The latter's task is to nourish the spiritedness of the *andres* who will sooner or later dismantle the universal and homogeneous state in a "nihilistic revolution." By unfettering the mind, philosophy can liberate the real men from the subjugation of modern tyranny. With the utmost care, philosophy must foster the truth about the "politically relevant natural differences among men."[57] This is a very dangerous truth at any time, let alone at the end of history, so it must be disseminated with utmost caution. Strauss's despair at modernity is so exaggerated that it borders on melodrama. And if the splendid isolation of the philosopher meant the renunciation of action in the world, then Straussianism would be laughable but not politically menacing. But alas, there is a radical activism operating among the cloistered.

Strauss has not escaped the influence of such romantic reactionaries as Oswald Spengler, Carl Schmitt, Ernst Jünger, Martin Heidegger, and others.[58] These romantic radicals are conservative outcasts of an enchanted but fictitious past. They blame modernity for having disenchanted the world and robbed it of meaning. Their abhorrence of secular, liberal, and industrialized civilization is not so much rational as aesthetic. In their view, modernity has replaced the splendor and rhapsody of high culture with unabashed mediocrity. So loathsome a world cannot profit from criticism. Only extraordinary measures could possibly have any effect. Only something cataclysmic could offer hope for a new rebirth. These disenchanted conservatives are simultaneously prophets of doom as well as hope. While pointing to dark and formless premonitions of disaster, they also hold out a remote possibility of a new apocalypse.[59]

It may be objected that Strauss could not possibly belong to the tradition of romantic radicalism. He was too moderate a man to endorse something as cataclysmic as a nihilistic revolution intended to return us to the primitive horde. Strauss has always taught that the function of philosophy is to uphold the myths of the age, not to incite revolution. Strauss's response to Kojève must be understood as hypothetical. The gist of his reply is that the universal and homogeneous state is not a reality; nor can it ever be a reality. It is as impossible as it is intolerable. But if, *per impossible*, it were to become a reality, then it is the case that the *andres* of this world would dismantle it, and it is only right that they do. But insofar as the universal and homogeneous state is not a reality, Strauss's impassioned call to nihilistic revolt is a fiction.

On the whole, Strauss thinks that the function of philosophy is to uphold the myths and illusions of the age, and not to challenge the salutary prejudices of convention. But this is the case *only* when the philosopher approves of the regime. However, when he does not, then he must use philosophy as a weapon to undermine it. This is the gist of Strauss's commentary on Rousseau, and it is the reason that he praised him for restoring ancient wisdom, which alone fathomed the power of philosophy.[60]

It is true to say that Strauss is using the fiction of the universal and homogeneous state to speak more freely about liberal democracy, or the regime required by modernity.[61] However, it is a mistake to believe that the universal and homogeneous state is simply fiction. On the contrary, Strauss understands it as the project that has animated modernity, East and West. Modernity aims to conquer nature, as well as human nature. It seeks to destroy the "order of rank" in nature and to re-create the world in its own egalitarian image.

Far from being an abstraction concocted by philosophers, the universal and homogeneous state, the state of Nietzsche's "last man," is for Strauss the disturbing reality in which we live; it is the nightmare to which modernity has inexorably led us. There is no place in this world for men like Simonides or Hiero. And although he does not put it this way, modernity has the technological might to exterminate such men (if they don't die out as a result of genetic engineering). This is how Strauss perceived the Holocaust. He regarded Hitler's regime as the democratic regime par excellence, and Hitler as the personification of the mass man. Unlike other writers, Strauss did not think that the Holocaust was an aberration in the history of the West; he saw it as the logical conclusion of modernity. Armed with technological might, the rule of the mob aims at the global extermination of the higher types. America could not have been much of a refuge for Strauss. It must have been like trying to escape modernity by fleeing to the heart of the universal and homogeneous state.[62]

Strauss scores some excellent points against Kojève. But Kojève does not lose this round simply on the strength of Strauss's arguments. He loses because he does not tell us what is good about the universal and homogeneous state. He does not give reasons why respect for "human dignity" is the best foundation of political life. He does not explain why equality of opportunity is *not* a plot against excellence. He does not tell us why a classless society is just.

Strauss is triumphant because Kojève's conception of the end of history cannot be distinguished from Nietzsche's abysmal prophecy and from Strauss's abhorrence of modernity. In comparison to the past, both Kojève and Strauss experience the present as an age of hitherto unsurpassed worthlessness. In this post-historical present, they are convinced that nothing great is possible. Kojève's concept of the end of history expresses a mood of cosmic melancholy about the present that dovetails handsomely with Strauss's anguish in the face of modernity. The two concepts—modernity and post-history—are a single explanatory tool that divides history into the glorious past and the abysmal present. In the final analysis, Kojève and Strauss share the same antipathy to modernity. That antipathy is so total that it cannot be harnessed toward constructive criticism. When a civilization is deemed to be completely devoid of redeeming qualities, there is nothing left to do but despair or destroy. Kojève's gratuitous suicide and Strauss's nihilistic revolt are the result. This is politics at its radical worst. What is ironic is that such radicalism passes for conservatism in America.

THE COMMISSAR AND THE SUPERMAN

The debate between Kojève and Strauss is not what it is generally believed to be. It is not a debate between a rabid modernist who has faith in progress and the future of mankind and an antimodernist who is pessimistic about the future and nostalgic for a lost golden age—they were both equally repelled by the modern world, which they saw in terms of Nietzsche's last man; they both longed for the "aristocratic virtues" of "real men" who risked their lives for "glory." Nor is it a debate between a Stalinist who is attracted to "modern tyranny" and a classicist who condemns tyranny *tout court*—both men pay tribute to tyranny. Nor is it a debate between one who believes that philosophers should be engaged in making history and one who thinks that they should retire to the seclusion of the academy—both men believed that ideas make history, and that philosophers must influence the powerful. Nor is it a debate between a radical revolutionary and a moderate conservative—neither was politically moderate. They were both cloistered intellectuals vulnerable to the excitement of political action on the world stage.

What then is at issue in what Allan Bloom called the "profoundest public confrontation between two philosophers in this century"?[63] It is my contention that the debate between Kojève and Strauss is best understood as a debate between a people's commissar and a Nietzschean superman. So regarded, it is indeed the debate of our time—a time full of commissars and supermen. At first blush they may seem very different, but in truth they are the same human type.

The people's commissar starts out as an idealist and a lover of humanity; he is selfless, compassionate, and motivated by an insatiable desire for social justice. But in time, he discovers, as Kojève did, that a man who plans to serve humanity must be hardened against the debilitating effects of moral scruples. He must be one of those extraordinary few who does not suffer the slings and arrows of a good conscience. He must transcend the ordinary ranks of humanity and live beyond good and evil. Paradoxically, he must become "dead to all human things" if he hopes to serve mankind. No one understood this better than Lenin. He knew that revolution was a brutal and bloody affair, and that one had to be cold and heartless to measure up to the task at hand. Being a real commissar, Lenin had to struggle against his own softness: he loved Beethoven, and knew nothing greater than the *Appassionata*, and would have enjoyed listening to it every day. But he realized that a people's commissar could not afford too much exposure to such "superhuman music" because it "makes you want to say kind, silly things, to stroke the heads of the people who, living in a terrible hell, can create such beauty."[64] The commissar cannot afford to be soft and sentimental. His warm "attachment to human things" must give way to cold indifference; his passion for justice must give way to calculations of utility; and his compassion must give way to cruelty when the need arises. As the self-appointed savior of mankind, the commissar must sacrifice his humanity for a future heaven on earth.

The drama takes an unexpected turn when the commissar begins to despise the very utopia for which he has labored so tirelessly. It is at this moment that the whispering of the superman has its greatest appeal. The superman bids him forget about humanity. Instead, he teaches the commissar to become intoxicated with his own "self-admiration." In time, the commissar abandons the grand mission that set him on his perilous course, in favor of his own self-aggrandizement. He begins to realize that it is sheer lunacy to go about sacrificing himself, his superb and extraordinary self, for commonplace humanity. He starts to acknowledge what he has always known—that nature contains a "rank order of beings." He becomes convinced that history is nothing but a stage on which this "hierarchy of beings" displays itself. He begins to regard the *journey* as more significant than the final destination. He stops thinking of his own life—a life beyond good and evil—as a means to the attainment of the grand finale and begins to think of it as an end in itself. In this way, the people's commissar slides into the persona of the Nietzschean superman. And far from being a grand transformation, this is a small step.

The story resembles the psychological drama of Dostoevsky's Raskolnikov. Raskolnikov begins by justifying his crime in terms of all the benefactions he will bestow on his family and mankind, but later in the novel, he abandons his altruistic ends in favor of a simple desire for self-aggrandizement and the perverse notion of glory through crime.[65] But unlike Dostoevsky's story, our story lacks a happy ending. Neither Kojève nor Strauss can escape the delusions of their conceit. It never occurs to them that the commissar-superman is someone who has sunk even lower than the ordinary rogues and scoundrels who acknowledge the validity of the moral laws they transgress.

Kojève and Strauss deceive themselves into thinking that history has conspired against the "higher types." They are convinced that the apotheosis of the masses has all but annihilated the extraordinary few. They believe that they are the last vestiges of a noble breed that has been left adrift and forsaken. This myth allows them to fancy themselves as the sensoria of cosmic despair, the marvels of post-history, and the living specimens of an extinct humanity. In the final analysis Kojève unwittingly joins Strauss in embracing the snobbish lunacy of the cloister, for which he had so brilliantly castigated Strauss.

In truth, history has not abandoned the "higher types." It has simply made them commonplace. If our world looks like a Hobbesian state of nature, it is because so many believe themselves exempt from the moral law that binds the rest of humanity. Terrorism, a suicidal and nihilistic rebellion that has become prevalent in our world, is not the work of ordinary criminals, but of extraordinary scoundrels and their gratuitous crimes.

As we shall see in the next two chapters, American writers such as Allan Bloom and Francis Fukuyama, who were influenced by Kojève as much as by Strauss, experience life in America as life at the heart of the universal and homogeneous empire. They regard Americans as last men wallowing in a meaningless animality at the end of history.

CHAPTER

▪ 11 ▫

Allan Bloom's Last Men

Allan Bloom considers Alexandre Kojève to be one of his greatest teachers.[1] He tells us that he studied with Kojève from 1953 to his death in 1968. Leo Strauss sent him to study with Kojève, even though the latter did not hold an academic post, and was not teaching his famous course on Hegel during that period. Bloom went to see him in his office at the French Economic Ministry, where Kojève was busy "presiding" over the end of history. The administration of things is no doubt a heady business, but as Bloom reports, Kojève was always ready to "close his door and talk philosophy."[2]

Bloom's *Closing of the American Mind* has been much more discussed than understood. In my view, those who came closest to understanding it were those who recognized the book as a jazzy version of the work of Leo Strauss.[3] But as we shall see, Bloom's book also bears witness to the influence of Alexandre Kojève. For Bloom understands America in Kojèvean terms as the historical return to animality.

Even though Bloom's book often reads like the meandering of an undisciplined mind, it nevertheless expresses a clear and recurrent theme—the contrast between *culture* and *brutishness*. This distinction is expressed variously as the difference between Europe and America, art and trash, tragedy and its absence, the arduous and the easy, sublimation and satisfaction, class and classlessness, hierarchy and equality. I believe that Bloom's distinction between culture and brutishness is an elaboration of Kojève's antithesis between the historical and the post-historical. Culture is for Bloom what history is for Kojève—a glorious interregnum between man's primitive animality and his return to brutishness at the end of history as represented by America. Following Kojève, Bloom paints America as the incarnation of the post-historical society, which is populated by last men—men who are comfortable in their animality. In what follows, I will explore Bloom's conception of culture and its demise. I will argue that Bloom's view of culture is postmodern, which is to say that it depends on the Nietzschean idea that all cultures are "horizons" and the Kojèvean assumption that in a post-historical world, all horizons have been exploded.

Bloom has been sorely misunderstood as a classical objectivist who heaps abuse on Nietzsche and modern relativism.[4] But as will become apparent below, Bloom's criticism is not directed at Nietzsche, but at the democratization, popularization, and bastardization of Nietzsche's thought in America. Bloom objects to the "Nietzscheanization of the Left," which has the effect of making Nietzsche into a spokesman for American liberalism. Bloom believes that properly understood, Nietzsche belongs to the right. As I will show, Bloom is the classic Right Nietzschean.[5] I will argue that there is no reason to regard his Nietzschean conception of culture as either good or desirable.

THE CHARMS OF CULTURE

Culture is another word for history, civilization, convention, civil society, country, city, or what Bloom likes to call "the horizon of the cave."[6] In Bloom's view, the word *culture* is of fairly recent extraction. It emerges as a reaction to the rational, calculating, and commercial society that is a result of Enlightenment thought. It was necessary for anti-Enlightenment philosophers, like Rousseau and Nietzsche, to invent a new term, because civilization itself had become so defiled by Enlightenment rationalism. Culture is a rediscovery of ancient wisdom, on the part of the critics of Enlightenment. Because he sides with the latter, Bloom uses the term, while objecting to the fact that it is not ancient enough for his liking.[7]

Bloom regards culture as a supremely magical charm by which natural man is transformed into a father and citizen. By its captivating artifices culture humanizes man. It weds him to a particular people with its distinctive way of life, its loves and hates, its language, its gods, and its conception of good and evil. Culture joins every man to his community by a bond of love. It transforms his natural self-love into love of his own offspring and motherland. Bloom does not fully divulge the means by which this transformation of natural man into father and citizen is accomplished. But he tells us that it has a great deal to do with sex.[8]

Sex is natural man's strongest passion. The object of culture is the sub-limation or transfiguration of sex into love.[9] The family is a vital instru-ment in this process (hence Bloom's lament of the decline of the family). Women are the accomplices of culture in its transformation of man. They allow men sexual access to themselves only under the conditions required by culture. Men must pay a high price for sexual satisfaction. They must work and sacrifice to rear and educate their offspring. The postponement of sexual gratification, coupled with the difficulty of its attainment, intensifies sexual pleasure in such a way as to weld the low-est aspects of man's being with the "highest reaches" of his soul. So, through the love of "one's own" (i.e., wife and offspring) man is linked to the greater community. Culture extends love outward from the fam-ily and attaches it to the motherland. The ingenuity of this process of sublimation is its capacity to preserve the original strength and vigor of the sexual passion while attaching it to the motherland. Sex is no longer a casual affair; it's a big deal.

Culture can accomplish this glorious metamorphosis of natural man because of her power to attract. As Bloom puts it,

> a culture is a work of art, of which the fine arts are the sublime expression. . . .
> Culture as art is the peak expression of man's creativ-ity, his capacity to break out of nature's narrow bonds. . . .
> Culture as a form of community is the fabric of relations in which the self finds its diverse and elaborate expression. It is the house of the self, but also its product.[10]

Culture is seductive; she surpasses nature in beauty and grandeur. Culture offers man something loftier and more exalted than anything he could find in nature. She rescues man from his natural solitude; she gives him refuge from his alienation; she furnishes him with a home and with roots. Man therefore experiences culture as fulfilling a deep-felt need or yearning. In this way, culture succeeds in making man feel incomplete in her absence.

Culture wages a war against chaos, nature, and brutishness. Culture is the triumph of order over chaos, art over nature, and humanity over brutishness. The purpose of culture is to give man dignity by raising him above the beasts. She teaches him to despise himself and his brutish-ness and worship something majestic and magnificent. Culture decides what a people bows before and regards as sacred. She teaches men worth and worthlessness, honor and contempt, love and hate. These are not questions of reason. Nature and reason are universal, but culture is particular. Culture is neither rational nor natural: we cannot choose between cultures on the basis of reason or nature. A plurality of cultures necessarily come into conflict with one another—a conflict that cannot be resolved by rational means. Therefore, it is not enough for culture to wage war against chaos, nature, and brutishness, she must also wage war against other cultures. She must defeat other cultures if she is to triumph.[11]

For all her particularity, culture insists on being the ultimate source of values, and the final court of appeal. Culture refuses to recognize any source of allegiance higher than herself. There can be no authority above culture.[12] To insure her authoritativeness, culture insists on the identity between the good and "one's own." She cannot tolerate a distinction between those two things. For such a distinction would undermine her authority and weaken the attachments of citizens to what is their own—i.e., their ready preference for their own children as opposed to the children of others, their fellow citizens as opposed to the citizens of the world, and their own motherland as opposed to any other piece of the earth.

In order to justify these attachments, culture needs "myths."[13] Myths are necessary for providing a people with an exalted sense of their place in the cosmos, or their mission in history. Myths teach people to take pride in their heritage, and this in turn allows them to develop a "collective consciousness." This may involve a "very great narrowness," but as Bloom explains, such a narrowness is not incompatible with "the health of an individual or a people."[14] Myths are the stuff of culture, and culture is the cement of society.

Bloom has no objections to the closed society. It would be unreasonable to protest against what he believes is the logic of political life—it would be like denouncing the sun for rising. A cultured society is necessarily a "closed" society. As Bloom puts it, "culture is a cave."[15]

According to Bloom, reason, science, and philosophy are a threat to culture. Philosophy discovers a standard outside of culture and uses it to judge the latter. It insists on the distinction between the just and the legal, the naturally or genuinely good and the conventional. Philosophy weakens the hold that culture has on men, because it undermines the "wholehearted attachment to one's own."[16] It substitutes truth for myth, and nature for convention.[17] It has an "uprooting charm" that destroys the spell of culture; it is therefore a very "dangerous business."[18]

For Bloom, culture is antithetical to philosophy, reason, and science and their claims to universality.[19] Culture abhors the universal because it believes that what all men share in common is not their humanity, but their *brutishness.* The modernist quest for the universal and homogeneous state is the antithesis of culture. As Kojève himself realized, the universal and homogeneous state is the demise of all culture and the return to animality. This is why a universal culture is a contradiction in terms.

Bloom thinks that liberal democracy, the regime required by modernity, epitomizes this contradiction. He asserts that there is a "fundamental conflict between liberal society and culture."[20] Liberal democracy is born of the belief in universal human rights, rights belonging to man *qua* man, rights grounded in nature rather than society. Modernity inherits its universalism from Christianity; in fact, it is the heir of Christianity —a religion that Bloom regards as very deleterious to culture.[21] Bloom rejects natural rights and denies that there is any universal morality. Right and wrong are products of particular cultures. He thinks that the belief in a universal morality is a fiction which afflicts men like Othello, whose devotion to the universalistic principles of Christianity is, in Bloom's view, the flaw in his character that leads to his downfall.[22]

Bloom follows Nietzsche and Strauss in thinking that it is preposterous to found society on reason (as opposed to myth) and populate it with natural men (i.e., men unadorned by culture). This is what Hobbes, Locke, and the moderns tried to do.[23] The result is bourgeois man, which Bloom thinks is indistinguishable from Nietzsche's last man. Bloom's admiration for Rousseau lies in the fact that he was able to see the decadence and depravity of modernity at the very moment of its greatest triumph. Rousseau was able to see that Enlightenment rationalism gave birth to "a certain low human type" that he was first to identify as the "bourgeois."[24] Rousseau had to rediscover the ancient understanding of culture.[25] He denounced reason and science as bad for man (at least for most men). He rediscovered the creative genius behind the myths of culture in his figure of the Legislator. In short, he recovered ancient wisdom while anticipating Nietzsche.

Bloom praised Nietzsche as one who not only recovered ancient wisdom, but went beyond Rousseau to provide the most penetrating diagnosis of the malaise of Western civilization.[26] Nietzsche detected a fearful "spiritual entropy" or an "evaporation of the soul's boiling blood."[27] He knew that culture had been eclipsed, and that man's humanity was threatened. Nietzsche wanted to discover a cure. He wanted to know how culture may be revitalized. Nietzsche understood that culture was the product of creative genius. No matter what conservatives tell us about tradition, every culture has a beginning. The makers of culture are great artists (Nietzsche usually calls them supermen, but Bloom avoids the term). They are master craftsmen who have the power, strength, courage, and personality to establish new modes and orders. What distinguishes these great creators is not the truth of their thought, but their creativity, which is manifest in their capacity to invent the horizons of culture. These makers of culture are also the makers of the myths that inspire and enchant, for "myths are what animate culture."[28] The makers of myth are also the makers of man. For man, so understood, is Greek, Indian, Jewish, Christian, or Moslem. What Bloom means by myth is what Kojève meant by ideology. The end of history is the end of ideology, the triumph of reason and the *death of man*. But Bloom was not yet ready to believe that the disease of the West was terminal.

Nietzsche surmised that if the West was to be saved, great creativity was needed. But the problem was not simple. Enlightenment sapped the energy from human originality and inventiveness; it destroyed the conditions of creativity itself, and made the restoration of culture highly problematic. This is why Enlightenment, with its concomitant devotion to democracy and egalitarianism, was Nietzsche's target.

Bloom accepts both Nietzsche's diagnosis of the malaise of Western civilization as well as his remedy. Enlightenment rationalism is the source of decline. The attempt to replace myth with reason, and culture with nature, necessarily ends in the death of man. Artistic genius, seductive myths, and magnificent illusions are necessary to restore the "soul's boiling blood" and to relieve the current entropy.

In summary, Bloom's conception of culture contains a philosophy of history that (with some help from Rousseau and Nietzsche) elaborates on Kojève's theme of the death of man. Briefly stated, the story is as follows. In the beginning, man lived in the bosom of nature. This natural savage was solitary, self-centered, strong, proud, and spirited.[29] Then came the culture creators—men like Homer, Moses, Jesus, and Buddha who succeeded in taming "the lion in the soul" and civilizing man.[30] Solitary man was wedded to a family, and through the mediation of a family, to a particular people. In time, the planet came to be inhabited by peoples, each having its distinctive way of life, its peculiar gods, its unique loves and hates, its characteristic language, its own conception of good and evil, and its special charm—none of which its neighbors understood.[31] History is the story of the clash of cultures. For love and pride in their own cultures, men were willing to die. Culture gave meaning to man's life and death. This was a glorious period in human existence. It was the age of war and heroism. Then came the culture destroyers: these were the moderns, with whom Kojève was once allied. They were not so much evil as unwise and misguided. They were Prometheans, bent on furnishing man with happiness. For love of man, they set out to bring history and its wars to an end. They dreamed of a single universal and homogeneous state of free, equal, peaceful, and prosperous men and women. In order to reach this goal, they had to destroy the distinctiveness of peoples; they had to demythologize and demystify life; they had to liberate man from the charms of culture; they had to replace the closedness of culture with openness; they had to unbend the "bow" of the spirit. However, they did not know that the effect of this project was to leave man permanently unstrung. They did not understand that the modern project was identical to the death of man. For man, properly so-called, is the fruit of culture.[32] The demise of culture, therefore, returns man to the bosom of nature. Ironically, progress brings man full circle back to animality. In short, culture is what Kojève meant by history. It is an interregnum period between man's primitive animality and his return to brutishness at the end of history. Culture represents the age of ideology, prejudice, and struggle. The demise of culture, or the explosion of all horizons, is the end of history and the death of man.

The story is breathtaking for its simplicity. Nevertheless, it is worth noting that it contains a certain incoherence. If natural man, spurred by the desire for recognition, is wild, capricious, and violent, and is only tamed by culture, then we should expect that when culture is extinguished, man would revert to his natural savagery. However, the story tells us that at the end of history, man is preoccupied with commerce and consumption, rather than with war and conquest; and the storyteller finds this disgracefully passive, submissive, and inert. He complains that man has been emasculated. It seems that we are compelled to reach the following conclusion: man is not by nature savage, but culture makes him so. In which case, there is no reason to lament the eclipse of culture. If all of the hateful things about man are the products of culture, then it would be a good thing if man were to be unstrung.

We cannot understand Kojève and Bloom's indictment of America unless we recognize that she is the incarnation of the historical return to placid animality—to commerce and consumption rather than war and struggle. For Bloom as for Kojève, America is the heart of the universal and homogeneous empire, and is the leader in the world process of animalization. She represents the demise of culture, the end of history, and the death of man.

Bloom is under the mistaken illusion that there are only two choices for mankind: either a mad devotion to the myths of our culture, or a collapse into commerce, meaninglessness, and animal consumption. What he forgets is that due to the wealth and leisure it makes possible, commerce is the necessary precondition for the development of the arts and sciences that give culture its distinctiveness.

One of the most pervasive themes of Bloom's book is that America is the ghost of Weimar and Nazi Germany. Bloom follows Strauss in thinking that Weimar is the prototype of liberalism—one step from complete barbarism. He therefore transposes the Weimar experience onto the American setting. As a result, his book is full of vague and formless premonitions of disaster. But one cannot help notice the irony of this critique, since Bloom contributes to the Weimarization of America that he denounces. His conception of culture, with its contempt for liberalism, pluralism, individualism, and diversity, and its emphasis on supermen concocting myths and illusions intended to mesmerize the masses into a single and belligerent "collective consciousness" is itself replete with fascistic resonances.

ROCK: MUSIC OF THE UNIVERSAL AND HOMOGENEOUS STATE

According to Bloom, American music or rock is the music of the universal and homogeneous state. Moreover, it is fully conscious of the fact. Its lyrics are full of longing for the universal, classless, prejudice- and conflict-free society.[33] "We are the world," pretty much sums it up. Rock "knows neither class nor nation."[34] Its universal appeal has its source in the fact that it panders to the only thing that human beings have in common—their animality. Rock manages to reach the whole world only by using the "common currency of the body." Rock is the expression of pure animal sexuality.

Bloom's portrait of the typical American adolescent with his headphones listening to rock while doing his homework is intended to epitomize the irony of historical progress. Lounging in his comfortable living room, he takes for granted liberties won by the "blood of martyrs." He is equally oblivious to the fact that science has "penetrated the secrets of nature" to provide him with the electronic sound he enjoys. Bloom declares him the symbol of the progress of civilization: "And in what does progress culminate? A pubescent child whose body throbs with orgasmic rhythms."[35] In Bloom's America all that is left are the rhythms of pure animal sexuality. What could better simulate the shrills of cicadas?

Bloom denies that rock music constitutes a genuine art form because no genuine art could have universal appeal. Genuine art is rooted in a particular soil; it must be the expression of the distinctive spirit of a people; it must be like Wagner's *Gesamtkunstwerk*.[36] But rock is not the expression of "collective consciousness." It is the universal music, the music of man's return to animality.[37]

I think it is worth noting that *Gesamtkunstwerk* is Wagner's notion of an all-inclusive multimedia art form, the crown of artistic excellence, which he believed to be exemplified by his own operas. Both Heidegger and the Nazis were very enthusiastic about this Wagnerian conception of art. They believed that art must be understood as a totality; it must penetrate every dimension of life; it must be a reflection of the nation; it must serve the purposes of what the Nazis called the *Volksgemeinschaft*.

It is clear that *Gesamtkunstwerk* is a recipe for turning art into propaganda. It robs art of its freedom; it also robs it of its capacity to transcend the narrow and parochial. As a result, art loses its standing as a social critic; it loses its ability to portray human experiences that are sublime, grand, elevating, and universal. It seems to me that *Gesamtkunstwerk* is a fancy excuse for making art the pimp of the established order.

It is no wonder that Wagner, this prodigy of culture, wore gloves whenever he conducted Felix Mendelssohn's music. He had to make sure that his cultural and racial purity was not contaminated by the music of the Jew. And why did he bother conducting Mendelssohn? He was paid for it.

BLOOM'S LAST MEN

In his preface to the translation of Kojève's *Introduction to the Reading of Hegel*, Bloom expressed the opinion that the value of Kojève's work rested in its ability to interpret "our" situation and to "paint a powerful picture of our problems as those of post-historical man"—with no worlds to conquer, no gods to revere, and no truths to discover.[38] Several years later, when he wrote *The Closing of the American Mind*, Bloom described his American students in the same terms he used to describe Kojève's post-historical men.

In the early stages of his professorial career, Bloom was attracted to his American students. Even though he thought of them as noble savages, he believed that they nevertheless held out great potential for cultivation. At the hands of the right professor (one who knows just what their souls long for) they could become flowers of culture.[39] Here is where Rousseau's *Emile* came in handy.[40]

Bloom does not speak abstractly on these issues. He provides poignant personal anecdotes. When he was four years old, a precocious boy told him bluntly that there was no Santa Claus. Bloom remarks cynically that the boy no doubt wanted him to "bathe in the brilliant light of truth."[41] This was clearly one of Bloom's worst childhood memories. Bloom compares this boy to a professor he met who thought that his duty as an educator was to undermine the prejudices of his students. Bloom remarks that such a professor does not know what he is doing; he does not understand what his students yearn for; he has no idea how destructive his activity is to the soul. Bloom is certain that depriving the soul of its cherished myths and illusions "lobotomizes" and "cripples" it.[42]

We are led to conclude that Bloom is a professor who leaves the prejudices, myths, and illusions of his students intact. But this is not altogether accurate. Being products of the "open" society, Bloom's students are startling for their *lack* of prejudices.[43] They are unhinged, unstrung, uncultured. The professor of culture must provide them with the nourishment for which their post-historical souls yearn. He must "dish out" Plato, Shakespeare, and more. As Bloom puts it, he must be at once a "pimp and midwife." Supposedly, he should seduce them with a little Nietzsche, then let Socrates help them give birth to their ideas. In this way, they come to believe that they have discovered for themselves what they have been taught by the master. The final goal is to make sure that students are furnished with the appropriate myths, attitudes, tastes, and prejudices.

As Bloom got older, he became more pessimistic, not just about the universities, but about his students. He was no longer charmed by their "natural savagery."[44] No longer did he regard them as diamonds in the rough. His efforts to turn them into paragons of culture were to no avail. He started to think of them as post-historical men—the last men. He described them as "naked animals" without the "trappings of civilization."[45] He compared them to a "herd" that was "grazing together."[46] Their music and their sexuality were especially despicable, and supremely illustrative of the depths to which they had descended.

In my view, Bloom's attitude to his students indicates either a growing resistance on their part to his seductions or a decline in his own powers to charm and bewitch them. It marks a definite transition from a Nietzschean optimism in his own culture-creating abilities to a Kojèvean resignation to the end of history and the triumph of the last man.

NIETZSCHE: OPIUM OF THE LAST MEN

In educating his students, Bloom hoped to lift them out of the universal and homogeneous quagmire. But as time went by, the task seemed more and more difficult. The first step was to get them to acknowledge, at least to themselves, that they were indeed last men. If they refused to recognize their lives as symptomatic of post-historical decadence, then they could not be shamed into exchanging their all-American prejudices (or lack thereof) for Bloom's cultured ones. Bloom surmised that their resistance to his art had its source in the uncanny way in which the Left has stolen Nietzsche—the wind from Bloom's sails.

In Bloom's view, the Left has democratized, Americanized, vulgarized, and trivialized Nietzsche. It has turned Nietzsche into a spokesman for all the leftist or post-historical things he despised—democracy, freedom, and equality. But properly understood, Nietzsche belongs to the Right.[47]

According to Bloom, Max Weber is the one who is responsible for introducing Nietzsche to America. Weber made Nietzschean concepts the common fare of American social science. The ideas of Nietzsche could not have taken root in America without his mediation, because Nietzsche was much too tainted with the crimes of fascism to be reputable.[48] According to Bloom, all of Weber's most significant concepts, the very concepts that have become the daily fare of American social science, are thoroughly Nietzschean. Weber's concept of charisma is a case in point.[49]

The "routinization of Weber" was the first step in the Americanization of Nietzsche. Then, with a little help from the leftists of the Frankfurt School, Woody Allen finished what Weber began. The result is the complete absorption of Nietzsche into American popular culture.

Bloom considers Woody Allen the architect of pop relativism. The latter is the trivialization of Nietzsche for the purposes of popular consumption. In *Zelig*, Woody Allen portrays a man in the grip of the nothingness of nihilism. Zelig is a man without a self or a fixed identity. He routinely takes on the identity of those around him—he is a Republican, a mafioso, a woman, a dancing rabbinic Jew, and even Hitler. Zelig is not comfortable in any of the roles he feels compelled to play. As a result, he becomes aware of his nothingness, which is a source of some angst, but not for long. Too much angst is un-American. Psychiatric therapy allows Zelig to discover a cure for his nihilistic afflictions. The solution is for Zelig to become the creator of his own being and his own values. Once cured, Zelig is happy; he no longer feels compelled to play the parts that others desire or expect. Zelig has achieved Heideggerian authenticity. When someone casually remarks "Nice day," Zelig disagrees, even if it really is a nice day. Zelig is now comfortable with nihilism.

Zelig is a parody of existentialism. In my view, the shepherd in Nietzsche's Zarathustra is a paradigm of existential transfiguration. He was choking on a big black snake that had crawled down his throat. Death seemed imminent. Then the solution came to him—bite! And when he bit down with all his might, the shepherd was transfigured— no longer shepherd, but Übermensch. If the snake is nihilism, then the superman is not the one who runs away, but the one who devours it with relish. The existential hero is not the one who despairs, but the one who realizes that nihilism is an opportunity for self-making. In his own ridiculous way, Zelig undergoes that transformation. However, Bloom does not like the American style of "digesting European despair." He misses the humor of it.

Bloom heaps abuse on Woody Allen for having so trivialized the abyss as to make Americans comfortable with nihilism.[50] Bloom resents this trivialization of his hero. Nietzsche's concepts are not meant for the common consumers of culture. The masses are not supposed to regard their beliefs as "values," but as eternal and unchangeable truths. Nor are they intended to regard their social functions as "roles."

So, thanks primarily to the efforts of Max Weber and Woody Allen, America has colonized Nietzsche and compelled him to serve as the "opium of the last men." This was accomplished by applying Nietzsche's standards for creative genius to every mediocrity. Apparently, Chicago has her own "Charisma Cleaners." The result is that America refuses to be realistic about herself. She fails to acknowledge her mediocrity. She refuses to see herself as a nation of last men. Instead, she fancies herself a nation of unique, autonomous, self-made, value-creating supermen.

The absorption of Nietzsche into America's popular culture is the source of Bloom's own troubles as an educator. Making Nietzsche commonplace has usurped Bloom's charms. Nietzsche seems less profound, abstruse, exclusive, outrageous, clandestine, and forbidden. In the face of so much smugness on the part of his last men, the "pimp and midwife" rolled into one finds himself powerless. His students are as unreceptive to the riches he has to offer as the last men were to Zarathustra.

There is no doubt that the Americanization of Nietzsche has taken the wind out of Bloom's sails. But to my mind, the real source of Bloom's troubles is that his conception of educating the young is seriously flawed.

Instead of appealing to their rational faculties, instead of providing them with reasons why truth, honesty, and justice are likely to contribute to their well-being, instead of giving them reasons why promiscuity is debilitating, he appeals to them on a subliminal level. His book is a subtle process of intimidation meant to inculcate prejudices and cultivate specific tastes, likes and dislikes. Every page whispers his unmistakable message: if you don't share my opinions and preferences, you are an uncultured, ignorant slob, comfortable in your animality like Nietzsche's last men.

THE CAVE OR THE VOID?

I hope to have made it clear that Bloom does not dissent from Nietzsche's analysis of culture. It is the democratization of Nietzsche by the Left and his colonization by American pop culture that he rejects.

Bloom thinks that Nietzsche and Plato taught the same facts about culture: the charms of culture have their source in the myths and illusions created by artists and poets; philosophy undermines myth in the name of reason, hence the legendary battle between poetry and philosophy. Insofar as these facts go, Bloom reckons that Nietzsche and Plato were perfectly agreed. However, he thinks that they parted company when it came to deciding whether to give their allegiance to poetry or philosophy. Plato sided with truth against myth, and with philosophy against poetry, whereas Nietzsche sided with myth and culture against truth, and with art and poetry against philosophy.[51]

Bloom is uncomfortable with Nietzsche's repudiation of philosophy. Nietzsche denounces Socrates. He regards the myths of culture as more worthy of love and devotion than the truth. He denounces the life of the philosopher because it is uncommitted and hence inhuman. Bloom does not deny that philosophy demythologizes and demystifies life. Nor does Bloom deny that the void outside the cave is dehumanizing. Nevertheless, he decides to embrace it. Bloom thinks that he is following Plato.[52] But in truth, his position is incoherent.

In my view, the reason that Plato and Nietzsche reached different conclusions is that *they started from different premises*. At the very least, they had opposite conceptions of culture, or "the cave." The Platonic cave is stupefying, herdlike, and glum. In contrast, the truth outside is blazing, brilliant, and beautiful. Unlike Plato's gloomy cave, Nietzsche's cave is luminous, alluring, and captivating. It is adorned with a plethora of noble illusions and life-giving myths concocted by poets. Nietzsche's cave glitters with the dazzling light of chandeliers crafted by artistic genius. It is a cave to end all caves. In contrast, the truth outside is grim— nothing but void, darkness, and brutality. For both Plato and Nietzsche, reason is the way out of the cave. But in view of their conflicting conceptions of the cave and what lies beyond it, it is not surprising that Plato chooses the way out, whereas Nietzsche does not.

The trouble with Bloom's position is that he accepts Nietzsche's premises while rejecting Nietzsche's conclusion. This is an incoherent position.[53] Anyone who believes, with Nietzsche, that art and culture are humanizing, while reason is brutalizing and dehumanizing, cannot side with reason against art. If reason is what Nietzsche says it is, then it is right that it be shunned. If the cave is the only place where there is light, there is no reason to leave it in search of darkness. Nietzsche's conclusion follows naturally from his premises. In light of the latter, Nietzsche is quite justified in denouncing the ignobility of philosophy. In contrast, Bloom's decision to embrace the dark and inhuman is monstrous. Of course, he could justify his choice by resorting to obfuscations borrowed from Leo Strauss: he could point to some occult affinity between the high and the low, the god and the beast, Socrates and Alcibiades. But this sort of obscurantism cannot *convince* anyone. Only someone under the spell of the Pied Piper would leave the glittering cave and wander out into the darkness.[54]

The most disturbing theme of Bloom's book is the comparison of America and Nazi Germany: America is enchanted with the same relativism that led Germany to Nazism. Bloom is suggesting that the Nazis are an example of what happens when all the horizons of the cave have been exploded, when all the humanizing myths of culture have disappeared, when the protective veil of biblical religion has been lifted: men who have pierced through the illusions of the cave are not necessarily afraid of the infinite spaces. On the contrary, they see the void as an opportunity to display their own creative powers and to remake the world in their own image. This insight notwithstanding, Bloom bids his philosophers leave the cave. But what is to guarantee that they will not behave just like the Nazis? Indeed, if Bloom's conception of culture is to be their guide, they would very likely act just like the Nazis did. They would denounce commerce and leisure as the eclipse of culture and the return to animality; they would concoct myths and illusions for the consumption of the herd; and they would insist that death and struggle in defense of these myths is the hallmark of humanity.

IS CULTURE GOOD?

The difficulty with Bloom's conception of culture is that it provides no standard by which culture may be evaluated. His Right Nietzschean understanding of culture is vulnerable to the same criticism that is often directed against Weber's conception of charismatic leadership. Just as charisma is charisma, so culture is culture. Bloom realizes that this criticism is commonly used against Weber, and he uses it himself, but he cannot deal with the same criticism when applied to the Nietzschean conception of culture that he endorses.

As Bloom himself admits, there is no denying that Hitler had charisma. But he adds that anyone who clings to charisma as an exalted idea is bound to regard Hitler as a "parody of charisma." But how are we to tell the real from the fake? What is the difference between Moses, Jesus, and Hitler? On the Nietzschean theory of culture, they cannot be distinguished. For they are all inventors of myths and illusions; they are all consummate liars; they have all imposed order on chaos; and they have all managed to acquire a following. The difference is that Bloom doesn't like Hitler, and Nietzsche doesn't particularly like either Moses or Jesus—but in their scheme of things, they cannot deny them the status of supermen. In the final analysis, Bloom's conception of culture is simply a question of taste.

Even if it is difficult to tell whether culture is good, it is easy to see that it is socially and politically advantageous. There is no doubt that the hypnosis of culture is useful for the preservation of society, both against external enemies as well as the internal winds of change. But it is also the case that the closed society is one that fills its citizens with hatred and prejudice regarding other cultures. And those who believe that their way is the *only* right way, and that all other ways and all other cultures are inferior, if not damnable and depraved, will not hesitate to destroy others if they have the power and opportunity to do so. In this atmosphere, conquest becomes a service to those conquered. Culture forges the illusion that the vanquished are being civilized. Bloom is aware of the fact that culture fosters fanaticism, but he defends it, saying:

> Fanaticism, although dangerous and distorting, could at least produce selfless and extraordinary deeds. But now fanaticism gives way to calculation.[55]

Bloom prefers fanaticism to indifference and the calculation of self-interest. He objects to enlightenment because it dispels the illusions and dampens fanaticism. He would have us count among the civilized only those who are completely trapped by the spell of their own culture. For him, only such a spell could spur men to great deeds; because in his account, men could not possibly take pleasure in doing anything grand and selfless. In the final analysis, Bloom's position encourages a warmongering disposition. Strauss calls it waspishness and praises it as a necessary component of civil society.[56] For Bloom, any attempt to undermine waspishness threatens culture, and brings us closer to the precipice—to openness, pop relativism, nihilism, indifference, the last men, and the end of history. All this assumes that there is nothing noble that transcends culture.

In contrast to Bloom, I believe there is a *noble* truth that transcends culture, access to which is necessary to humanize those in the grip of culture. What human beings share in common is not just their *animality*, but a common understanding of right and wrong to which they appeal in disputes among themselves. If this were not the case, then there would be no room for diplomacy or argument. The only exchange between two totally insulated cultures would be war. However, observation and experience testify to the contrary. Human beings belonging to radically diverse cultures do not just fight, as animals do, they *quarrel*, which means that they use speech to appeal to principles that the other is bound to recognize. They might say "we were here first," or "you fired the first shot."[57] And even when they do wrong, they pretend to justify their misdeeds by appealing to universal moral principles. Of course, these are often seen for what they are—smokescreens. Nevertheless, it means that nations do not simply go about boasting of their crimes and conquests. They recognize a moral order that they transgress at their peril. A nation that becomes too bloodstained will lack luster; and it will be unable to elicit the allegiance of its citizens.

In order to explain what I mean, I will take the liberty of using a personal example. One of my students was a soldier in the Israeli army and was studying in Canada on a student visa. He read Bloom's book, and found it compelling. He felt that he had personally experienced the truth of what Bloom said about culture—a wholehearted commitment to culture was humanizing. However, thanks to his education, he was now able to make the distinction between the good and "one's own." He recognized, as he had not before, that the interests of Israel were not identical with justice and goodness. He feared that he could not go back to the occupied territories and face the *Intifada* with the same equanimity he had before. He was worried that he could no longer be as good a soldier as he once was. As a result, he was convinced that his education had contributed to making him a worse human being and a worse citizen. So enchanted was he by Bloom's message that he blamed his enlightenment for making him less human. For individuals as for history, enlightenment leads back to animality. It seemed to me that this student had understood Bloom very well.

This example vividly illustrates the importance of the distinction between the good man and the good citizen. Only someone who is completely stupefied by the charms of culture will fail to experience an inner conflict between man and citizen. By the same token, the greater the gulf between man and citizen, the greater the danger of social disintegration. It is not just culture that makes a society strong, but justice. Moreover, justice is not simply a matter of being good to friends and evil to enemies—good to fellow citizens and belligerent to outsiders. Justice requires equitable relations between citizens and outsiders. I thought that my student might still go back and fight, but he would be unlikely to do it with the same zeal that he had done before. And far from thinking that he was less human because he was less "waspish," I thought that his education had made him a better man. This is not to say he was no longer a good citizen; only that he was no longer a zealot. Nor does the prevalence of nonzealots make a nation weak. On the contrary, *only* thinking citizens have the ability to improve their nation. Only such citizens can ensure that the gulf between the good man and the good citizen does not become greater than humanity can bear. Only such citizens can make it possible for a nation to elicit allegiance from its citizens without forcing them to surrender the humanizing attachments to truth and justice. This does not mean that there can ever be a society free of injustice. It does not mean that the gulf between the ideal and the actual can ever be transcended. Hegel was keenly aware of this gulf as the source of human unhappiness. In my view, it is the sort of unhappiness that man must live with, and soften. But the gulf cannot be obliterated without terror and tragedy. By the same token, we need not abandon the cave to the proverbial darkness. Nor should we depend exclusively on artificial forms of illumination. Instead, we should discover skylights.

It behooves us to keep in mind that if culture is neither good nor humanizing, then there is no reason to bewail its demise. The truth of the matter is that we are stuck with "culture" because human beings will always be narrow-minded, partisan, ignorant, and unjust. The end of history understood as the end of ideology or culture is not possible.

In conclusion, *culture* is Bloom's word for what Kojève called history and its plethora of ideologies. It refers to that period in human affairs after man's emergence from his primal animality, and before the reanimalization of man at the end of history. The founders of modernity spoke of the first state of nature before the existence of civil society. Now, Bloom declares that we have arrived at the second state of nature. The first state of nature was prior to the advent of historical civilization; the second state of nature comes at the end of history, after the demise of culture.[58] The end of history arrives when all of the horizons of culture have been exploded and culture has become a relic of history. Because culture alone is responsible for the humanization of man, the demise of culture is equivalent to man's return to animality. America is the symbol of the dissolution of culture or the end of history. Her triumph on the world stage fills those who are in the grip of the Kojèvean scheme of things with foreboding. Francis Fukuyama, a former student of Allan Bloom's, is one of those who is prone to post-historical despair. In the next chapter, we shall see how he deals with his unhappiness.

CHAPTER

▪12▫

Francis Fukuyama's Unhappy Consciousness

F rancis Fukuyama's book *The End of History and the Last Man* is first and foremost a popularization of the ideas of Alexandre Kojève.[1] The very title of Fukuyama's book captures the paradoxical nature of Kojève's thought. On one hand, *end of history* smacks of the bright optimism of Marx, on the other hand, *last man* refers to Nietzsche's pessimistic prognostications.

At the hands of Kojève, the end of history has become an expression of the unhappiness that grips those who are convinced that history, understood as the domain of significant events and glorious actions, has become the casualty of the modern world. At the end of history, in a world defined and shaped by liberal democracy, *nothing significant is possible.*

In what follows, I will show that Fukuyama has uncritically absorbed the ideas, tastes, and intellectual errors of Kojève's thought. Fukuyama's thinking displays the same absence of dialectic, the same dualism between master and slave, the same endowment of mastery with all the genuinely human attributes, the same view of history as the triumph of slavery, the same account of liberal democracy as the progressive animalization of man, the same abhorrence of equality, the same romanticization of the warrior ethic, the same fascistic celebration of violence, and the same crisis of manliness. I will argue that, far from ennobling political life as Fukuyama believes, Kojèvean notions pervert, debase, and diminish it.

The collapse of the Soviet Empire and the demise of communism around the globe have led Fukuyama to marvel at Kojève's prescience.

Kojève was right in thinking that history ends with the global realization of liberal democracy.

Fukuyama's book has puzzled and perplexed its reviewers. How could a thesis that is so simple-minded and puerile be advanced?[2] Why has it received so much attention? In light of the rise of nationalism and Islamic fundamentalism, how could anyone think that liberal democracy has triumphed once and for all? With environmental catastrophe looming so large, how could anyone assume that the earth can support the globalization of a technological culture?[3] And how can a book that allegedly celebrates the triumph of American liberal democracy contain so much gloom?[4]

END OF HISTORY VS. END OF IDEOLOGY

Fukuyama's end of history thesis is often compared with the end of ideology thesis propagated in the 1950's and 60's by American political scientists such as Seymour Martin Lipset and Daniel Bell. But as I will show below, the similarities are extremely superficial. The end of ideology thesis emerged in the context of the Cold War; its goal was to export American liberty to the world and to counteract the seductions of Soviet propaganda. It was firmly rooted in the tradition of American liberal democracy. These theorists would be delighted to see America as the single superpower around the globe. They did not conceal their enthusiasm for making America the model for the world.

Bell and Lipset believed that, within the advanced industrialized countries, the political ideologies of the Right and the Left had become exhausted.[5] The Right no longer believed that laissez-faire capitalism was viable—a certain degree of government intervention was necessary. By the same token, the Left realized that complete socialization of the economy posed too great a threat to freedom, as the Soviet example made clear. As a result, a new "consensus" was forged that effectively brought an end to the age of ideology. Good riddance. Ideology will not be missed; for it is the stuff of politics, and politics is the domain of values, conflict, and unreason. In view of their anticipation of the eclipse of politics, it is not surprising that Lipset and Bell decided to move into sociology. They surmised that all of the interesting problems of domestic life would be sociological. This turned out to be something of a self-fulfilling prophecy. Their influence on political science turned the latter into a pedestrian discipline that had nothing to do with questions of truth, justice, or the good. The disappearance of ideology also meant the disappearance of competing conceptions of the good. The study of politics became as mundane as it was "scientific." Of course, the political science that they inspired was far from neutral, on the contrary, it enshrined the values of the American status quo.[6] The latter became the yardstick against which every political order around the globe was to be measured by the science of politics.

All this is not to say that politics disappeared from the face of the earth. As Bell and Lipset acknowledged, politics remained a matter of great concern in international affairs. The international arena continued to be the domain of struggle between American liberalism and Soviet communism. The end of ideology theorists were not confident in the triumph of American liberalism. They believed that the conditions of poverty and hopelessness in the Third World made the apocalyptic character of communist ideology almost irresistible. The problem of American foreign policy, as they saw it, was to devise strategies that might prevent Third World countries from falling prey to the seductions of Soviet ideology.

In contrast to the end of ideology thesis, the end of history thesis has its roots in the European tradition of *Kulturpessimismus* that Fukuyama inherits from Kojève and Strauss. It is profoundly antiliberal and antidemocratic; and far from hoping to export American culture to the world, it regards America's supremacy as the global triumph of mediocrity. Its mission is to save the world from increasing Americanization and to save America from herself.

THE COLLAPSE OF THE SOVIET UNION

For Kojève, as for many European intellectuals who followed Heidegger, the collapse of the Soviet Empire would not have been considered a world historical event. As we have seen, Kojève and Heidegger did not consider the differences between American liberalism and Soviet communism to be decisive. On the contrary, they thought that both Washington and Moscow shared the same goals of modernity. They were both secular, materialistic, technological, efficient, egalitarian, and universalistic. Both the United States and the Soviet Union represented the modernist uprooting of people from their soil or homeland in a quest for universalism and homogeneity. They both aimed for a global society of equal and prosperous men and women. They wanted to create a global human community that was devoid of the old class hierarchies. The difference between them was one of means, not ends. It was a difference of style—the style with which they set out to conquer the world. The Americans used seductive psychological and commercial techniques, whereas the Soviets specialized in systematic terror.

For those who regard America with so much contempt, the collapse of the Soviet Empire and the emergence of the United States as the undisputed military power around the globe is not a reason for celebration. For them, the preeminence of American power and influence spells the end of European high culture, refinement, and good taste. What makes these high-minded Europeans particularly gloomy is the fact that American military might is accompanied by the undisputed appeal of what they see as America's tinsel culture, brazen commercialism, rampant technology, mechanism, utilitarianism, and general all-around vulgarity.

FUKUYAMA'S INTELLECTUAL BAGGAGE

Francis Fukuyama stands in the privileged position of knowing that America's soapy advertising has won out over Soviet terrorism. As a student of Allan Bloom's, Fukuyama is well versed in European *Kulturpessimismus*. But despite his intellectual baggage, Fukuyama is much too American to wallow in European despair or to wax nostalgic for a lost and irretrievable past. This is not to say that there is not a great deal of despair and nostalgia in the book, but only that Fukuyama's first instinct is to tackle the conditions of modernity with aplomb.

At one level, Fukuyama's book can be read as a heroic response to the despair and despondency of his intellectual mentors. He agrees with them that the universal and homogeneous state is here. Life no longer has the fullness it once had when it was anchored in that "complex of ethical habits and customs" called culture.[7] Now culture is no more. Democratic institutions and market economics have been erected on the grave of culture. But it is cowardly to lament. There is no going back. We cannot reinvent the old myths and religions. We are post-historical men. We cannot expect to live in the comfort of the old horizons because philosophy has exploded all horizons. Neither can we live in expectation of new gods or supermen to save us. All we can do is to make the best of an inevitable situation—a situation that is the product of historical "progress." When Fukuyama talks of progress, he puts the word in quotation marks because he thinks that it does not constitute an improvement from lower to higher forms of human life, but the reverse—from the first man to the last man. Let us turn to his account of history.

HISTORY AS A THYMOTIC AFFAIR

Fukuyama begins with the Kojèvean assumption that politics, properly understood, is a struggle for recognition. Following Allan Bloom, Fukuyama thinks that Plato also acknowledged the importance of the desire for recognition, which he attributed to that part of the human soul he called *thymos*, or spiritedness. Fukuyama is one of those writers who has to find a Greek word to dignify his discourse, for fear that it could not be sufficiently elevated otherwise. *Thymos* is the word he appropriates; he uses it as a synonym for the human desire for recognition. Later, I will explain why adopting this term is particularly inappropriate. But for now, I will use the term as Fukuyama uses it.

Thymos plays a critical role in Fukuyama's dialectic. History begins with two different manifestations of *thymos*, which he dubs *megalothymia* and *isothymia*.[8] The difference between these two "thymotic" passions is stark. *Megalothymia* is the *thymos* of great men; it animates the few, as opposed to the many, the masters, as opposed to the slaves. It is the desire to dominate others in order to be recognized as a superior. Fukuyama identifies it with the desire for glory, the desire to be Caesar, Napoleon, or Stalin.[9] It leads to domination and conquest. In contrast, *isothymia* is the humble demand for equal and mutual recognition. It is the *thymos* of the many, as opposed to the few, the ordinary, as opposed to the extraordinary, the mediocre as opposed to the great. It is not the desire to dominate or to be superior, but the humble self-respect of common folk who refuse to be dominated, exploited, manipulated, or treated like objects. In short, *megalothymia* is the desire for mastery whereas *isothymia* is the desire for mutual and equal recognition.[10]

Politics is a thymotic affair. It is a clash of two conflicting and incompatible manifestations of *thymos*—*megalothymia* and *isothymia*. History is the story of this conflict. It comes to an end when or *if* this conflict is resolved. The thesis of Fukuyama's book is that the conflict may be coming to an end because *megalothymia* has been defeated, rechanneled, redirected, or sublimated into economic life. History is moving in the direction of the victory of *isothymia*. Insofar as liberal democracy is responsible for the triumph of *isothymia*, it is appropriate to think of it as the final chapter of the historical drama.

To understand why the outcome of history is not a cause for celebration, it behooves us to examine the story and its protagonists more closely. We will find that it is the same story as told, not by Hegel, but by Kojève.

In the earliest ages of mankind, *thymos*, in its youthful form as *megalothymia*, is the motor of history. The "first man" is intensely social because he is preoccupied, above all else, with what others think of him. He wants to be "recognized as a man."[11] To prove himself, he embarks on "a violent struggle to the death for pure prestige."[12] He thinks that he can gain prestige, preeminence, and recognition, *not* by acting in a way that is sociable, affable, civil, gracious, and just, but by trying to conquer, crush, subdue, vanquish, and enslave others. Hegel would say that he was most unwise, that these sorts of tactics will not give him the recognition he longs for. Like Kojève, Fukuyama believes that risking life in a battle for pure prestige is a distinctively human characteristic, which sets man apart from animals. It proves that, unlike animals, men are free to thwart the animal instinct for life and self-preservation by risking their life for something that transcends the merely biological.

Man's desire for recognition therefore leads to bloody battles in which each man tries to impose himself on others as an object of supreme value. These battles are the foundation of class stratification; they determine who will be master and who will be slave. Needless to say, the winners become the masters, and the losers their slaves. The earliest societies are therefore aristocratic.[13]

Fukuyama does not simply conclude that the aristocrats displayed superior strength or brutality. Instead, he concludes, as did Kojève, that the masters deserve to win because they are *"more human."*[14] The masters are superior to the slaves because they display the human characteristic par excellence in great abundance—they risk life for the sake of pure prestige. It is the latter that "constitutes man's identity as man."[15] The success of the master is connected to his ability to transcend his animal instinct for self-preservation and to live according to the "warrior ethos," which is to say, conquer or die. This ethos is proof of his manliness. It demonstrates that his commitment to prestige is much greater than his commitment to life. The master therefore deserves to win, and the slave deserves to lose. Fukuyama tells us that he admires Hegel for finding something "morally praiseworthy in the pride of the "aristocrat-warrior" and something "ignoble" about the slave.[16] This is not surprising since Kojève is the only Hegel he knows.

For Fukuyama as for Kojève, the slave is not a slave just because he has lost the battle. He is a slave because of his own failings. His slavery is a result of his inability to adopt the aristocratic contempt for life. He has not been able to live up to the aristocratic ethic, or warrior ethos. He could have chosen death, if he was man enough. Instead, he succumbs to the animal instinct for self-preservation and chooses a life of slavery. The slave is therefore inferior *as a human being,* and therefore *deserves* to be a slave. Even though the slave succumbs to the animal instinct for life, he is not completely lost to humanity. He retains a degree of his humanity insofar as he continues to long for recognition. But he modifies and tempers this longing. Instead of yearning to be preeminent, or to be recognized as a superior, he longs merely to be recognized as an equal. This desire for equal and mutual recognition is the slavish manifestation of *thymos,* but it is *thymos* nevertheless.

Isothymia is the slave's demand for equal recognition.[17] It is the demand to be treated as an end, not a means. As is the case of all thymotic passions, the concern is not with what one is, but merely with how one is regarded or treated by others.

Christianity, which Kojève and Fukuyama regard as the slave ideology par excellence, is the great inspiration behind this slavish manifestation of *thymos.* Christianity teaches that all men are equal before God because they are all moral agents who are free to choose between good and evil. This claim to equality is understood to be totally universal—every human being supposedly qualifies because the claim is not dependent on merit.

Liberalism, as understood by Kojève and Fukuyama, is the secularization of Christianity. It tries to implement in the political domain what Christianity proclaimed in the theological.

The true spiritual father of liberalism was Hobbes. He was the real enemy of aristocratic pride, which is the "virtue" of the warrior ethic.[18] Hobbes did not realize that the desire to dominate others on the basis of a "superior virtue" was ennobling.[19] Hobbes saw nothing praiseworthy in the pride of the aristocrat-warrior. Instead, he dubbed it "vainglory" and maintained that it was the root of all human misery. Consciously, deliberately, and methodically, Hobbes proceeded to root out the aristocratic ethos from the depths of man's soul. Fukuyama echoes Kojève and Strauss in maintaining that history has conspired against the "higher types"—against the master.[20]

Insofar as liberalism was a revolution against traditional aristocracy, it had to "declare war" on the "aristocratic warrior."[21] The plan was to make politics a rational affair.[22] This was to be accomplished by turning the animal part of the psyche against the noble or human part. Liberalism therefore unleashed animal appetites and allowed them, with the help of reason, to conquer the spirited or thymotic part of the soul. By becoming the slave of the appetites, reason played a critical role in the conquest of *thymos*. In short, the human psyche was the battlefield of the liberal revolution.

Nothing represents this animalization of man better than the bourgeois. He is utterly devoted to life, which means that he has totally given way to the animalistic part of his nature.[23] He loves security, and shuns risk; he is selfish, self-satisfied, and materialistic. Nothing is more nauseating than this "last man" as Fukuyama calls the bourgeois. The animalization of man goes hand in hand with the "economization of life."[24] Liberalism turns politics into economics. It depoliticizes the aristocratic world of mastery. War is central to aristocratic life. But war is "economically suboptimal," so, liberalism transforms the aristocratic warrior into a peaceful businessman.[25] Liberalism swindles the noble warrior into sacrificing his aristocratic pride in exchange for peace, material comfort, and security.[26] In this way, liberalism replaces the "noble contempt for `mere' life" with the plebeian concern for self-preservation.[27]

It is not clear how liberalism managed to swindle these noble warriors. It sounds highly unlikely that such manly lovers of war and risk could be so easily seduced by the prospect of mere peace and security. But in any case, Fukuyama believes it happened, and is continuing to happen around the globe. Noble warriors are everywhere being transformed into successful businessmen. Throughout the Third World, descendants of warriors are hanging up their swords as "family heirlooms" and taking their place behind the computer terminal![28] The globalization of liberalism turns noble savages and samurai into businessmen and computer jockeys. This is the human tragedy that political scientists casually refer to as the process of "modernization."[29]

Nowhere has this process been more successful than in America. Nowhere has the bourgeois emerged as victorious; and nowhere has the economization of life been more complete. American politics is a conspiracy against greatness. It gives no scope to the noble *thymos* of the few—they are decisively hemmed in by a system of checks and balances. American politics will not permit a Caesar or a Napoleon, but only a Jimmy Carter or a Ronald Reagan—the people's servants, not their masters. The result is the wholesale emasculation of men and the creation of a society of "men without chests."[30]

According to Fukuyama, Nietzsche was the "greatest and most articulate champion of *thymos* in modern times" and "the prophet of its revival."[31] Even when it might have seemed hopeless, Nietzsche manfully asserted the primacy of *megalothymia* and sought to undo the "damage" that modern liberalism has done to man's pride. Fukuyama makes a valiant effort to escape from Nietzsche's conclusions—the return to *megalothymia* and all the horrors that may entail. By turning to Hegel, he thinks that he might discover the "noble" core of liberalism. But alas, the only Hegel he knows is Kojève, and as we have seen, Kojève's ideas are little more than a Nietzschean inversion of Hegel. Fukuyama makes an effort to put the best light on the human predicament. He surmises that the master's quest for recognition ends in an "impasse." The "tragedy of the master" is that he is "deeply human" *only* in the act of risking his life.[32] Once they settle down and experience a few years of peace and tranquillity, the aristocrats "degenerate into pampered and effeminate courtiers."[33] The implication is that the manful quest for recognition requires conditions of perpetual turmoil and belligerence.

History must therefore turn to the slave. Following Kojève, Fukuyama thinks that the slave must accomplish two things. First, he must master nature, and second, he must overcome the fear of death that led to his enslavement. Again, the French Revolution is the key to the slave's emancipation. In the revolution the slaves risk their lives, and in so doing, overcome the fear of death that originally defined them as slaves.[34] The result is the realization of universal recognition. Once again, history is the triumph of the slave. Now, the slaves are the new masters.

The problem is this. The society of masters that has been established by the victory of the slaves in the French Revolution is open to the same objection as the former society of masters. Once the revolution is won, and peace and tranquillity are entrenched, then the humanity of the new masters is in question. Those who no longer fight are not human. Decadence sets in and the preoccupation with consumption and material security returns us to the contemptible world of Nietzsche's last men, embodied in the American bourgeois. Once again history leads to the animalization of man—this time on a mass scale.

Fukuyama tries to make the case for Hegel, but by relying on Kojève he is forced back to the Nietzschean conclusions he hoped to escape. History ends in the animalization of man, the eclipse of manliness, and the triumph of the slave morality. But is this predicament inescapable?

KOJÈVE OR STRAUSS?

Fukuyama wavers between two alternative positions. Either the conflict between *megalothymia* and *isothymia* has conclusively and irreversibly ended with the defeat of *megalothymia*, or the struggle between the protagonists continues, which is to say that history is not over. As we have seen above, these two alternative positions belong to Kojève and Strauss respectively. Stephen Holmes is quite right in thinking that Fukuyama is strung out between the two thinkers, and that this tension accounts for many of the contradictory elements of his work.[35] However, the two positions are not as far apart as is generally believed to be. They both exalt mastery and understand history as the eclipse of this manly virtue. They do not differ in their assessment of the present, only in that of the future. Kojève thought that a return to history, properly speaking, was unlikely, and that we had better make the best of the dehumanizing end by being self-consciously playful and frivolous, or by mimicking the glory of history's beginning through the *acte gratuit*. Strauss anticipated the eternal recurrence of the same. He thought that the "real men" and their desire for glory (or *megalothymia* as Fukuyama would have it) will not remain shackled forever, and that they will plunge us back into history, to repeat the process all over again.

There is no doubt that Fukuyama is nostalgic for the lost *thymos*. His book ends with a warning as well as a plea on behalf of *megalothymia*. He tells us that our only hope of hanging on to liberal democracy is to give scope to the manifestations of *megalothymia*. Otherwise, thymotic passions will plunge us back into history. Back into history? What happened to the end of history? Fukuyama hedges on whether the end of history is decisive or not. He ends up saying that we are moving inexorably toward greater freedom and democracy—but that could change.

What are we to do to escape the possible wrath of *megalothymia*? Fukuyama counsels us not to listen to the demands of *isothymia*—the demands for increasing democratization. In other words, we must take seriously the criticisms of liberal democracy that issues from the Right. We must give scope to *megalothymia* within liberal democracy. The very least we can do is to allow those with extraordinary ambition to become exceedingly wealthy. Needless to say, this is precisely the sort of idea that endears Fukuyama to the neoconservatives. But they are not aware of the extent to which this position constitutes a colossal compromise on Fukuyama's part. After all, the sublimation of *megalothymia* into economics transfigures it almost beyond recognition. And there is no doubt that Fukuyama longs for the real thing.

In fairness to Fukuyama, we must acknowledge that he did not set out to glorify *megalothymia*. On the contrary, he was more or less resigned to its defeat. He set out to discover something ennobling in *isothymia* that would confer a certain dignity on liberal democracy. However, the gurus he chose to follow made that impossible. The only thing of value that he was able to attribute to *isothymia* is that it was *thymos* nevertheless, and for all its slavish humility, contained vestiges of pride that were reminiscent of the lost aristocratic ethos. Like Kojève, he did his utmost to present the unhappy predicament in its best light; he did his best to be cheerful; he made a heroic effort to convince himself that the slave morality has a special dignity after all. But in the final analysis, his fate was the same as Kojève's. Like the latter, his cheerfulness was a thin veneer that could not conceal his unhappiness.

KOJÈVE'S LEGACY AND ITS TROUBLES

History

The view of history as moving purposefully toward the satisfaction of man's deepest desires presupposes a set of highly questionable assumptions that neither Kojève nor Fukuyama are able to sustain. It assumes that (*a*) human desires are universally homogeneous rather than being mutually incompatible and irreconcilable, that (*b*) human desires are in principle satisfiable, and that (*c*) they are actually satisfied by liberal democracy. So, assuming that there are only one set of nonconflicting desires as the motor of history, and assuming that these desires are inherently satisfiable, and that liberal democracy is successful in accomplishing the satisfaction in question, then the thesis is plausible. But as we have seen, Kojève and Fukuyama are unable to sustain any of these assumptions. Far from being homogeneous, man's deepest desire, the desire for recognition, is divided into two mutually incompatible and irreconcilable passions—the quest for dominance and the quest for equality. So, far from proceeding toward the satisfaction of human desires, history is a perennial conflict between conflicting and irreconcilable ends.

Dualism and Dialectic

The Kojèvean view of history is not Hegelian or dialectical in any meaningful sense of the term. In a dialectical account, the opposites are reconciled in a synthesis that transcends the opposition—just as a child is identical to neither parent, yet incorporates aspects of each. Anyone who is eager to ennoble liberalism by bestowing upon it the mantle of Hegelianism must argue that liberalism is a synthesis of the demands for equality and those of inequality. He must argue that liberalism is a compromise between equality and hierarchy—formal equality before the law and material inequality in proportion to merit and achievement. But

Fukuyama does not make this point. Instead, he presents us with a dualism that cannot be resolved unless one of the protagonists is completely vanquished. Like Kojève, he believes that history has all but vanquished everything he considers great and noble. And naturally, he is nostalgic for what has been banished.

Fascistic Resonances

Kojève and Fukuyama have fallen in love with the dialectic; they are enthralled by negativity, struggle, diremption, war, and death. In the absence of the dialectic, life lacks luster—it is static, stagnant, slavish, and unmanly. Man is a political animal, and politics is a dialectic of struggle and death. The dialectic cannot afford a moment's rest without threatening man's humanity. Peace, prosperity, and tranquillity are anathema to the lovers of dialectic. They are political junkies in Jon Elster's sense of the term.[36] They cannot get enough of politics. They believe that politics alone gives life meaning. They see it not as a means to an end, but as an end in itself. Political junkies despise liberalism because they think that it depoliticizes the world. Liberalism turns politics into a mere means, rather than an end. And what is worse, it subordinates politics to *life*. Liberalism does indeed turn politics into a vehicle for creating a sufficient degree of order, peace, and prosperity that would make it possible for human beings to live and laugh, dance and sing, buy and sell, read and write, worry and worship, and a host of other mundane and majestic activities that make up human life. But such love of life is anathema to the devotees of death and dialectic.

In contrast to the liberal tradition, the republican tradition has always regarded politics as an end, and not as a means. But Kojèveans like Fukuyama cannot hide behind republicanism. Republicans do not define politics as war, negativity, struggle, and dialectic. Instead, they see politics as an exercise in the arts of speech, decision-making, and compromise. They believe that participation in politics educates citizens and makes them more public-spirited, less isolated, atomic, and powerless. The best-known adherents of this tradition in our time are Hannah Arendt and those who have followed in her trail—such as G. J. A. Pocock and Charles Taylor. But the Kojèvean mind glorifies politics understood as war, violence, and death.

The Kojèvean may be in love with the dialectic, but he cannot fathom it. The latter is a purposeful movement toward harmony, reconciliation, resolution, and synthesis. Kojèvean thought is undialectical; history is a battle that culminates in winners and losers, victors and vanquished, masters and slaves. But even the winners cannot be winners for long, for it is only the fight that gives meaning to their existence.

The Kojèvean dialectic is a dualism between two incompatible and irreconcilable protagonists. History ends with the victory of the slave; while the master is completely vanquished.

Having endowed the master with everything genuinely human, free, noble, and great, Fukuyama waxes nostalgic over that noble warrior of old who has been effectively exorcised from our world. Having noted the humanity of the master in relation to the slave, the nobility of *megalothymia*, and the eclipse of that "superior virtue" at the hands of liberalism, it is now possible to understand why Fukuyama *cannot* regard the victory of liberal democracy as a cause for celebration.

Equal Recognition

At the end of the historical drama, the principle of equality is victorious. But all his efforts notwithstanding, Fukuyama cannot see anything worthy in the quest for equal and mutual recognition. Fukuyama regards even the most modest demands for equality as having no legitimate foundation whatsoever. And even worse, he believes that they spring from the resentment of the inferior many toward the superior few. For example, he is convinced that what ignited the revolution against communism in East Germany was not just its economic inefficiency, or the long-standing grievances of the people against the communist regime, but the "thymotic anger" that was the response of the average East German to seeing the opulence of Erich Honecker's residence on television.[37] Fukuyama sees the triumph of *isothymia* in terms of the victory of resentment. Fukuyama has so thoroughly absorbed Nietzschean tastes that he is unable to learn any lessons from Hegel.

The trouble is that *isothymia* has no status in Fukuyama's scheme of things. In the case of *megalothymia*, the master's demand to be recognized as a superior rested on his ability to risk life, to contravene his natural instincts, and to defy death. These are not the most admirable qualities in a human being, but if we assume that they are, then we would have to admit that the master's claim to recognition is not completely vacuous. But this is not the case in the slavish manifestation of *thymos*. It seems that the demand of the many for recognition has no basis other than their own sense of self-worth, and at most, the Christian belief in the equality of all before God—an equality that is understood to be totally indifferent to merit.

Fukuyama believes that this relatively vacuous universal claim is the foundation of liberalism and the main inspiration behind the civil rights movement in America. This allows Fukuyama to advance a rather bizarre interpretation of both Christianity and the civil rights movement. When Martin Luther King says in his famous "dream speech" that he had a dream that his children and their children will live in a world where they are judged by the content of their characters rather than the color of their skin, Fukuyama thinks that he is pleading for equal and mutual recognition *independent* of merit. But King takes it for granted that some people are morally superior to others or have better characters. A man of character is not bent on conquering, crushing, and subduing others for his own self-aggrandizement; he does not regard members of the opposite sex simply as territory for his "sexual conquests";[38] he is civil, gracious, and just; he cares about the well-being of others; and he keeps his word even when it is not convenient for him to do so. He is therefore more worthy of trust, more fit for responsibility, and more deserving of recognition. Martin Luther King wants to be judged by the quality of his character. It does not occur to Fukuyama that there can be distinctions among people on the basis of their character. The only distinction he recognizes is between those who flirt with death and those who opt for slavery.

Fukuyama's perspective is inimical to the most modest demands of equality. He associates the simple demand for the equality of all citizens before the law with a nightmarish egalitarianism of sameness and homogeneity. This radical egalitarianism is achieved at the expense of all those who excel in beauty, music, art, science, or sports. Fukuyama's interpretation of Martin Luther King's "dream speech" is a case in point. His understanding of the civil rights movement in America conjures up the wild fictions of Kurt Vonnegut. A comparison between Vonnegut's "Harrison Bergeron" and Fukuyama's picture of America explains what I mean.

In "Harrison Bergeron," Vonnegut imagines a society where:

> Everybody was finally equal. They weren't only equal before God or before the law. They were equal every which way. Nobody was smarter than anybody else. Nobody was better looking than anybody else. Nobody was stronger or quicker than anybody else. All this equality was due to the 211th, 212th, and 213th Amendments to the Constitution. . . .[39]

In that society, anyone who was more intelligent than average was required by law to wear a "mental handicap radio" in order to keep his or her brains scrambled. Likewise, anyone with exceptional good looks had to wear a red rubber ball for a nose, keep her eyebrows shaved off, and her teeth randomly covered with black caps. In extreme cases, good-looking people might have to wear a grotesque mask. These precautions would ensure that these people would not take advantage of their good looks or superior intelligence. Nor was talent appreciated and enjoyed. Ballerinas of ethereal beauty and grace were required to wear hideous masks and dance with heavy bags tied to their ankles, which allowed them to do little more than hobble awkwardly on stage. In this oppressively egalitarian society, Harrison Bergeron, the incarnation of *megalothymia*, is born. He wants to become Emperor, and chooses the ballerina with the most grotesque mask as his Empress. In an inspired flash, they tear off their handicaps—their noses, their masks, their bags, and their legislated brain scramblers. And for an exhilarating moment, they dance in defiance of the laws of the land as well as the laws of gravity. Quickly, the Handicap General puts an end to this alarming scene, and shoots them dead. This is the picture of America that Fukuyama shares with Kojève, Strauss, and Bloom.

Plato's Thymos vs. Desire for Recognition

At the heart of the end of history thesis is the assumption that the quest for prestige is distinctively human. Even if this is the case, it does not follow that it is either noble or admirable. In truth, those who pursue recognition above all else are not the most savory types. Fukuyama is totally uncritical of the desire for recognition. He uses it both as a description of human nature *and* as an account of what constitutes manliness. It does not occur to Fukuyama that the preoccupation with recognition is a human failing. People who seek recognition above all else care little about what they are or what sorts of excellences they possess. Such people generally invest all their energies in making the right impression; they are concerned more with appearances than with reality. They do not strive to be honest, but only to appear honest. Nor is their desire for recognition a desire to be excellent or to excel at something—music, diving, painting, or dancing. If they surpass others in anything, it is only in their desire for self-aggrandizement, preeminence, and prestige. Moreover, such persons rarely attain the regard of others they seek. The truth has a way of tripping them up.

Fukuyama's appropriation of the word *thymos* shows how oblivious he is to the distinction between those who pursue excellence and those who merely desire recognition. Plato used the word to refer to the "spirited" part of the psyche as opposed to the appetitive and rational parts. Someone who is spirited has lots of spunk, for good or for ill.[40] *Thymos* is therefore not an "innate sense of justice," as Fukuyama maintains,[41] it is connected to justice only when the person is already just, and pursues the just course with the typical vigor of a spirited person. *Thymos* is connected to self-esteem, but only in the just person. Fukuyama is mistaken in thinking that self-esteem is the same as the desire for recognition, or that Plato's *thymos* is indistinguishable from the desire for recognition.[42]

Plato's example of Leontius is as clear as Fukuyama's reading is stupefying.[43] Leontius is a just and honorable man in the Platonic sense of that term. In that sense, justice is first and foremost (though by no means exclusively) about one's relation to oneself. Justice is a psychic condition in which reason, or the best part of the psyche, rules over the appetites with the help of the spirited part. In the just man, the spirited part sides with reason and champions its cause. Plato uses Leontius to explain what he means. One day, Leontius was coming up from the Piraeus when he saw some corpses left behind by the executioner. He was overwhelmed by an urge to look at them. He tried to fight his morbid curiosity, but to no avail. Finally he gave way to his desire. He was so disgusted with himself that he railed against himself, and speaking to his eyes, he shouted, "Now have your way, damn you. Go ahead and feast at this banquet for sordid appetites."[44] Plato uses the story to illustrate that desire and spirit are two distinct parts of the psyche. There is no doubt that the incident damaged Leontius's self-esteem. But this Platonic account of self-esteem has nothing to do with having others recognize you—it is not an intersubjective phenomenon. It does not depend on the perceptions of others, but only on your own perception of yourself. Nor does it imply that the latter is just a function of the extent to which others esteem you. Others may esteem you very highly, but they don't know that you regularly feast your eyes on corpses. It is your own knowledge of your conduct that fills you with contempt for yourself. Nothing else is necessary. Plato's model is an objectivist model that ill fits the Kojèvean paradigm, which is intersubjective. In other words, the Kojèvean desire for recognition makes your own self-esteem dependent on the extent to which you are esteemed by others. It is a desire for "another consciousness" to share your own supposedly high evaluation of yourself. It is not a desire to change yourself, or insist on a higher standard of conduct for yourself; it is merely the desire to change the way others regard you. But Leontius was not concerned with the way others regarded him. He was concerned with the sort of person he was. He was not happy with himself and was determined to change his conduct. For all these reasons, the marriage between Plato's conception of *thymos* and Kojève's desire for recognition is one that cannot be consummated.

Far from ennobling liberal democracy, the understanding of politics as a struggle for recognition debases it. Fukuyama's understanding of the conflict over abortion as a struggle for recognition is a case in point. In his understanding, the antiabortionist believes that a climate in which abortion is readily available will undermine the status of the family, and along with that, the recognition accorded to her as a mother in society. She does not want to lose that recognition, so she takes a stand against abortion. On the other side, the prochoice woman wants to be the equal of men in society, and considers her capacity to bear children as an obstacle that may interfere with her desire for recognition as the equal of men. So she takes a stand in favor of abortion. We are left with two equally illegitimate (or is it legitimate?) demands for recognition. The concept of recognition does not begin to fathom the politics of abortion, let alone ennoble it.

For all his preoccupation with recognition, Fukuyama has not thought about what it is that people admire. People do admire strength; and they do admire courage; and courage does involve a willingness to risk one's life. But people don't admire strength for its own sake, or strength that is badly used. They admire the strength of those who use it for good purposes. Therefore, some account of what sorts of ends are good is necessary to understand what it is about strength that people admire. The same is true for courage. Courage is not fearlessness, nor is it a desire to contravene nature for the very sake of that contravention. Courage is not a desire to risk life just to prove you have an "aristocratic" contempt for it. Courage is, at the very least, the ability to risk life and limb for the sake of something other than one's own selfish quest for prestige.

Crisis of Manliness

The source of Fukuyama's unhappiness at the end of history is his longing for the lost *thymos*. I do not wish to argue about whether history has or has not ended in the nauseating specter of the last man. I believe that those who are so persuaded will not be convinced by any facts to the contrary. What I wish to address is the underlying assumptions that lead to the fashionable melancholy of those superior few who believe that history has conspired to emasculate them.

What is at stake is not a thesis about history, but deeply inculcated and unexamined assumptions about the high and low, noble and base, manly and bestial. It is no exaggeration to say that the end of history thesis contains a crisis of manliness of monumental proportions. Like Kojève, Fukuyama labors under the impression that to be a real man is to be animated with a desire to conquer and dominate others. The whole book is a subtle, but unmistakable, celebration of death and violence, on the ground that they are inseparable from masculine virility. Wittingly or unwittingly, Fukuyama follows Kojève in celebrating the "master morality" understood in the crudest sense of the *libido dominandi*.

What is it about *megalothymia* that fills Fukuyama with so much rapture? What is it about the master that makes him the symbol of true manhood in the Kojèvean scheme of things? What makes Kojève and Fukuyama think that risking life in a battle for pure prestige is the manliest of qualities?

There is no basis for thinking that risking life needlessly is distinctively human. Fukuyama acknowledges the claims of modern biologists, according to whom animals also fight battles for prestige.[45] They do not just seek their own self-preservation, or the preservation of their young, they stake out territory and fight battles for dominance. But Fukuyama dismisses this as "instinctual behavior," which is to say that it is itself part of nature, and not a contravention of it. But why can the same thing not be said of the human propensity to risk life for the sake of recognition and prestige? Fukuyama does not say. The only response he gives is that engaging in these battles makes man a "moral agent" and this cannot be said of any animal. But he does not explain why it can be said of man.

One of the difficulties of the Kojèvean way of thinking is that it unconsciously and uncritically identifies nobler or higher ends with nonmaterial ones. Moreover, it proceeds to establish a dichotomy between the low, materialistic, animalistic, and ignoble on one hand, and the high, nonmaterialistic, genuinely human, and noble on the other. It may well be the case that human beings are characterized by nonmaterial pursuits. But there is no reason to conclude that all nonmaterialistic pursuits are noble. The pursuit of prestige may be nonmaterial, but that does not make it noble. Fukuyama speaks nonsense when he says that the willingness to risk life in a bloody battle for pure prestige is a "moral phenomenon," or that it is the stuff of man's "moral fibre," or that it proves that man is a "moral agent."[46] If fighting battles for prestige makes man a moral agent, then we must conclude that animals who engage in this sort of behavior must also be moral agents. So understood, moral agency does not set men apart from animals.

Fukuyama's effort to distinguish men from animals also relies on the human capacity for freedom. Following Kojève, Fukuyama believes that the desire for recognition raises man above the animals because it illustrates that man is *free* to thwart nature and act contrary to her commands. But the Kojèveans have a curious conception of freedom. On one hand, they reject the liberal or "negative" account of freedom as absence of external restraint, to do as one pleases. But they also reject the "positive" view of freedom as the capacity to exercise internal restraints, using reason to choose among our desires, acting according to some, and suppressing others. Instead, they regard freedom as the capacity to act contrary to *all* of our natural, or biological, desires, especially the desire for self-preservation. Man's freedom is understood in terms of the capacity to *contravene* nature, to act unnaturally, or contrary to naturally given needs or purposes. In the Kojèvean view, freedom is nothing other than the capacity to *thwart* the animalistic instinct for life, by risking death. The quest for recognition, the risk of life for pure prestige, becomes the symbol of man's humanity because it is the sort of conduct that cannot be accounted for in terms of need or any other natural purpose. It is a *free* action precisely because it seems purposeless and unmotivated, at least from nature's point of view.

The Kojèvean conception of freedom is not only opposed to nature, but also to reason. Kojève regards reason as being allied to nature, to the animal and the biological. As we have seen, the Kojèvean understanding of freedom has its roots in the existential conception of the *acte gratuit*. Like Kojève, Fukuyama assumes that reason is merely instrumental to animal desires. Insofar as reason is allied to nature, or ministers to animal desires, freedom must consist in acting unnaturally and unreasonably or with no regard to biological needs.

Fukuyama therefore reaches the conclusion that human nobility is linked to *megalothymia* or the desire for conquest because the latter is nonbiological, nonrational, and nonnatural. He laments the fact that *megalothymia* has been deprived of its legitimate claim to rule.[47] But has it ever, in any world, been able to make a legitimate claim? Has anyone, at any time, been able to make a claim to rule over others simply on the ground of having a contempt for reason, nature, and life itself?

In our pacified world, Fukuyama thinks that the only real men left are those who belong to gangs like the Bloods or Crips. They prove their manliness by risking their lives in bloody battles over a name or a flag, or some other useless thing. They alone are "willing to kill and be killed over something of purely symbolic value, over prestige or recognition."[48] And all their drug dealing notwithstanding, Fukuyama insists that it must be said that they are more "deeply human" than more sensible folks who submit to "peaceful arbitration or to the courts."[49]

The Kojèvean historical drama, subtly but unmistakably, inculcates a low and ignoble conception of manhood. Its message is that a real man, a great and noble man, is one who has a passionate desire for recognition. He is willing to risk his life to conquer and subdue others; he displays an overbearing contempt for life; he takes every opportunity to thwart nature; and his actions are spontaneous, unmotivated, and irrational. These are the essential qualities of manhood. It is my contention that this conception of manhood contributes more to the animalization of man than does liberal democracy.

There is no doubt that liberal democracy on the American model leaves much to be desired. But it is absolutely deplorable to find it criticized by those who believe themselves to be taking the high moral ground against materialism, consumerism, selfishness, and frivolity, when the "virtues" they champion are in fact so low. As I have shown, the celebration of struggle, violence, and death as ends in themselves are at the heart of the thesis. I believe that, like so many of the students who fall prey to the seductions of Strauss, Fukuyama was a hapless victim. There is no doubt that this sort of thinking has a certain appeal, not the least of which is its high-minded rhetoric. But this is not to exonerate these students altogether. They uncritically absorb this way of thinking not just because it sounds glorious and high-minded, but because they are not clever enough to see through the haze. For example, Fukuyama is unable to see that the distinction between nonmaterial and material pursuits is not necessarily identical to the distinction between the high and the low, the moral and nonmoral, the human and the animalistic. There is absolutely nothing moral, just, elevated, or peculiarly human about the master's nonmaterial desire for conquest, dominance, prestige, and self-aggrandizement. The latter is not to be confused either with morality or with excellence and virtuosity.

More than anything else, the end of history theorists fear the liberal pacification of the world by economics. Instead, they long for the sheer excitement of battle. And so far, the world is eagerly obliging.

For all its contempt for America, the Kojèvean sensibility panders to the most vulgar aspects of her culture—her violent and anarchic qualities, and above all, her Rambo conception of valor. Ironically, Kojèvean conceits contribute to the very animalization of man that they ostensibly decry.

Part IV

CONCLUSION

CHAPTER

■13□

The Roots
of Postmodern Politics

Postmodernism marks the beginning of a new age that is profoundly disenchanted with modernity. Kojève is a pivotal figure in this disenchantment, for he has historicized it, dramatized it, and given it cosmic significance. Kojève thought that history was a tragedy in which man struggles to realize his fondest dreams, and when he actually succeeds, he realizes that he has created a world fit for passive, domesticated animals. Accordingly, Kojève announced the end of history and the death of man. Nevertheless, he thought that this calamity should be borne with equanimity, since it is the inevitable consequence of the triumph of reason and science in the world.

Kojève's account of man's historical journey had the effect of romanticizing the past almost beyond recognition. Kojève turned history into a personal tale told by an old man who had some fabulous adventures in his youth, but had nothing left but his memories. Kojève was convinced that history was a tragedy and that he had witnessed it because he was living in the old age of mankind. Kojève's historical tragedy has a remarkable similarity to the story told by Hans Christian Andersen in "The Little Fir Tree." All her life, the little fir tree dreamed of being a Christmas tree—decorated, beautiful, and admired by all. So she struggled long and hard in the forest trying to reach the sunshine and grow as tall and straight as she could. After many years, the little fir tree eventually got her wish. But she soon discovered that being a Christmas tree was not what she expected. The wax from the candles dripped on her branches and caused her great pain, but she dismissed this discomfort as a small price to pay for greatness. With Christmas over, the little fir tree was abandoned in the attic to dry up, then crushed and burned for fuel in the spring. Only at the end of her journey, when all her desires have been fulfilled, does the little fir tree understand that her days in the forest were her most glorious. In Kojève's historical drama, man is like the little fir tree: he struggles long and hard for equality and prosperity, but having realized everything he struggled for, he (or the sages in his midst) becomes aware that the historical struggle was by far the best part of the journey. Wisdom comes at the end of history. But ironically, so does death. As Bataille would have it, history is like life—an exuberant expenditure of energy toward a summit that is death.

In Kojève's historical drama man was the beautiful and virile protagonist. He was free, dynamic, and totally exhilarating. He defied nature, he risked life, and he transformed the world. His death, his cries, and his "negativity" put an end to the drabness and predictability of nature and animality. But now that the struggle is over, risk has given way to security, adventure has given way to routine, and youth has given way to old age. But there is a small comfort in this tale. Wisdom is the reward of old age. Living at the end of history, Kojève tried to console himself with wisdom, but it was not always enough to make up for the lost dynamism of youth.

In Kojève's view, history is ironic. Having struggled long and hard to achieve a universal society of equal and prosperous men and women, man discovers that progress has led to the spiritual impoverishment of the last man. Kojève inverts the Hegelian dialectic. Instead of guiding us to the summit, the dialectic ushers in the night of the world. History is a circle that begins in the darkness, silence, and indifference of animality, and returns us once again to the bosom of nature. In short, history is but a brief interregnum in the eternal darkness of the world.

I have argued that there is nothing dialectical about Kojève's conception of history. Kojève transfigured Hegel's dialectic into the genealogy of the slave morality. He replaced the dialectic with a stark dualism of master and slave, masculine and feminine, man and nature, life and death, Being and Nothingness. Moreover, he allied reason with nature, biology, femininity, and the slavish love of life. He therefore understood the march of reason in history as the eclipse of manliness, death, war, and struggle. For Kojève, history was a tragedy in which a cold, instrumental, and uninspired rationalism has conquered and disenchanted the world. Every trace of masculine madness, lightning, and frenzy has been banished by this global tyranny that is as soft and unobtrusive as it is complete and totalitarian.

It is possible to regard postmodernism as a rejection of rationalism and objectivism and a resurgence of relativism. But this account cannot begin to capture the novelty of this particular reincarnation of relativism. Whereas the arid relativism of old dismissed reason as impotent, the new relativism depicts reason as an implacable tyrant. I have shown that this postmodern transfiguration of relativism is largely the work of Kojève. Postmodernism has its roots in a historicized version of Nietzsche's epistemology. It imagines that history itself has vindicated Nietzsche; and it regards our world as living proof that reason and its devotion to truth is destructive of human life. This new brand of relativism is more dramatic, tragic, and beguiling.

Kojève painted the modern world not only as the tyranny of reason, but as the actualization of truth. History is a tale in which ideology gives way to truth. At the end of history, all ideologies are exploded. The fate of man is like the fate of Oedipus; having solved the riddle of the Sphinx, he brought destruction upon himself. Accepting Kojève's logic led his postmodern followers to repudiate truth as well as reason.

The postmodern dilemma is this: Can we live in a world in which reason and its truths have proven to be the source of the greatest tyranny? Can we live in a world in which all horizons have been exploded? Can we live in a world in which all belief systems are deemed to be fictions? Can we live in an utterly disenchanted world without myths, illusions, or religions? Can we live in a world without the taboos and prohibitions that heighten and intensify human experience? Can we live in a world characterized by the tyranny of Woman and the eclipse of manhood? Can we live in this twilight of history? Both the French and American writers who were bewitched by Kojève agreed that they could not. So, what is to be done? Starting from the same Kojèvean assumptions, Kojève's admirers reached different conclusions.

It is my contention that postmodernism is best seen as a reaction to the historical drama as described by Kojève. Starting from Kojève's premises about our historical predicament, it is possible to reach three equally plausible conclusions—each representing an alternative posture of postmodernism. First, we may conclude with Queneau that we should adopt an attitude of playful resignation in the face of a meaningless world. The idea is to rejoice in this "Sunday of life" and spend our time laughing and frolicking in a world in which nothing new or significant is possible. This is the posture most characteristic of the postmodern celebration of meaninglessness. It is an attitude that delights in self-conscious contradiction, incoherence, fragmentation, eclecticism, haphazard promiscuity, and unqualified superficiality. It is the sort of attitude that is reflected as much in literature, films, videos, literary criticism, architecture, fashion, and even psychoanalysis. For example, postmodern architecture is a parody of the glorious forms of the past—Doric columns, Byzantine domes, and Gothic arches are combined in a meaningless eclecticism that defies the utilitarian and efficient principles of modern structures. The same attitude is reflected in the fashions of Jean Paul Gaultier, the architect of global-village chic. Indian nose-rings, African tatoos, Eskimo hair, harem pants, tribal jewelry, and body painting, are combined in a rootless nostalgia for rootedness. Meanwhile, postmodern psychoanalysts like Gilles Deleuze and Félix Guattari reject the search for identity as the wellspring of fascism, and espouse a global nomadic spirit. Multiple identities, schizophrenia, and madness are endorsed as a therapeutic escape from sanity.[1]

However, Kojève's depiction of the post-historical predicament need not lead to a wholesale commitment to zany eclecticism. On the contrary, another attitude is more likely to be fostered. As I have shown, Bataille, Foucault, Strauss, Bloom, and Fukuyama rejected Queneau's playful resignation. Instead, they insisted on reinvesting the meaningless world with meaning, intensity, or significance. Bataille and Foucault longed for the delights of the forbidden and the glory of transgression. Strauss and Bloom felt that it was the social duty of philosophers to restore the fabric of myth and meaning—but not before the megalothymic few destroy the meaningless hedonism of the last man. These are the different options that Kojève's heirs adopted, and they are representative of the political alternatives that postmodernism offers.

Kojève's admirers were more likely to abhor the modern world. They accepted Kojève's depiction of the world as the incarnation of reason and science—homogenized, normalized, and routinized. They found modern life predictable, meaningless, frivolous, drab, and inglorious. They thought that man had been domesticated, pacified, and animalized. They longed for discontinuity and diremption. They longed for difference and diversity. They longed for the excitement of battle and the anguish of death. They longed for solidarity and struggle. They longed for risk and glory. And though they shared Kojève's conception of humanity and virility, they refused to resign themselves to the death of man. They insisted that even though man has been castrated and crushed, he could still rise from the ashes and inaugurate a new dawn. Accordingly, they lived in anticipation of the overthrow of the tyranny of reason by the return of Dionysus or the ascendancy of a few "real men" whose thymotic passions can plunge the world back into history and all its enchantments.

Having accepted Kojève's view that the modern world was the product of reason, Kojève's admirers could not repudiate modernity in the name of reason. They had to launch their revolt against reason itself. They had to side with madness against reason and with Dionysus against Apollo. They were led to champion everything that reason had banished—the criminal, the mad and the tyrannical—Gilles de Rais, Pierre Rivière, Hiero, the Bloods and the Crips. And despite their veneration of Plato, Strauss and his followers yearned for the lost Dionysus. Strauss's intensive study of Plato's *Laws*, with its protracted discussion of wine, led him to conclude that Plato "likens philosophy to madness, the very opposite of sobriety and moderation."[2] Even the divine Plato was a secret adherent of the cult of Dionysus.

I believe that Kojève's picture of the world has given birth to a dark romanticism that manifests itself in a profound nostalgia for what reason has banished—myth, madness, spontaneity, instinct, passion, and virility. In my view, Kojève's conception of modernity as the fateful triumph of arid rationality is the cornerstone of postmodern thought; it explains its negativity, its dark romanticism, and its Dionysian frenzy.

If we set aside those who are eager to wallow in meaninglessness, then we can regard postmodern politics as a dispute between the right- and left-wing disciples of Nietzsche. The Right Nietzscheans are eager to construct the imaginary edifices that account for order and dominion, while the Left Nietzscheans are eager to defy, transgress, and unmask these fictitious edifices of power. Both groups regard politics as a project of domination. And while one group glorifies mastery, the other glorifies revolt. And far from being mutually exclusive, the two positions are mutually dependent.

The French admirers of Kojève are self-styled leftists, even though this posture is, as I have shown, difficult to sustain. Despite his overtures toward communism, Bataille was unable to resist the attractions of the Fascists. And as we have seen, Foucault, the supposed liberator of the oppressed and subjugated, longed for the overt forms of power that make transgression perilous and glorious. Nevertheless, Bataille and Foucault have a claim to being on the Left since they have an insatiable appetite for transgression and revolt. Foucault mobilizes philosophy, now transfigured into genealogy, in the service of the project of perpetual negation and ceaseless overturning. Genealogy unmasks power and paves the way for revolt and transgression. But to storm the Bastille, you need a formidable prison. Bataille and Foucault are not enemies of power, but quite the contrary. A "limit" is necessary if the exhilaration of transgression is to be experienced. In days gone by, God used to provide the limit. But now that God is dead, man must invent his own limits and his own mortifications.

Finding the modern world a numbing experience, Bataille and Foucault hoped to intensify life by keeping man in a heightened state of anguish and ecstasy. Accepting Kojève's conception of negativity as the essence of man's freedom and humanity, they embarked on a project of perpetual negation. But as I have argued, the effort to intensify experience through perpetual negation is doomed to failure. Far from intensifying life and experience, it is bound to breed a profound indifference. Moreover, its delight in transgression leads it to celebrate everything forbidden regardless of its character—crime, madness, and sexual license are some examples.

Foucault's leftist posture is misleading. The Nietzschean Left bears little resemblance to the traditional Left. The latter advocates revolt not as an end in itself but as a means to the realization of liberty and justice. In contrast, Foucault believes that liberty is impossible and that justice does not exist. Liberty is impossible because the self cannot be defined independently of power. On the contrary, the self defines itself only in an act of defiance against the power that frames and formulates it. Power defines the self and reduces it to a predictable thing. But transgression affirms man's no-thingness; it celebrates his spontaneous and surprising capacity for negation. So understood, the existential demand for self-making or self-definition becomes heroic. This heroic revolt is "sovereign" in Bataille's sense of the term, which is to say that it mimics the Kojèvean drama of lordship as opposed to bondage. Heroic transgression requires the negation of the given and the risk of life. I have argued that Foucault's primary objection to disciplinary power is that it is so unobtrusive that it robs man of the opportunity for heroic transgression and revolt. Far from being a liberator and an enemy of power, Foucault longed for power that was arbitrary, oppressive, and awe-inspiring—only such a power can provide the necessary conditions for heroic revolt.

In contrast to the traditional Left, the postmodern Left does not look forward with optimism toward the future. With the exception of those, like Queneau and others, who enjoy frolicking in the meaninglessness of an eternal present, postmodernism is backward-looking—it is filled with nostalgia for the past, and gripped by an exaggerated melancholy about the modern world.

Postmodernism is generally regarded as a left-wing political movement. This is particularly true in America where it has been adopted by left-liberals and Marxists. But it is a mistake to assume that postmodernism is necessarily leftist in character. If there is no preexisting or given reality, if there is no truth, then man is free to make and unmake the world at will. The Left Nietzscheans opt for the project of making and unmaking, asserting and unmasking power after power. But this project of perpetual revolt is not required by the Nietzschean epistemology. Kojève's American admirers offer a more conservative and apparently more sober solution.

Kojève's Straussian admirers would no doubt repudiate my characterization of them as postmoderns. For they regard postmodernism as the last gasp of modernity—radical, liberal, and individualistic. But their objections notwithstanding, it is clear that they share the postmodern assumptions of Nietzsche and Kojève. However, they insist on keeping Nietzsche as the preserve of the few. In their view, the fact that political reality is an arbitrary construction of power is no reason to embark on a deconstructive project of genealogical unmasking. This could only lead to rabble-rousing, mayhem, and barbarism. Instead, philosophy must use all the rhetorical powers at its disposal in order to restore the fragile fabric of myths and illusions on which political order depends. This is not a simple matter, for the myths on which culture rests are like a house of cards: they cannot withstand too much scrutiny. To camouflage the political fact of domination requires splendid lies and spectacular frauds. For in the absence of the enticing illusions of culture, humanity will inevitably descend into barbarism, since man is by nature a savage animal. The harsh truth about truth must remain, like philosophy itself, the exclusive preserve of the few. So the argument goes.

I have argued that the Straussian reasoning is flawed because it exempts itself from the barbarism it attributes to the rest of humanity when the latter is unduped by the illusions of the cave. Strauss and Bloom suggest that the Nazi Holocaust was the result of the destruction of the protective veil of illusion. They imply that the Nazis discovered the truth of nihilism—they knew that reality is a void, and this dangerous knowledge led them to remake the world in their own image. But despite the dangers of nihilism, Strauss and Bloom bid their disciples to leave the cave and embrace the void. But what is to prevent them from behaving just like the Nazis? All we have is Strauss's assurances that his philosophers "will hurt no one." This may be true in a world that the philosopher thinks is worth preserving. Modernity is not such a world;

it is a tyranny of the rabble—a world in which "real men" like Hiero and Simonides have been banished. It is time for these banished *andres* to resurface and to destroy the egalitarian and animalistic world of the universal and homogeneous state in a nihilistic revolt. The postmoderns on the Right deny that society can have its foundation in the dark and savage truth—the truth of the void. Yet they cling to one fact of nature, one datum of reality—the superiority of the megalothymic few and their overabundant passion for mastery. That is the single truth that must inform the mythical constructions of political reality. If the myths of culture are intended to banish the darkness of nature, then why not banish this particular dark truth along with all the others? And who is to say that it is an irreducible truth and not itself a fiction? In my view, the superiority of the megalothymic few is indeed a fiction inherited from Kojève's lowbrow conception of valor.

It is clear that the politics of postmodernism, whether Left or Right, is deadly. And what is deadliest of all is the confrontation of the two. Both regard politics as a project of domination. While the Right seeks to reinvent the horizons of the cave, the Left is eager to unmask them. The two projects are mutually reinforcing. One group glorifies mastery, the other glorifies revolt. One spins the webs of fictions intended to conceal the reality of domination while the other deconstructs them to reveal the naked power they conceal. Together they turn the postmodern conviction that politics is a project of arbitrary power into a reality. In a world where all claims to truth and justice have been exploded as manifestations of the will to power, all political conflict becomes a clash of mutually incompatible claims for dominion. There can be no hope of coexistence—one must destroy the other.

Postmodernism explodes the traditional political distinction between Right and Left. Postmodern politics is not a dispute between those who love order and those who prefer liberty. The Nietzscheanization of the political Right and Left has replaced the contest between liberty and order with an endless dialectic of domination and transgression. The deadly nature of postmodern politics will no doubt intensify existence, which is precisely what it is intended to accomplish. For what the Right and the Left share in common is the Kojèvean conviction that the modern world is the apotheosis of the disenchanted and pacified world of Nietzsche's last man. They are therefore determined to reinvent the myths and illusions that they believe gave life its enchantment in the dawn of history.

Kojève had no use for the postmodern efforts to remythologize the world. He balked at the idea that one could regress from science back to myth. He thought that we must content ourselves with a disenchanted world since that is the inevitable legacy of science. This is the picture of the world that Kojève's admirers inherited. It made them gloomy not just because they had unwittingly romanticized war and death, but because the prospect of a deathless unchanging world, especially one dedicated to material satisfaction above all else, is bound to rob the human spirit of hope and foster nihilism and despair. The question remains: is Kojève's picture of the modern world plausible?

Kojève focused on the "success" of the modern project. He pointed to the prosperity of the advanced industrial countries; he thought that they had for all intents and purposes overcome scarcity and offered their citizens lives of ease in which they worked as little as possible. The Third World is eager to follow in their footsteps and is quickly adopting the ways of the advanced countries. The technocratic culture of the West has become a universal culture because it has proven to be the most successful at satisfying the universal needs and desires of mankind. Technology has not only provided prosperity, it has also homogenized ideas, values, and culture around the globe, and in so doing, it has undermined the ideological as well as the material grounds for war. Our world is pretty much free of the bloody struggles for domination, which have been the hallmarks of human history. Global peace will soon prevail. Of course there will be problems, but Kojève thought that they would be practical difficulties to be solved by science. He was certain that the world that was taking shape before our eyes cannot rationally be surpassed.

It can be argued that Kojève's depiction of our world is not compelling. The prevalence of war, Islamic fundamentalism, nationalism, and ethnic cleansing are proof that the universal and homogeneous state is not a reality. Besides, the environment and the natural resources of the world cannot possibly sustain a global technological culture. So, the universal and homogeneous state is not even a possibility. However, empirical evidence to the contrary is not enough to refute those who experience modernity as the insipid reality of the last man. And one must admit that there is much in our world that fuels the Kojèvean imagination. In light of the collapse of the Soviet Empire and the end of the Cold War, Kojève's thesis seems prescient. Liberal democracy has triumphed over communism. And as Kojève predicted, it was not a military victory. Our world is increasingly becoming a "global village" linked together with global networks such as CNN, fast foods such as McDonald's and Pizza Hut, microcomputers such as Apple and IBM, global stars such as Michael Jackson and Michael Jordan, global sex symbols such as Cindy Crawford and Naomi Campbell. There are also GATT talks, free trade, multinationals, global commodities, money markets, and a World Bank.

When McDonald's opened its doors in Moscow, everyone knew that the Cold War was really over. And when McDonald's moved into Saudi Arabia, journalists speculated that the liberation of Saudi women was imminent. When Pizza Hut appeared in Damascus, reporters yielded to Kojèvean logic and said: with Pizza in Damascus, can peace be far behind? By the same token, given that *The Cosby Show* was recently the most popular television situation comedy in South Africa, could there have been any doubt that apartheid would be abolished? When everyone watches the same television shows, hums the same tunes, loves the same sports, and shares the same conception of the good life, can there be anything to fight about? Kojève thought there would not be anything to fight about, but surely he was mistaken. There is no reason to assume that war is necessarily rooted in ideological conflict. Two nations who share the same conception of the good life may fight over their respective shares of scarce resources. Kojève's reasoning is flawed by the assumption that technology will bring an end to scarcity.

Whatever its shortcomings, Kojève's vision cannot simply be dismissed as fiction. The trend to globalism is very real, as evidenced by the breathtaking developments in global technologies. However, the globalizing trend is not the only one that is steadily gaining strength around the globe. There is at the same time a trend toward tribalism and parochialism. It can be argued that these two opposite and mutually exclusive forces are fighting a battle unto death for the soul of the world. The globalizing forces appeal to our desire for peace, order, prosperity, and pleasure; while the tribalizing forces appeal to our desire for identity, community, and solidarity.[3] But far from thinking that these are mutually exclusive forces, I believe that they are mutually supportive and reinforcing. The more the universal and homogeneous state looms like a threat, the more anxious the tribalizing forces become. It is as if they feared a conspiracy to rob the world of all its color, character, and distinctiveness. At a recent round of GATT talks, the French insisted that their films were part of their "national soul" and that they would continue to use tariffs and surcharges to fight the infiltration of American films. Kojève would have dismissed the gesture as futile. But Kojève's postmodern admirers would applaud it as a victory against the juggernaut of the universal and homogeneous state.

The celebration of difference and the rise of multiculturalism is the hall-mark of postmodernism. And not surprisingly, the American melting pot is its target. America itself is now regarded as an insidious homogenizing force. Instead of giving people a new identity as Americans, it is perceived as robbing them of their identities and leaving them with nothing but cit-izenship in the insipid universal and homogeneous state. This is a dan-gerous trend that may well be the undoing of America since it threatens to turn it into a stage on which the struggle of ethnic rivalries takes place. Allan Bloom's indictment of America is rooted in the refusal to see lib-eralism as a culture like any other, and insists that it is the eclipse of cul-ture, the end of history, and the ascendancy of the last man.

The postmodern repudiation of truth and justice and its claim that every truth is someone's truth and every justice is someone's justice pro-vides fertile soil for the tribalizing forces to flourish. There is nothing that postmodernism finds more ominous than the "hegemonic" discourses of science and technology. Postmodernism is characterized by an instinc-tive distrust of everything universalistic as a tyranny disguised in the lan-guage of reason and science. By sowing such a strong aversion to everything global, including reason itself, Kojève has unwittingly con-tributed to the current appeal of the tribal and parochial.

The aversion to everything global is part of the legacy of Kojève. The trouble is that some of the most elevating and humanizing aspects of life are universalistic. Science, religion, art, poetry, and dancing are not intended to be slaves of the national interest or manifestations of col-lective consciousness, but the expression of the beauty and strength of the human spirit and its capacity to triumph even under the most dire circumstances. If we succumb to the horror of everything universal, we will also succumb to the attractions of the tribal and parochial. Those who sing the praises of community, identity, and solidarity tend to ignore the fact that the price of so much coziness is xenophobia, hatred, and suspicion. The only human virtue it cultivates is loyalty, which is a mafioso virtue that is as indifferent to justice as it is to truth.

What is troublesome about the globalizing forces is that they have become a mind-set. They have spawned a breed of politicians and tech-nocrats who perceive the globe as their domain of action. They regard politics as a technical endeavor of manipulation and control in which mankind is part of the stuff to be arranged. When the rule of men gives way to the administration of things, men themselves become the things to be administered. This is the source of the dismay about the universal and homogeneous state. The technological preoccupation with control and mastery has had the opposite effect to what was anticipated. Instead of making man free and self-reliant, it has made him helpless and dependent. Refusing to be turned into a thing, refusing to give in to helplessness and despair is, as it has always been, the test of the human spirit and its mettle.

When Kojève came upon the idea of the *négativité gratuite*, he thought that it was a solution to the unbearable homogeneity of the world and a way to affirm man's no-thingness—a way to prove that he was not a thing to be managed and manipulated. But as I have argued, there is no reason to stop at suicide. Gratuitous murder, violence, and crime would be even more effective. But far from affirming the freedom and resilience of the human spirit, the *négativité gratuite* is an expression of despondency and despair. And far from being a protest against the modern world, it reflects its powerlessness. Kojève's "unemployed negativity" is not the invention of eccentric intellectuals. It has become a common malaise of industrial societies. Our world is teeming with the inarticulate rage, senseless crimes, and gratuitous violence of skinheads in Germany, aggro-punks in Britain, and drive-by gangs in America. In other words, the postmodern world tacitly affirms Kojève's conception of freedom as the capacity to risk life and flirt with death in a fit of capricious, incomprehensible, and purposeless negativity.

In short, our postmodern politics has its roots in the Kojèvean conviction that nothing great is possible and the Kojèvean understanding of man as a negative being. These two assumptions celebrate the gratuitous violence so rampant in our world—the world that Kojève's heirs paradoxically regard as the incarnation of placid animality.

∎ 14 ◻

Politics and the Plurality of the Good

In concluding, I would like to respond to Kojève and his postmodern heirs by suggesting an alternative way of understanding political life. I will not defend this position fully, but will merely provide a sketch of its salient features. I will begin with the following premises. First, there is absolutely no reason for conferring eternity on any political order. Every political order, no matter how grand, is doomed to decay and degenerate. The universal and homogeneous state is no exception. Second, there is no reason for thinking that modern technological culture is the logical outcome of reason. On the contrary, there are a plurality of political orders that are compatible with reason. Third, there are no grounds for thinking that human history has been shaped by a single set of human desires and aspirations. While it is true that the most basic human needs are the same, human beings have different conceptions of the good life, and strive to satisfy different desires and aspirations. These diverse desires and aspirations are often mutually exclusive, and hence come into conflict with one another. History is the story of the triumph of some and the defeat of others. Fourth, there is nothing in the historical process that guarantees that only the good or the rational will succeed. Fifth, political conflict is not always a conflict between good and evil. More often than not, it is a conflict between competing goods. Sixth, political order is not founded on lies and frauds concocted by philosophers and supermen, but on genuine goods that human beings recognize as worthy of pursuit. Seventh, reason is in most cases insufficient for choosing among a plurality of incommensurable goods. As long as human beings continue to live together in society and pursue certain excellences to the inevitable exclusion of others, there will be conflict. These are the assumptions that will inform my reply to Kojève and his postmodern heirs. The position I am defending is pluralistic as well as objectivist, Hegelian as well as Platonic.

My philosophical position is Hegelian insofar as it is not content with the absolute transcendence of the good. I believe that goods that are distant and unattainable in this world are pernicious fictions that are destructive of life. By positing all value in some unattainable beyond, they not only render life in this world worthless, but they turn philosophy into an apology for the vilest practices of mankind. St. Augustine's defence of the Roman practice of torturing witnesses in an effort to make them tell the truth is a case in point. Although he realized that the practice had the effect of making witnesses say whatever their tormentors wished to hear, he nevertheless defended it as the way of the world in which we are compelled to live as a punishment for original sin. In this way, Augustine rendered all his lofty Christian ideals altogether worthless in guiding life; he never tired of telling us that justice is not of this world. In contrast, Hegel was the philosopher of immanence. Only a good that can be realized in this world is real. What is the meaning of history and its struggles if it is not about the efforts to realize some good or other. The tragedy of human life is that in their sometimes fanatic efforts to realize some good, human beings are willing to commit the most unspeakable atrocities. But these latter have the effect of tarnishing the beautiful edifice they hoped to erect. And even when they succeed, their success is only partial and the good they seek eludes complete actualization. In my view, both Plato and Hegel are right. Hegel is right in thinking that absolute transcendence renders human life worthless and history meaningless. And Plato is right in thinking that every incarnation of the good is but an imperfect imitation of a perfect ideal that exists only in the mind. And this is precisely why every political order, no matter how successful it is in realizing some good or other, is bound to fail. In time, its imperfections rise to the surface and become too obvious to be ignored. In short, I believe that Hegel's optimism needs to be dampened by the sobriety of Plato's realism.

Prior to the popularity of historicism, political philosophy was preoccupied with understanding the secret of the longevity and stability of civilizations. In uncovering the secret of success, political philosophy also aimed to discover the causes of decay. It was assumed that understanding the dynamics of health and disease in the body politic may reveal the mechanisms by which the inevitable process of decay and degeneration can be delayed.

We cannot begin to understand political order—its emergence, its success, and its degeneration—unless we abandon the postmodern notion that politics is primarily a matter of domination. All his efforts notwithstanding, Foucault could not escape the negative analysis of power. Even when he thought he had discovered the "positivity of power," he understood the latter as an expression of disciplinary power's devious techniques of domination. But there is nothing either particularly new or particularly devious about the positive mechanisms of power. The positive aspects of power are those by which it seduces us into compliance. To be successful, power must turn us into active participants in our own seduction. Far from being the latest scam of disciplinary power, positivity has been integral to political power from time immemorial. Repression cannot possibly account for the active collaboration and acquiescence of citizens with power. Something else must be at work. The success of any power rests on the affirmation of something genuinely good to which human beings can be drawn. For whatever they seek, human beings seek something they believe to be good. Even when Bataille celebrates evil, he does so in an effort to rediscover the vitality of life. Ruling simply by coercion is a very difficult affair. Resorting to massive doses of violence is usually an indication of impending failure.

When power is successful, it can dispense with violence, and rule its subjects from within. Freud expressed this in terms of the internalization of authority and the creation of a superego that dominates, represses, and chastises us from within. But such "domination" is not deserving of the name. When the one who dominates and the one who is dominated are the same person, domination has become transfigured. Power does not simply internalize domination. It creates ideals, goals, and aspirations that individuals struggle to live up to or realize. Every successful social order, every social order that is strong enough, delightful enough, or beautiful enough to win the devotion of a sizable portion of its population will display features of the positivity of power. Power displays its vitality when it is able to trigger the mechanisms of self-motivation and self-discipline. The magic of political power lies precisely in its capacity to trigger this mechanism of self-control.

The success of any power lies in its ability to make its vision of human excellence so alluring that all other visions pale in comparison. Power, used in this broad sense, cannot be eradicated from human life. The dream of liberation from power is indeed an impossibility. Nay, liberation would be death, for life and power are one. Or, as Nietzsche put it, life and injustice are the same. For every power, every society, every order, every culture, every discourse must practice "mechanisms of exclusion." Every affirmation of some excellence inevitably excludes other contenders. And such exclusion, insofar as it is exclusion of other equally valid human goods, is unjust.

These mechanisms of exclusion must be brought to bear in every system of power, in every culture and in every vision of how human life should be ordered. In liberal societies there is supposed to be more diversity and less exclusion, at least in theory, if not in practice. But even liberal societies must exclude certain contenders for excellence. This is necessarily the case because these contenders are mutually exclusive. The trouble with liberalism is that it pretends to celebrate all excellences. But this is impossible, and it leads to the inability to affirm anything at all. Societies, like individuals, must choose between alternative goods and excellences to pursue. And while this choice can be rational in view of the circumstances and available opportunities, it could also be a matter of taste, inclination, and proclivities. A zealous allegiance to the values and institutions of one's society is a natural human tendency, but it is also narrow-minded and irrational.

Let me use a few examples to illustrate what I mean. In theory, reason cannot tell us which of two institutions of marriage—say polygamy and polyandry—is inherently superior to the other. What reason *can* tell us is that some institution of marriage or other is good because it is a way of avoiding promiscuity, developing deep attachments, affirming the priority of love and friendship, and creating the conditions for the care and education of offspring. Under historical circumstances in which there is a shortage of women in a population, polyandry would be reasonable, and every effort should be made to make it look as pleasant and as attractive as possible. By the same token, if there is a shortage of men in the population, then polygamy would be deemed a reasonable arrangement, and every effort should be made to make it seem attractive. And while institutions of marriage may have their origins in arrangements that are rational in view of the circumstances in which they emerge, they usually continue to exist long after the conditions in which they emerged have disappeared. And on the whole, gender trouble sets in when one sex and its contribution to society is valued above the other. For it is the case, as Kojève never tired of repeating, that human beings seek recognition. And this is as true for women as for men. The unhappiness of women in modern society is connected to the devaluation of their labor and their social functions. Only a search for recognition can explain why they have left their homes in pursuit of the meaningless and unsatisfying work that modern society has to offer.

The choice between an economy based on free enterprise and one based on socialist modes of production is also one that cannot be determined by reason in abstraction. Each economic system affirms genuine human goods. Free enterprise affirms the values of independence and self-reliance, while socialist modes of production affirm the values of mutual dependence and cooperation. It is very difficult for a society to affirm both equally. One set of values is bound to triumph over the other. If independence and self-reliance are deemed to have priority over mutual dependence and cooperation, then a system of free enterprise is likely to be chosen. Trouble sets in when the system fails to promote and enhance the values that made it popular from the start. Capitalism is a case in point. In its early inception, it promised freedom and independence; and it continues to appeal to us as the means to freedom from big government. But in the twentieth century, we know that it frees us from big government only to leave us at the mercy of big business. And despite its current historical success, it is bound to decline if it is unable to revitalize the original source of its appeal.

The success of modernity as a whole cannot be separated from its ability to appeal to genuine human goods and excellences. Its postmodern enemies are mistaken in presenting it as a sickness that emerges on the historical scene full-blown in all its perversity. But it must be admitted that modernity's inception and its decline are like those of any other set of political and cultural ideals. In its early inception, modernity contained something good and beguiling. It was a revolution against the darkness and prejudice of the Middle Ages. It was a revolution against the authority of the Church, its taboos, repressions, inquisitions, and witch burning. It was a new dawn of the human spirit—celebrating life, knowledge, individuality, freedom, and human rights. It bequeathed to man a sunny disposition on the world, and on himself. Gone were the days when man would bear life like a cross and wait patiently for his salvation. Gone were the Gothic cathedrals with their enormous arches that were intended to intimidate man and make him look small and paltry. A new proportion emerged that was intended to give man self-confidence and make him at home in his world. The new spirit fueled scientific discovery, inventiveness, trade, commerce, and an artistic explosion of great splendor. But as with every new spirit, modernity has gone foul.

Ironically, success sows the seeds of decay. Man's self-confidence gave way to megalomania. He embarked on a project to remake the world. He thought that he could conquer nature and bring an end to scarcity, misery, and disease. But instead of enhancing man's freedom, the scientific conquest of nature has reinforced the lust for conquest and domination. Technology has made death camps and other instruments of mass destruction a reality. It has given some men enormous power over others. Genetic engineering has made scientists into new gods who can decide what sort of people there should be. Modernity lost the freshness and innocence of its early promise because its goals became inflated, impossible, and even pernicious. Instead of being the symbol of freedom, independence, justice, and human rights, it has become the sign of conquest, colonialism, exploitation, and the destruction of the earth. And while Kojève and his followers despaired at the materialistic wasteland that modernity engendered, it must be admitted that their thought valorizes mastery and conquest as the most divine essence of man's humanity—the very thing that sets him apart from the animal world.

The idea that modernity is the embodiment of the only values compatible with rationality, and that the ills and excesses of modernity are themselves part of the logic of reason and science, is a gross exaggeration. Yet this belief has led Kojève's followers to reject reason as a legitimate ground of social order. It has also led them to follow Nietzsche in portraying social life as an arbitrary construction. But surely Nietzsche tells us what is only a half truth when he portrays different moralities as a matter of aesthetic taste or preference inculcated either by artistic genius or by sly and clever fellows like Socrates. Postmoderns on the Right and the Left are equally convinced that social prohibitions and taboos are arbitrary constructions.

The attraction of the postmodern assault on truth has its source in the fact that it is an antidote to the singularity of the traditional conception of good that is imbedded in the rationalist and objectivist tradition of the West. It is also an antidote to the pretensions of rationalism that imply that reason alone can yield a single good that is supreme and unsurpassable. This posture ignores the plurality of goods and the powerlessness of reason in choosing among them.

The postmodern assertion that discourse creates truth *ex nihilo* is a wild exaggeration. Truth, reality, or nature are not a formless chaos on which man imposes order. Rather, nature, and human nature in particular, is abundant with possibilities. Reason is indispensable for sifting out the potentialities for good from amid the plethora of other possibilities.

But the choice among goods is not a function of reason alone. For there are a plurality of goods that are equally compatible with reason and nature. And it is these potentialities for good that are the ground of human struggle at the level of theory as well as practice. Human struggles are not simply struggles between good and evil or knowledge and ignorance, but struggles between competing goods. If we are to learn any lessons from postmodernism, then the rationalists and objectivists, among whom I count myself, must acknowledge that a cold, dissecting rationalism is not enough to suffice us. How we choose to live as human beings is not just a matter of rationality, but also of art and beauty. The aesthetic appeal of art, myth, and fantasy are indispensable in eliciting the devotion and solidarity that are characteristic of groups of people who share a common set of values. The word *values* as opposed to the word *good* is the proper one in this case. For there are a plurality of *goods* not all of which can be simultaneously *valued* by any given group or social order. A purely rationalistic account of values denies the artistic and aesthetic component involved. It fosters the illusion that our values are the only ones that could possibly be hallowed by reason. It encourages a moral absolutism that is the heart and soul of political imperialism. Yet it is an illusion to which mankind is prone. Ironically, the very forces that civilize us also account for our unsurpassed barbarism.

The trouble with postmodernism is that its repudiation of reason is so radical and its rejection of the modern world is so total that it cannot affirm anything as genuinely good and worthy of pursuit; it regards every affirmation as a form of domination or a manifestation of the will to power. Postmoderns on the Right celebrate the artistry of domination, while those on the Left celebrate the art of deconstructing the mechanisms of power. The result is a deadly confrontation.

L·I·S·T O·F A·B·B·R·E·V·I·A·T·I·O·N·S

ILH   Alexandre Kojève, *Introduction à la lecture de Hegel*, edited by Raymond Queneau, (Paris: Gallimard, 1947).

IRH   Alexandre Kojève, *Introduction to the Reading of Hegel*, edited by Allan Bloom and translated by James H. Nichols, Jr. (New York: Basic Books, 1969). I will refer to this edition whenever possible, but since it is not complete, I will also be referring to the French edition.

OT   Leo Strauss, *On Tyranny* (Ithaca: Cornell University Press, 1963). Includes a debate between Kojève and Strauss on tyranny and wisdom.

CORR   Leo Strauss, *On Tyranny*, edited by Victor Gourevitch and Michael S. Roth, (New York: Free Press, 1991). This recent edition includes the correspondence between Alexandre Kojève and Leo Strauss. I will refer to this edition *only* when referring to the correspondence, otherwise I will use the more accessible edition cited above.

N·O·T·E·S

PREFACE

1. Mark Lilla, "The End of Philosophy: How a Russian émigré brought Hegel to the French," *Times Literary Supplement*, (April 5, 1991), p. 3.

2. Some believe that Sartre was also in attendance, others say he was not, and others believe that he *should* have attended. Kojève's lectures were collected, edited, and published by the poet and novelist Raymond Queneau as *Introduction à la lecture de Hegel* (Paris: Gallimard, 1947). I will refer to this work as *ILH*. The English edition, *Introduction to the Reading of Hegel*, was edited by Allan Bloom and translated by James H. Nichols, Jr. (New York: Basic Books, 1969). I will refer to the English edition as *IRH*.

3. Victor Gourevitch and Michael S. Roth, who recently published the correspondence between Alexandre Kojève and Leo Strauss in a new edition of Strauss's *On Tyranny* (New York: Free Press, 1991). I will refer to this edition as *CORR* and will use it only for references to the correspondence. Otherwise, I will use the more accessible edition of *On Tyranny* (New York: Free Press, 1963), which I will refer to as *OT*.

4. See Raymond Aron, *Memoirs: Fifty Years of Political Reflection*, translated by George Holoch, with a foreword by Henry A. Kissinger (New York: Holmes and Meier, 1990), p. 67. The influence of Kojève in the French ministry is explored in depth by his biographer, Dominique Auffret, *Alexandre Kojève: La Philosophie, l'état, la fin de l'histoire* (Paris: Bernard Grasset, 1990).

CHAPTER 1

1. For a detailed biography of Kojève see Dominique Auffret, *Alexandre Kojève: La Philosophie, l'état, la fin de l'histoire*. Auffret focuses on his work at the French ministry and tries to link it to his intellectual life.

2. Ibid., p. 10: Auffret reports that Kojève was suspected of being a communist spy who managed to infiltrate the French government and become one of its most influential officials. The fact that Kojève was deeply moved by Stalin's death in 1953 probably added fuel to the fire.

3. Ibid. See also the review of the book by Mark Lilla, "The End of Philosophy," in the *Times Literary Supplement* (April 5, 1991), pp. 3–5. Like his biographer, Lilla is totally charmed by Kojève; he thinks that Kojève is among the truly superior minds of this century, comparable only to the likes of Leo Strauss.

4. These included Allan Bloom, Hilail Gildin, Stanley Rosen, and Victor Gourevitch.

5. Kojève, "Hegel, Marx et le christianisme," *Critique*, Paris, (August/September 1946), p. 366. English translation by Hilail Gildin, "Hegel, Marx and Christianity," *Interpretation*, Vol. 1 (1970), pp. 21–42.

6. Hyppolite must have been aware of the seductive power of Kojève's thought, for he is said to have stayed away from the seminar on purpose, to avoid the influence of Kojève. This is reported by John Heckman in "Hyppolite and the Hegel Revival in France," *Telos*, No. 16 (Summer 1973), p. 135. Hyppolite's translation of Hegel's *Phenomenology* appeared in 1947, the same year in which Raymond Queneau published Kojève's lectures. However, a sizable portion of Kojève's lectures were already published in *Mesure*, Vol. 1 (January 1939). It is unlikely that Hyppolite was unfamiliar with this work. Despite his efforts to avoid the influence of Kojève, Hyppolite's commentary on Hegel in the more than six hundred pages of his *Genesis and Structure of Hegel's Phenomenology of Spirit*, translated by Samuel Cherniak and John Heckman (Evanston: Northwestern University Press, 1974), tends toward the same anthropological and materialistic view of Hegel that characterizes Kojève's interpretation. Like Kojève, Hyppolite emphasizes the master-slave dialectic and the unhappy consciousness. He also shares Kojève's Marxist or anthropo-

logical interpretation of Hegel. But unlike Kojève, he is more hesitant, less bold, and less Heideggerian in his approach. In an effort to give a more "impartial" interpretation of Hegel, he tended to leave the text with all its ambiguities intact. In comparison to Kojève, he was a plodding scholar. This assessment of Hyppolite is shared by Gaston Fessard, "Two Interpreters of Hegel's Phenomenology: Jean Hyppolite and Alexandre Kojève," in *Interpretation*, Vol. 19, No. 2 (Winter 1991–92), pp. 195–199, translated from the original review in *Études* (décembre 1947), pp. 368–73. Fessard was a Catholic priest who championed the Right Hegelian interpretation of Hegel, which emphasized the theistic element in Hegel's thought. Fessard thought that the dialectic begins with alienation and finitude and ends with the reconciliation of man and God in beatitude. He was a very faithful listener at Kojève's seminar, and was no doubt impressed with Kojève's brilliance, even though he completely dissented from Kojève's anthropological, materialistic, and atheistic interpretation of Hegel. For Fessard, Hyppolite lacked luster when compared to Kojève.

John Heckman admits that Hyppolite's interpretation wavers and is not sufficiently developed. For all his effort to be true to the text, Hyppolite was accused of sneaking in an interpretation, without ever developing it or fully substantiating it. The generally wishy-washy reputation of Hyppolite is probably due to the fact that he did not take sides among the contending interpretations of Hegel. He did not take a stand on the fundamental questions of his time regarding the interpretation of Hegel—namely, does Hegel lead to Marx and to Marx's humanistic atheism, or is Hegel the last defense against Marx? Does Hegel's Spirit refer to man or God? Is it man or God that is the moving force of history? Yet when forced to choose, he usually came down in favor of Kojève's Marxist humanism. See Heckman's introduction to Hyppolite's *Genesis and Structure of Hegel's Phenomenology of Spirit.*

7. On the differences between Kojève and Hegel, see Patrick Riley, "Introduction to the Reading of Alexandre Kojève," *Political Theory*, Vol. 9, No. 1 (1981), pp. 5–48. See also Denis J. Goldford, "Kojève's Reading of Hegel," *International Philosophic Quarterly*, Vol. 22 (1982), pp. 275–294; George Armstrong Kelly, *Idealism, Politics and History: Sources of Hegelian Thought* (Cambridge: Cambridge University Press, 1969), esp. pp. 313, 333, 338, where he describes Kojève as "wilfully misreading" Hegel's whole philosophical method. See also George Armstrong Kelly's "Notes on Hegel's Lordship and Bondage," in *Review of Metaphysics*, Vol. 19, No. 4 (June 1966), reprinted in Alasdair MacIntyre (ed.), *Hegel: A Collection of Critical Essays* (New York: Doubleday, 1972), pp. 189–217.

8. The best introduction to Hegel's philosophy is his own introduction to his *Lectures on the History of Philosophy*, 1840, 3 vols., translated by E. S. Haldane (London: Routledge and Kegan Paul Ltd., 1892, 1955); Hegel makes this comment about Socrates, in Vol. I, p. 384.

9. Ibid., Vol. I, p. 2.

10. Ibid., Vol. I, p. 3.

11. G. W. F. Hegel, *Phenomenology of Spirit*, 1807, translated by A. V. Miller with foreword by J. N. Findlay (Oxford: Oxford University Press, 1977), p. 264. I admire Findlay's approach immensely, but have no desire to implicate him in my account.

12. Findlay makes this point very well in his foreword to Hegel's *Phenomenology*.

13. Judith Shklar develops this idea in her *Freedom and Independence: A Study of Hegel's Phenomenology of Mind* (New York: Cambridge University Press, 1976). This is a delightful and brilliant work, even for those who do not agree with its thesis.

14. This is why Hegel says that the philosophies of Plato and Aristotle cannot be revived; see *Lectures on the History of Philosophy*, Vol. I, p. 46.

15. Hegel, *Lectures on the History of Philosophy*, Vol. I, p. 387.

16. Ibid., p. 420.

17. Ibid., pp. 446, 447.

18. Ibid., p. 385.

19. Ibid., p. 409.

20. Ibid., p. 145.

21. Ibid., p. 446.

22. Ibid., p. 402.

23. Hegel, *Phenomenology*, p. 277.

24. See Hegel's preface to the *Philosophy of Right*, 1821, translated with notes by T. M. Knox (Oxford: Oxford University Press, 1952), p. 13. Hegel makes the same point in the *Lecture on the History of Philosophy*, Vol. I, p. 52. Knox explains (p. 304) that the expression "grey in grey" is a reference to Goethe's *Faust* where Mephistopheles says:
    My worthy friend, grey are all theories
    And green alone life's golden tree.

25. This interpretation was popular among Jesuits and Christians such as Gaston Fessard, Jean Wahl, Henri Niel, and others who contributed to the journal *Dieu Vivant*. These Hegelians believed that far from being an atheist, Hegel enriched Christianity. They were also rabidly anticommunist. Jean Wahl, *Le Malheur de la conscience dans la philosophie de Hegel* (1929), is the richest articulation of this position. I certainly believe that Wahl is right in thinking that Hegel tried to combine the spiritual depth of Christianity with the physical lightness and beauty of Greek culture. But Wahl tended to make history somewhat inscrutable, since it depended on an unpredictable God. While waiting for his final redemption, man had to deal with extremes of loneliness, alienation, unhappiness, and diremption. Wahl's interpretation reflects a certain existential influence, and it is not surprising that he went on to write *Études Kierkegaardiennes*. For discussion of Jean Whal, see Michael Roth, *Knowing and History: Appropriations of Hegel in Twentieth-Century France* (Ithaca and London: Cornell University Press, 1988).

26. Mark Poster recognizes Kojève's importance in the development of Sartre's existential Marxism in his *Existential Marxism in Postwar France: From Sartre to Althusser* (Princeton: Princeton University Press, 1975), pp. 9ff.

CHAPTER 2

1. Hegel, *Phenomenology*, pp. 113ff.

2. In his classic essay, "Notes on Hegel's Lordship and Bondage," *Review of Metaphysics*, Vol. 19, No. 4 (June 1966), reprinted in Alasdair MacIntyre (ed.), *Hegel: A Collection of Critical Essays* (New York: Anchor Books, 1972), pp. 189–217, George Armstrong Kelly rightly complains that reading the *Phenomenology* as social history obscures its inner, phenomenological, and psychological dimension. He regards Kojève's exposition to be typical of Marxist readings, but he is unaware of its existential dimension. Nevertheless, he is quite right in thinking that Kojève's exegesis is a work of our time. Kelly sheds light on Hegel's master-slave dialectic by linking it to the ideas of contemporaries such as Schelling and Fichte. Like Shklar, he tends to emphasize Hegel's admiration for the Greeks. He suggests that for Hegel, as for Plato, the psychological dimension of the soul corresponds to the outer, external, and interpersonal relations between individuals in society.

3. Kojève, *IRH*, p. 4.

4. Ibid., p. 112.

5. Ibid., p. 61.

6. Ibid., p. 28.

7. Ibid., p. 5, and Kojève, "Hegel, Marx and Christianity," p. 26.

8. Kojève, *IRH*, p. 6.

· 9. Kojève, "Hegel, Marx and Christianity," p. 29.

10. Kojève, *IRH*, p. 27.

11. Ibid., p. 6.

12. Ibid., p. 6.

13. Ibid., p. 5.

14. Ibid., p. 38, and Kojève, "Hegel, Marx and Christianity," p. 26.

15. Kojève, *IRH*, p. 38.

16. Ibid., pp. 6, 23.

17. Ibid., pp. 11, 12, 16.

18. Ibid., pp. 7–8.

19. Ibid., p. 26.

20. Kojève, "Hegel, Marx and Christianity," p. 32. Needless to say, the unpredictability of human freedom will prove to be an obstacle to Kojève's end of history thesis.

21. Kojève, *IRH*, p. 9.

22. Kojève, "L'Ideé de la mort dans la philosophie de Hegel," Appendix II of Kojève's *Introduction à la lecture de Hegel (ILH)*, English translation by Joseph J. Carpino, "The Idea of Death in the Philosophy of Hegel," *Interpretation,* Vol. 3, Nos. 2 & 3 (Winter 1973), p. 131.

23. Ibid., p. 140.

24. Ibid., p. 143.

25. Kojève, *IRH*, p. 16.

26. Ibid., p. 21.

27. Kojève, *ILH*, p. 89; see also Kojève, *IRH*, pp. 58–62.

28. Hegel, *Phenomenology,* pp. 111–119.

29. In a superb essay, Dennis J. Goldford has taken Kojève to task on this point. He has argued that Kojève's master-slave dialectic makes no sense. There can be only one master, not a society of masters since mastery leads them to continue the fight until one of them emerges supreme. Even granting a plurality of masters, they could not coexist in a condition of mutual recognition without undermining the

master-slave dialectic itself. To be the moving force of history, the dialectic must result in death or slavery, not in mutual recognition. If mutual recognition is the result of the fight, then there is no reason for history to continue; the goal has already been reached. See his "Kojève's Reading of Hegel," *International Philosophical Quarterly*, Vol. 22 (1982), pp. 275–294. Although Goldford's essay is excellent, it is shockingly blind to certain aspects of Kojève's thought. For example, while he recognizes the fact that Kojève turns Hegel's quest for recognition into a quest for dominance, he concludes that Kojève's view of human nature is classical because it identifies the essence of man with his gregariousness. It seems to me that the desire to dominate and subjugate others hardly qualifies as a manifestation of gregariousness (p. 281). Goldford also fails to see the existential dimension in Kojève's thought, emphasizing only the Marxist and materialistic one.

30. Kojève, *IRH*, p. 22.

31. Ibid., pp. 60–62.

32. Ibid., p. 62. Compare Kojève's treatment with that of Hegel in the *Phenomenology*, pp. 267ff, as well as *The Philosophy of Right*, sec. 166. See also Kojève, *ILH*, p. 105:
   La contradiction l'intrieur de l'État antique est aussi "naturelle": c'est la separation des sexes. Ainsi lorsqu'il y a lutte entre l'Universel et le Particulier, le Citoyen et la Femme, la Loi humaine et la Loi divine, l'État et la Famille,—l'État, en détruisant le Particulier, détruit sa propre base (Wurzel) et se détruit donc lui-même; et si c'est le Particulier qui triomphe, l'État est encore détruit par cette activité criminelle. . . . La Femme est la réalisation concrète du crime. L'ennemi intérieur de L'État antique est la Famille qu'il détruit et le Particulier qu'il ne reconnaît pas; mais il ne peut se passer d'eux. L'État antique périt par la Guerre (=manifestation exclusive de l'Universel).
Kojève understands the drama as a struggle between the universal and the particular, the male citizen and the female who is not a citizen, human law and divine law respectively. In this struggle, the feminine and particular eventually triumphs over the masculine and universal. It is interesting to compare this interpretation to more orthodox Marxist interpretations like that of Georg Lukács in his *The Young Hegel*, translated by Rodney Livingstone (London: Merlin Press, 1975), p. 412. In Lukács's account, Antigone represents the matriarchal order of tribal society that is higher morally and humanly to the class societies that followed it; moreover, the collapse of tribal society was brought about by the release of base and evil passions and impulses. On the other hand, Lukács argues that Hegel recognizes that this collapse of tribal society was inevitable and "signified a definite historical advance." In contrast to Kojève's interpretation, Lukács rightly reads Hegel's story as a story in which the state and the masculine order triumphs, not the feminine one.

33. Kojève, *IRH*, p. 61.

34. Hegel, *Phenomenology*, pp. 274, 275.

35. Ibid., pp. 274, 275.

36. Ibid., p. 276.

37. Ibid., p. 278.

38. Jean-Paul Sartre's novel *Nausea* (Paris: Gallimard, 1938), translated by Robert Baldick (London: Penguin Books, 1965), is a superb illustration of the intensity of the awareness of being a no-thing. A man contemplating the trunk of a tree becomes literally ill at its thingness—the absence of self-consciousness, the inability to be other than it is, the fact that it is formulated, given, and unfree. But what really makes him nauseous is not that inertness of thinghood, but the prospect that he will end up a thing himself—a corpse.

39. Jean-Paul Sartre, *Being and Nothingness*, translated by Hazel E. Barnes (New York: Washington Square Press, 1966), Part I, Chapter 2 on "Bad Faith."

CHAPTER 3

1. Kojève, *IRH*, p. 28.

2. Ibid., p. 30.

3. Ibid., pp. 47–48. Kojève is convinced that this idea of man as a nothingness is the foundation of Hegel's anthropology.

4. Ibid., pp. 32–33, 53.

5. Ibid, p. 33.

6. Ibid., p. 53.

7. Hegel also criticizes Stoicism for being indifferent to natural existence; its freedom exists only in thought and lacks "the fullness of life." See Hegel, *Phenomenology*, p. 122.

8. Kojève, *IRH*, p. 54.

9. Notice that Hegel does not think of Christianity as a slave morality or ideology. Hegel's own analysis of Stoicism and Skepticism is followed, not by a discussion of Christianity, but a discussion of the "unhappy consciousness." See Hegel, *Phenomenology*, p. 126.

10. Kojève, *IRH*, p. 55.

11. Ibid., p. 55.

12. Ibid., p. 56.

13. Ibid., p. 56.

14. Ibid., p. 56.

15. Ibid., p. 57.

16. Ibid., p. 66.

17. Ibid., pp. 62–63.

18. Ibid., p. 64. Because the juridical person is also a property owner, Kojève declares the Roman Empire to be the beginning of the bourgeois world, with its emphasis on property or capital, which becomes the new master to whom everyone is a slave.

19. Ibid., p. 57.

20. Ibid., p. 68.

21. Kojève, "La Métaphysique religieuse de Vladimir Soloviev," *Revue d'histoire et de philosophie religieuses*, Vol. 14 (1934), pp. 534–554, and Vol. 15 (1935), pp. 110–152.

22. See for example Vladimir Soloviev, *Lectures on Godmanhood*, 1877-84, (London: Dennis Dobson, Ltd., 1943). Soloviev's optimistic picture of history darkened in the writing just preceding his death. See especially the "Short Narrative About Antichrist" at the end of his *War and Christianity*, 1899, (London: Constable & Co. Ltd., 1915), pp. 144ff. However, Kojève is not interested in this part of Soloviev's development.

23. Kojève praises the Christian idea of the Incarnation, but he is critical of the Resurrection. He thinks that the latter defeats the dialectic. This is part of what is at issue between him and Gaston Fessard, the Catholic priest who frequented his lectures on Hegel. See especially Kojève's review of Fessard's books, "Christianisme et Communisme," in *Critique* (1946), pp. 308–312, also included in the "Kojève-Fessard Documents," *Interpretation: A Journal of Political Philosophy*, Vol. 19, No. 2 (Winter 1991–1992), pp. 185–200.

24. Kojève, "Origine chrétienne de la science moderne," *Sciences*, Vol. 31 (May/June 1964), pp. 37–41.

25. Kojève, "Hegel, Marx and Christianity," p. 26.

26. Ibid., p. 26.

27. Kojève, *IRH*, p. 57.

28. Ibid., pp. 66, 67, 69; see also Kojève, "Hegel, Marx and Christianity," pp. 37–40, on Napoleon and Hegel.

29. Kojève, "Hegel, Marx and Christianity," p. 39.

30. Ibid., p. 40, note.

31. Kojève, "Entretien," an interview of Kojève by Gilles Lapouge, *La Quinzaine littéraire*, Vol. 53 (1–15 July, 1968), pp. 18–20.

32. Kojève, *IRH*, p. 69.

33. Ibid., p. 69.

34. Ibid., p. 69.

35. Vincent Descombes, *Modern French Philosophy*, translated by L. Scott-Fox and J. M. Harding (Cambridge: Cambridge University Press, 1980), pp. 15–16, and Kojève, *ILH*, p. 95.

36. Kojève, "Hegel, Marx and Christianity," p. 28.

37. Compare Kojève, *IRH*, p. 69, with Hegel's "Absolute Freedom and Terror," *Phenomenology*, pp. 355ff.

38. See the accounts of Hegel on the French Revolution by Charles Taylor, *Hegel and Modern Society* (Cambridge: Cambridge University Press, 1979), pp. 100ff, and Judith Shklar, *Freedom and Independence: A Study of the Political Ideas of Hegel's Phenomenology of Mind* (Cambridge: Cambridge University Press, 1976), pp. 174ff. See also Chris Arthur, "Hegel and the French Revolution," *Radical Philosophy*, Vol. 52 (Summer 1989), pp. 18–21.

39. Kojève, "The Idea of Death in the Philosophy of Hegel," p. 156, note.

40. Kojève, "Hegel, Marx and Christianity," pp. 28–29.

41. Ibid., p. 27.

42. This formal recognition of the individual by the state is hardly distinguishable from the understanding of the individual as a juridical person in the Roman Empire. Nor would Kojève deny this; but he would add that at the end of history, *everyone* is recognized by the state, not just the citizens and propertied classes.

43. Kojève, "Hegel, Marx and Christianity," pp. 28–29.

CHAPTER 4

1. Kojève, *IRH*, p. 156.

2. Ibid., p. 159, note.

3. It may be worth noting that Hegel did not anticipate a classless society. And, if we are to go by his *Philosophy of Right*, he certainly did not think that it was a good idea. On the contrary, he maintained that a society needs differentiation or "estates"; these latter correspond to social and economic classes—the peasantry, the landowners, the businessmen, and the professionals. There is nothing classless or homogeneous about this scheme. Nor did Hegel believe that a universal society free of war was either possible or desirable. See for example, *Philosophy of Right*, sections 324, 372. See also Steven B. Smith, "Hegel's Views on War, the State and International Relations," *American Political Science Review*, Vol. 77 (September 1983), pp. 624–632. Smith's reading of Hegel is clearly influenced by Kojève; while he realizes that Hegel did not anticipate an end to war, and did not even think that such a development would be desirable, Smith thinks that Hegel's views of war undermine his philosophy of history, which Smith understands in Kojèvean terms as a progress toward perpetual peace, homogenization, a withering away of the nation state, and the general bourgeoisification of the world.

4. Karl Marx, *The Communist Manifesto*, 1848, edited by David McLellan (Oxford: Oxford University Press, 1992), Ch. 2, p. 23.

5. The view of history as ending in capitalism has been more recently expressed in the work of Gilles Deleuze and Félix Guattari, *Anti-Oedipus* (New York: Viking Press, 1977). Deleuze and Guattari maintain that capitalism emerges as the universal truth of history because it is a process of "deterritorialization" or uprooting that supposedly destroys nationalities and this is the goal of history. Capitalism tears the peasantry from its origin in the land. In the primitive tribe, every aspect of human existence is governed by social "codes" or rules, but capitalism "decodes" the world. It brings liberation because it undermines all the myths and illusions that have kept humanity enthralled. Capitalism invents the detached, absolute, private individual disposing freely of his body, his organs, and his labor. It has the potential of creating a world of blissful, nomadic, rootless individuals who hold nothing sacred. But alas, capitalism has the tendency to undercut its own liberating tendency by creating new or artificial roots or "territories." The goal of the *Anti-Oedipus* is to undermine the family, which it regards as one of these artificial "territories." However, there are other targets, like psychoanalysts, who insure that the old beliefs survive even after they have been repudiated. Deleuze and Guattari were very influenced by Jacques Lacan, who was one of Kojève's devoted listeners and friends. Indeed, Lacan's philosophical-psychological *oeuvre* is best described as the application of Kojève's Hegel to Freudian psychoanalysis.

6. See Kojève's "Capitalisme et socialisme: Marx est Dieu, Ford est son prophète," *Commentaire*, Vol. 9 (Spring 1980), p. 136.

7. Vladimir Ilyich (Ulyanov) Lenin, *Imperialism, The Highest Stage of Capitalism* (Moscow: Foreign Language Publishing House, 1916).

8. Kojève, *IRH*, pp. 160–162, note; see also "Capitalisme et socialisme," pp. 135–137.

9. Kojève, "Entretien," an interview of Kojève by Gilles Lapouge in *La Quinzaine littéraire* (1–15 July 1968), pp. 18–20.

10. Kojève, *IRH*, p. 160, note.

11. Kojève, "Entretien," p. 19.

12. Ibid.

13. Kojève, "Marx, Hegel and Christianity," pp. 41–42.

14. This Kojèvean vision of the end of history has led scholars to argue that Kojève is a Kantian. See for example, Patrick Riley, "Introduction to the Reading of Alexandre Kojève," *Political Theory*, Vol. 9, No. 1 (February 1981) pp. 5–48. This is also the view of Stanley Rosen, *Hermeneutics as Politics* (Oxford: Oxford University Press, 1987). No doubt there are similarities between Kojève and Kant, but they are too superficial to warrant the claim that Kojève is a Kantian. See Kant, *On History*, edited by Lewis White Beck (New York: Library of Liberal Arts, 1963). Kant was both a rationalist and a champion of freedom. He railed against the self-appointed "guardians" of humanity who kept the rest (including the "entire fair sex") in a condition of tutelage. Far from thinking that freedom of thought will lead to anarchy and chaos, Kant believed that people will converge on a single set of universal principles, which will become the foundation of a universal republic characterized by liberty, rationality, and "perpetual peace." But for Kant, this was not the final end or goal of history, but merely the "womb where all the original capacities of the human race can develop" (p. 23). Uppermost among the latter are "goodness of heart" and a genuine morality to replace the "simulacrum of morality" and the preoccupation with "outward decorum" that dominates "mere civilization" (p. 21). As we have seen, morality and goodness of heart were no part of Kojève's concerns. And unlike Kant, Kojève valorizes war and struggle. And as I will show, Kojève drives a wedge between freedom and reason; his conception of freedom has its source in the existential understanding of freedom that departs dramatically from the rationalism of Kant or Hegel.

15. Kojève's letter to Strauss, September 19, 1950, in Leo Strauss, *CORR*, p. 255.

16. Kojève, "Entretien," p. 19.

17. Kojève, "Les Romans de la sagesse," *Critique*, No. 60 (1952), pp. 387–397. The essay is about the sages portrayed in Raymond Queneau's novels.

18. Kojève, *IRH*, p. 35.

19. Ibid., p. 32.

20. Ibid., p. 31.

21. Ibid., p. 35.

22. Kojève, "Hegel, Marx and Christianity," p. 37.

23. Kojève's letter to Strauss, September 19, 1950, in Strauss, *CORR*, p. 255.

24. Strauss's reply to Kojève on this matter is in "Restatement on Xenophon's Hiero," in Strauss, *OT*, pp. 189–226.

25. Reported by Stanley Rosen in *Hermeneutics as Politics*, p. 106.

26. Ibid.

27. Kojève, "Tyranny and Wisdom," in Strauss, *OT*, pp. 143–188.

28. Wassily Kandinsky, *Concerning the Spiritual in Art*, 1912 (New York: George Wittenborn, Inc., 1947).

29. See Peg Weiss, *Kandinsky in Munich: The Formative Jugendstil Years* (Princeton: Princeton University Press, 1979). The Jugendstil movement was an artistic movement that emerged in Munich in the 1890's and was intended to uphold liberal ideals endangered by the conservative, Catholic, authoritarian, and Bismarckian trends in Germany at the time. But it later became inspired by Volkish, Wagnerian, and anti-Semitic trends and started to use art for nationalist purposes.

30. Kojève, "Pourquoi concret," in Wassily Kandinsky (1866–1944), Écrit complets: La Forme, Vol. 2 (Paris: Denoël Gonthier, 1970), pp. 395–400.

31. I will examine the influence of Heidegger on Kojève's thought more fully in the next chapter.

32. Kojève, IRH, p. 158, note.

33. Ibid., p. 159, note.

34. Reported by Stanley Rosen, who knew him personally, in Hermeneutics as Politics, p. 93. Rosen's thesis is that postmodernism is not so much an attack on the Enlightenment as its last gasp. Rosen understands the Enlightenment project as an attempt to universalize radical individualism, and in so doing, undermine "politics." He regards Kojève as the clearest expression of Enlightenment rationalism. For Rosen, the intellectual demise of Kojève is a microcosm of the intellectual bankruptcy of the Enlightenment. This is also Strauss's view, and it partially explains the interest that Strauss and his students take in Kojève's work.

35. Kojève, IRH, p. 160, note.

36. Ibid., p. 159, note.

37. Ibid., p. 160, note.

38. Ibid., p. 159, note.

39. Ibid., p. 161, note.

40. Ibid.

41. See my discussion in Part III of this book.

42. Kojève, IRH, p. 161, note.

43. Ibid.

44. Ibid.

45. Ibid.

46. Ibid., p. 162, note.

47. Ibid.

48. Ibid.

49. Ibid.

50. He certainly regarded it as significant and wrote to Leo Strauss about it. In a letter of October 4, 1962, Strauss tells Kojève that he is "anxious to see the second edition of the book, especially the supplement on Japan." See Strauss, CORR, p. 310. Another reason for the significance of the trip is that Kojève had a love affair with a young Japanese girl. His biographer reports that Kojève confided in a friend a few weeks before his death that it was the most perfect love he had ever known. See Auffret, Alexandre Kojève, p. 342.

51. Yamamoto Tsunetomo, *Hagakure: The Book of the Samurai*, translated by William Scott Wilson (Tokyo: Kodansha International Ltd., and New York: Harper and Row, 1979). The book was used to inspire the *kamikaze* pilots of World War II. *Kamikaze* means "divine wind" and is the name of the winds that made it possible for the Japanese to defeat the Mongol invasions led by Kublai Khan in 1274 and again in 1281. Many copies of the book were destroyed before the American occupiers arrived.

52. Tsunetomo, *Hagakure*, p. 17.

53. Ibid., p. 18.

54. Kojève, "Entretien," p. 19.

55. Ibid.

56. Ibid.

57. Yukio Mishima, *The Way of the Samurai: The Hagakure in Modern Life*, translated by Kathryn N. Sparling (New York: Basic Books, 1977).

58. Ibid., pp. 22–23. Mishima claims that prior to the Americanization of Japan, the Japanese made a clear distinction between romantic love and sexual desire. They would satisfy their sexual desire in a brothel but would never lay a hand on the women they loved, such was the spirituality of their love. With more than a touch of melodrama, Mishima adds that this is the "tragic physiology of the human male." I found absolutely no evidence of this separation of sexual desire from love in the *Hagakure* itself, and the suggestion is bizarre, for it means either that the institution of the family did not exist among the Japanese, or that all wives were prostitutes. Mishima comes closer to the mark when he says that the *Hagakure* suggests knowing the beloved emotionally for several years before the love is consummated. This insures that the "voltage" of love is preserved.

59. Ibid., p. 24.

60. Kojève, "Le Dernier monde nouveau," *Critique*, Vol. 12, No. 2 (1956), pp. 702–708.

61. Sagan admits that all this is true about her life in *Réponses: The Autobiography of Franoise Sagan*, translated by David Macey (Godalming, Surrey, England: Ran Publishing Co., 1979), which consists of interviews with Sagan.

62. Sagan, *A Certain Smile*, translated by Anne Green (New York: E. P. Dutton & Co., 1956), pp. 14 and 16 respectively.

63. See for example, Aritha van Herk, *Judith* (Toronto: McClelland and Stewart-Bantam, 1979).

64. Kojève, "Le Dernier monde nouveau," pp. 702, 704.

65. Ibid., p. 705.

66. Ibid., p. 707.

67. André Gide's novel *Les Caves du Vatican*, 1914, has been translated as *Lafcadio's Adventures* by Dorothy Bussy (New York: Vintage Books, 1953).

68. *Lafcadio's Adventures*, p. 220.

69. Ibid., p. 219.

70. It seems to me that the full measure of the damage that Augustine has visited on the Western tradition has yet to be documented. Even reasonable men continue to paint him in glowing colors. See for example, Charles Taylor's *Sources of the Self: The Making of Modern Identity* (Cambridge, Mass.: Harvard University Press, 1989).

71. Gide's novels are filled with gratuitous actions. Gide learned his Augustinian lessons well. In *Strait Is the Gate*, translated by Dorothy Bussy (New York: Alfred A. Knopf, 1959), he uses the character of Alissa to paint a picture of Christian virtue: puritanical, ascetic, and self-abnegating. Alissa loves Jerome, her childhood sweetheart, who is totally devoted to her and wishes to marry her. But she loves God more, and decides that she can get closer to God only if she "sacrifices" Jerome. Her God is exacting and demanding and the gate to His abode is strait and narrow: it requires a solitary journey. Alissa makes this solitary journey through life. Having abandoned her family and her sweetheart, Alissa dies tormented and alone—even God seems to have abandoned her, and she begs Him to take her life quickly before she blasphemes. Alissa's puritanical virtue is an exaggeration of Augustine's. She rejects every hint of pleasure not only in this world, but in the next. She insists that her sacrifice is for love of God, and not for the sake of a greater happiness. Whereas Augustinian virtue merely delays gratification, Alissa's virtue renounces it altogether. The message is that virtue, if it is to be a truly grand achievement, must be pursued for its own sake and not for any pleasure it may give in the world beyond (that it gives no pleasure in this world is taken for granted). To be glorious, virtue cannot have a goal or motive, it must be altogether free and gratuitous.

    See also *Prométhée mal enchaîné*, translated by Lilian Rothermere as *Prometheus Illbound* (London: Chatto and Windus, 1919): Zeus explains his love of gambling as an *acte gratuit* because there is nothing he could win that he does not already have.

72. Hobbes thinks that he need only demonstrate that every good deed to which a man can lay claim hides an egocentric motivation in order to prove that man is evil. For Hobbes, even laughter cannot claim a spontaneity free of self-centered calculation: we laugh at jokes only to congratulate ourselves for having understood them. But the force of Hobbes's arguments depend heavily on the assumption that man is genuinely good only when his goodness is unmotivated by any desire, especially a desire for pleasure.

73. It has been argued that there is no such thing as a gratuitous action, and that every action is done for a reason. I think that this approach misses the mark because it implies that all actions are instrumental. But surely, there are actions that are ends in themselves—or at least are constitutive of the ends they seek, whether the latter is pleasure, prestige, or a feeling of superiority. Advocates of the *acte gratuit* assert that acting arbitrarily, capriciously, and inscrutably is proof of one's superiority. It is impossible to respond to this claim if one simply denies that there is any such thing as an *acte gratuit.*

74. Kojève, "Hegel, Marx and Christianity," pp. 26, 27, 33: Kojève defines "spiritual" as that which is "against nature." He therefore concludes that risking death and seeking prestige are "spiritual" pursuits, which are distinctively human. This reasoning is based on the fallacious assumption that animals do not fight battles for prestige and dominance. The same fallacious reasoning leads Francis Fukuyama to admire members of street gangs like the Crips and the Bloods as the few remaining examples of manhood in the postmodern world. See my discussion in Chapter 3 of Part III, below.

CHAPTER 5

1. See Stanley Rosen's review of Kojève's *Essai d'une histoire raisonnée de la philosophie païenne*, in *Man and World*, Vol. 3, (1970), p. 120.

2. See Jean-T. Desanti, "Hegel est-il le père de l'existentialisme?" *La Nouvelle critique*, Vols. 56 and 57 (1954), pp. 91–109 and 163–187 respectively. Desanti was a young communist student struggling to understand Hegel. He believed that Lenin was the key to Hegel, and rejected Kojève's "existential" interpretation. Nevertheless, he tells us that he was attracted to Kojève's Hegelianism in spite of himself.

3. Mark Poster recognizes the importance of Kojève in the development of existential Marxism. See his *Existential Marxism in Postwar France* (Princeton: Princeton University Press, 1975). Poster thinks that

Sartre's view of Hegel was shaped by Kojève. It is also important to remember that a sizable portion of Kojève's lectures were published in 1939 in *Mesure*, and that Sartre's *Being and Nothingness* was published in 1943.

4. See for example Nietzsche's *Twilight of the Idols*, 1889, translated by R. J. Hollingdale (London: Penguin Books, 1968), pp. 36 ff.

5. Despite its origin in Nietzsche's thought, existentialism lacks the *joie de vivre* of Nietzsche because of its emphasis on death and anxiety. Existentialism is vulnerable to what Nietzsche considered the greatest peril to confront Western civilization once God is dead—nihilism.

6. Martin Heidegger, *Being and Time*, translated by John Macquarrie and Edward Robinson (New York: Harper and Row, 1962), Part I, Sec. 40.

7. Jean-Paul Sartre, *Being and Nothingness*, 1943, translated by Hazel E. Barnes (New York: Washington Square Press, 1966), Part I, Ch. 2.

8. Heidegger, *Being and Time*, Part II, Secs. 51–53. See also Marjorie Grene, *Heidegger* (London: Bowes and Bowes, 1957), for an excellent introduction to Heidegger's existentialism. Grene describes vividly the "intensely felt finitude of a being cast strangely into an absurdly given world to face there the terror of his own non-being" (p. 67). I am inclined to agree with her that Tolstoy's *The Death of Ivan Ilych* accomplishes the same task as Heidegger's *Sein und Zeit*, but is more lucidly written and more readable. She explains the dual tension of being destined yet free by saying that even though heredity and environment have made me what I am, *they* in turn are what I make of them, and therein lies my freedom. This formulation may be too commonsensical to capture Heidegger's meaning, but it certainly rings true. Grene emphasizes the break between Heidegger's earlier and later work. George Steiner does the same in his beautifully written *Martin Heidegger* (Chicago: University of Chicago Press, 1978, 1979). Steiner's new introduction deals with Heidegger's Nazism.

9. Alexandre Kojève, "The Idea of Death in the Philosophy of Hegel," translated by Joseph J. Carpino, *Interpretation*, Vol. 3, Nos. 2 and 3 (Winter 1973), p. 131. For a discussion of "Being-toward-death," see Heidegger, *Being and Time*, Part II, Secs. 51–53.

10. Kojève, *IRH*, p. 155.

11. Ibid., pp. 212–213, note.

12. Alexandre Kojève, *Essai d'une histoire raisonnée de la philosophie païenne*, 3 vols. (Paris: Gallimard, 1968, 1972, 1973). The books were intended as part of a Hegelian encyclopedia of philosophy culminating in Hegelian wisdom, which includes all that has gone before it while recognizing that no new thoughts are possible. Kojève believes that a history of philosophy is the story of the march of reason in history culminating in wisdom.

13. Alexandre Kojève, *Kant* (Paris: Gallimard, 1973), p. 65.

14. Kojève, *IRH*, p. 213, note.

15. Ibid., p. 214, note.

16. Ibid., p. 215, note.

17. Ibid., p. 214–215, note.

18. Kojève, "The Idea of Death in the Philosophy of Hegel," p. 131.

19. Ibid., pp. 130ff.

20. Ibid., p. 138.

21. Ibid., p. 140.

22. Martin Heidegger, "Letter on Humanism," *Basic Writings*, edited by Farrell Krell (New York: Harper and Row, 1977), pp. 193–242.

23. Martin Heidegger, *An Introduction to Metaphysics*, 1953, translated by Ralph Manheim (New York: Anchor Books, 1959), pp. 3–4.

24. Heidegger, "Letter on Humanism," p. 225.

25. In Heidegger's view, even Nietzsche did not succeed in escaping the logic of Western metaphysics. On the contrary, he embodied its nihilistic finale.

26. Heidegger, "The Question Concerning Technology," in *Basic Writings*, pp. 308, 315.

27. Ibid., p. 289.

28. Heidegger, *An Introduction to Metaphysics*, pp. 31–37.

29. Friedrich Nietzsche, *Beyond Good and Evil*, 1886, translated by Walter Kaufman (New York: Vintage Books, 1966), Preface, p. 2.

30. Heidegger, "Letter on Humanism," p. 210.

31. Ibid., p. 193.

32. Some of Heidegger's critics have argued that far from transcending Western metaphysics, Heidegger has simply become entangled in its web. All his talk about falling out of Being, not being able to listen to Being, the silence of Being, the house of Being, the shepherd of Being, makes no sense unless Being is interpreted in theological terms—as it was by Paul Tillich, Rudolph Bultmann, Emmanual Levinas, or William Richardson. But Heidegger insisted that he was doing something new, that his conception of Being was thoroughly temporal. See Emmanuel Levinas, *Totality and Infinity*, translated by Alphonso Lingis (Pittsburgh: Duquesne University Press, 1969), or William J. Richardson, *Heidegger: Through Phenomenology to Thought* (The Hague: Martin Nijhoff, 1963).

33. Victor Farias, *Heidegger and Nazism*, translated by Paul Burrell and Gabriel Ricci (Philadelphia: Temple University Press, 1989); Hugo Ott, *Martin Heidegger*, translated by Alan Blunden (New York: Basic Books, 1993); see also reviews by Thomas Sheehan, "Heidegger and the Nazis," and "A Normal Nazi," in *New York Review of Books*, June 16, 1988, and January 14, 1993, respectively. See also the new introduction to George Steiner's *Martin Heidegger*. Steiner points to the affinity between Heidegger's *Being and Time* and Hitler's *Mein Kampf:* both were simultaneously dark yet full of promise and expectation. For a more detailed account of the connection between Heidegger's philosophy and his Nazi politics see Richard Wolin, *The Politics of Being* (New York: Columbia University Press, 1990). Wolin divides Heidegger's writings into three periods. In the early existential period Heidegger celebrated self-assertion, freedom, and making one's own destiny. In the middle period, he had a much gloomier outlook on the human condition but thought that leader-creators or Nietzschean supermen might save us—that was his Nazi period. In his late work, he lost all hope, took on an attitude of complete resignation, and announced that "only a god could save us." Wolin believes that Heidegger's "turn" was not just a change of emphasis, but a complete contradiction of his earlier work. My own view is that the difference between his earlier and later work is not as great as it is generally believed to be.

In his own defense, Heidegger insisted that he had always supported a spiritual rather than a biological version of the Nazi doctrine; see "Only a God Can Save Us," interview with *Der Spiegel*, 1966, in Richard Wolin (ed.) *The Heidegger Controversy* (New York: Columbia University Press, 1991), pp. 91ff.

34. There is an unmistakable affinity between Heidegger's philosophy and Nazism that has often been noted: the agrarian sympathies, the antipathy toward cosmopolitanism, capitalism, liberalism, America, and modernity; all these were regarded as part of a single phenomenon. The Nazis made the link between the Jews and the modern, cosmopolitan, capitalistic, liberal temper; for the Jews were defined by the diaspora, which meant that they were rootless vagabonds with no connection to the soil. This is why Jewish intellectuals like Leo Strauss, who shared the same likes and dislikes as Heidegger, had to argue that the Jews were not "modern." See for example, Leo Strauss, "Why We Remain Jews," a very important, widely circulated, but still unpublished manuscript.

35. Heidegger, *An Introduction to Metaphysics*, p. 31.

36. See Heidegger's *Der Spiegel* interview, 1966, in Wolin (ed.), *The Heidegger Controversy*.

37. Heidegger, *Being and Time*, Part I, Sec. 2, p. 28.

38. In his later work, Heidegger followed his beloved poet J.C.F. Hölderlin, who believed that the poet, not the philosopher, was best equipped to listen to the voices of nature, and to reveal reality; the poet was the chosen spokesman of the gods, and the mediator between nature and mankind. But in the last years before his insanity, Hölderlin called himself a false priest; he thought that his insanity was a divine punishment for his presumptuousness. In contrast, Heidegger never repented his presumptuousness.

39. See Kojève's *Essai d'une histoire raisonnée de la philosophie païenne*, Vol. 1, *Les Présocratiques* (Paris: Gallimard, 1968); Kojève acknowledges his profound debt to Heidegger but rejects the return to the pre-Socratics, p. 165. See also Heidegger's *Parmenides*, 1982, translated by André Schuwer and Richard Rojcewicz (Indianapolis: Indiana University Press, 1992). Both writers use the pre-Socratics for their own purposes. Heidegger wanted to show that before the corruption of Western metaphysics, before it was polluted by Socratic ideas, man was defined in terms of his search for Being or his relation to Being, and not as a rational animal. Reason is about dominance, control, and technology. Heidegger believed that the pre-Socratics had an immediate grasp of reality, and that the immediacy and freshness of their acquaintance with Being has been lost or forgotten by Western metaphysics since Socrates. Moreover, this "forgetfulness of Being" has left man in his current condition of "homelessness," which is inseparable from the crisis or decline of the West. Heidegger thought that by recovering the wisdom of the pre-Socratics, he would rediscover the vitality of the West.

40. Parmenides, Fragment No. 1, and "The Way of Truth," in Milton C. Nahm (ed.), *Selections from Early Greek Philosophy* (New York: Meredith Publishing Co., 1964), pp. 91ff.

41. Kojève, "The Idea of Death in the Philosophy of Hegel," p. 115.

42. Kojève considered the philosophies of Schelling and Spinoza to be recent versions of the Parmenidean view of Being.

43. Kojève, "The Idea of Death in the Philosophy of Hegel," p. 116.

44. See Sartre's preface to Frantz Fanon, *Wretched of the Earth*, translated by Constance Farrington (New York: Grove Press, 1963).

45. The extent of Sartre's involvement in the French Resistance is not as great as legend would have it. See for example, Paul Johnson's lighthearted book, *The Intellectuals* (London: Weidenfeld and Nicolson, 1988), Ch. 9.

CHAPTER 6

1. Georg Wilhelm Friedrich Hegel, *Lectures on the History of Philosophy*, 1840, 3 Vols., translated by E. S. Haldane (London: Routledge & Kegan Paul, Ltd., 1892), Vol. I, p. 402.

2. For Nietzsche, the Olympic gods represented the "only satisfactory theodicy ever invented," because "the gods justified human life by living it themselves." *The Birth of Tragedy*, translated by Francis Golffing (New York: Anchor Books, 1956), p. 30.

3. Nietzsche believed Socrates had the features of a criminal.

4. Friedrich Nietzsche, *Beyond Good and Evil*, translated by Walter Kaufmann (New York: Vintage Books, 1966), Part V, Sec. 191, p. 104.

5. Nietzsche, *Beyond Good and Evil*, Part V, Sec. 191, p. 104; *Birth of Tragedy*, pp. 4–5. See also Friedrich Nietzsche, *Human All Too Human*, translated by R. J. Hollingdale, with an introduction by Erich Heller (Cambridge: Cambridge University Press, 1986), Part II, "The Wanderer and his Shadow," Sec. 86.

6. Nietzsche, *Beyond Good and Evil*, Part II, Sec. 28, p. 41.

7. Ibid., Part V, Sec. 295, and Friedrich Nietzsche, *The Gay Science*, translated by Walter Kaufmann (New York: Random House, 1974), Sec. 340.

8. Nietzsche, *The Birth of Tragedy*, pp. 112, 113.

9. Kojève's reasons for thinking that Christianity and science have a special affinity are outlined in "Origine chrétienne de la science moderne," *Sciences*, Vol. 31 (1964), pp. 37-41. Kojève argues that science could have emerged only in the context of a Christian culture. His reason is that all other religions insist on a duality between God and the earth; but this duality is breached by the Christian idea of the incarnation. The latter makes God actually present in the world and this opens the possibility of its perfection. Inspired by Christianity, science assumes this task, but in time it no longer needs Christianity. So, while Christianity gives birth to modern science, the latter eventually transcends the need for Christianity and gives birth to a fully secular world.

10. Nietzsche, *Beyond Good And Evil*, Part V, Sec. 202, p. 116.

11. Ibid., Part III, Sec. 62, p. 76.

12. Ibid., Part V, Sec. 203, p. 118.

13. Friedrich Nietzsche, *The Use and Abuse of History*, translated by Adrian Collins (New York: Macmillan, Library of the Liberal Arts), Sec. VI, p. 44. But Nietzsche adds that life is higher than science, and nature is bound to revenge herself. For whatever destroys life will itself be annihilated (Sec. X, p. 70).

14. Friedrich Nietzsche, *Thus Spoke Zarathustra*, translated by Walter Kaufmann (London: Penguin Books, 1954), Prologue, Sec. 5, p. 17.

15. Ibid., Prologue, Sec. 5, p. 17.

16. Nietzsche, *Use and Abuse of History*, Sec. II, p. 15.

17. Nietzsche, *Zarathustra*, Prologue, Sec. 5, p. 17.

18. Nietzsche, *Zarathustra*, Prologue, Sec. 5, p. 18.

19. Ibid.

20. Ibid.

21. Nietzsche, *Beyond Good and Evil*, Part V, Sec. 199, p. 111.

22. Nietzsche, *Use and Abuse of History*, Sec. IX, p. 62, and Sec. VIII, p. 52. Nietzsche ridicules the idea that what comes after is necessarily superior, and the tendency to idolize success.

23. Nietzsche, *Zarathustra*, Prologue, Sec. 3, p. 14, and Nietzsche, *Beyond Good and Evil*, Part V, Sec. 199, p. 111.

24. See Strauss's letters to Kojève, especially the letters of September 11, 1957, and August 22, 1948, in Leo Strauss, *CORR*, pp. 291, 236, respectively. The same view is expressed by Allan Bloom in his introduction to Kojève's *IRH*.

25. Nietzsche, *The Birth of Tragedy*, p. 95.

26. Ibid., pp. 94-95.

27. Nietzsche, *Beyond Good and Evil*, Part V, Sec. 199, p. 111.

28. Nietzsche was apparently "terrified at the sort of people that would model themselves after his superman." See Eric Heller, *The Artist's Journey into the Interior* (New York: Random House, 1959), Ch. VI, "The Importance of Nietzsche," p. 175.

CHAPTER 7

1. See Kojève's review of three of Queneau's novels in "Les Romans de la sagesse," *Critique*, Vol. 60 (1952), pp. 387–397.

2. Ibid., p. 396.

3. Kojève, *Essai d'une histoire raisonée de la philosophie païenne*, Tome I, *Les Présocratiques* (Paris: Gallimard, 1968), p. 17.

4. In the early stages of the movement, Breton was primarily preoccupied with liberating what has been repressed by civilization, in the hope that he will find something redeeming buried deep in the subconscious of man. Like the Dada movement to which he first belonged, Breton rejected Western culture—society, morality, reason, and religion—as the sources of the sorry and sordid war of 1914 as well as the peace of 1918. But the Dada movement tended to be totally negative. The Dadaists were so busy "spitting on humanity" that they did not accomplish much else, and Breton became aware of their sterility. Later, Breton moderated his view because he did not want to forfeit his desire for truth, beauty, and justice. See André Breton, *What is Surrealism?* translated by David Gascoyne (London: Faber & Faber, 1936), p. 50; see also J. H. Matthews, *An Introduction to Surrealism* (University Park: Pennsylvania State University Press, 1965), p. 35.

5. Breton, *What is Surrealism?* p. 49.

6. According to Maurice Nadau, *The History of Surrealism* (New York: Macmillan, 1965), surrealism eventually took two parallel paths—one in the direction of political revolution (led by Louis Aragon, who participated in the Second International) and the other in the exploration of the unknown forces of the unconscious (led by Salvador Dalí). But Breton always tried to reconcile both aspects of the movement and for the most part controlled it authoritatively.

7. According to Breton's biographer, J. H. Matthews, *André Breton* (New York: Columbia University Press, 1967), p. 9, Breton used to leave his hotel room door open in the hope of waking up to find a strange woman by his side, chosen for him by chance. When Nadja was committed to an asylum, Breton felt that he should have helped her more, but as Matthews points out, he regarded insanity to be a liberation of the imagination—he had observed insanity during World War I while working in the Psychiatric Center at Saint Dizier while he was in the army. Breton had studied medicine, although his true vocation was literature.

8. *In L'Immaculée conception* (Paris: Pierre Seghers, 1961), André Breton and Paul Éluard maintain that love of a woman as well as revolutionary hope are mediators between the self, its dreams, deliriums, and neuroses on one hand, and the world on the other. The subtitles of the work are borrowed from Hegel's *Encyclopedia of Philosophy*, especially from the "Anthropology," where Hegel talks of adult life as mediating between the dreams and ideals of childhood and the hard realities of the world. Hegel also talks of the "hypochondria" of those who resist the adaptation; but Breton and the surrealists embrace hypochondria as a sign of well-being. The title refers to the Virgin Mary as a symbol of womanhood and the route to redemption, but there is nothing Catholic about it. The work reflects the profoundly antireligious sentiments of the surrealists.

9. Breton's words, quoted by Matthews, *André Breton*, p. 22.

10. See for example Elizabeth Grosz, *Jacques Lacan: A Feminist Introduction* (London: Routledge, 1990).

11. Raymond Queneau, *Odile* (Paris: Gallimard, 1937).

12. Automatic writing is writing whatever comes into your head without altering it in any way, because doing so would interfere with the creative process. An example is Paul Éluard and André Breton, *L'Immaculée conception.* The text was written in a fortnight. The two authors chose the titles from the start, then they wrote in parallel with one sheet written by Breton and another by Éluard and then the texts were combined to create a new and final text.

13. Thanks to the love and friendship of Odile, the young man in the novel manages to escape from this fraudulent intellectual circle and begin a meaningful life. Some commentators have rightly noted that Queneau ridicules the surrealists while borrowing one of their themes—self-knowledge through love of a woman.

14. Raymond Queneau, *Le Chiendent* (Paris: Gallimard, 1933).

15. See, for example, Martin Esslin, "Raymond Queneau," in John Cruickshank (ed.), *The Novelist As Philosopher* (New York: Oxford University Press, 1962), p. 84. The same view is expressed by Allen Thiher, *Raymond Queneau* (Boston: Twayne Publishers, 1985), p. 115.

16. *Les Fleurs bleues*, 1965, translated by Barbara Wright as *The Blue Flowers* (New York: New Directions, 1967).

17. Compare with Heidegger's abhorrence of tourism, in "The Question Concerning Technology," in *Basic Writings* (New York: Harper and Row, 1977), p. 297. Heidegger is filled with horror at the thought that Hölderlin's Rhine might be regarded as a "water-power supplier" or worse—a tourist sight!

18. Raymond Queneau, *Zazie dans le métro* (Paris: Gallimard, 1959), translated by Barbara Wright as *Zazie* (London: Bodley Head, Ltd., 1960, and New York: Harper & Brothers, 1960). The book was a best-seller that was translated into nine languages and also made into a film by Louis Malle. For an excellent overview of Queneau's literary career see Richard Mayne, "The Queneau Country," *Encounter*, Vol. 6 (1965), pp. 64–71.

19. Raymond Queneau, *Le Dimanche de la vie* (Paris: Gallimard, 1951), translated by Barbara Wright as *The Sunday of Life* (London: John Calder Publishers, Ltd., 1976).

20. Queneau, *The Sunday of Life*, p. 151.

21. This leads some commentators to think that Valentin is a saint and mystic. See Esslin, "Raymond Queneau," p. 93. It is not clear how Esslin can square this with his claim that Valentin is also a simpleton and an existentialist who enjoys the simple pleasures of the moment (p. 98).

22. Queneau, *The Sunday of Life*, p. 131. Even though Julia was never home in the daytime, Valentin never thought to ask her where she went or what she did all day while he was minding the haberdashery—that would have been too "husbandlike."

23. Kojève, "Les Romans de la sagesse," p. 397.

24. Raymond Queneau, *We Always Treat Women Too Well*, translated from the French by Barbara Wright (New York: New Directions, 1981). There is much controversy about this particular novel. It was originally published by Gallimard in 1947 under the pseudonym of Sally Mara, and published again by Gallimard under Queneau's name in 1962. Some have compared the novel to the pornographic American novel by James Hadley Chase, *No Orchids for Miss Blandish* (London: Robert Hale Ltd., 1971), which enjoyed great popularity in France in 1946. But as Barbara Wright and others have pointed out, the difference between the two novels is stark: Miss Blandish is a helpless captive who is repeatedly drugged, beaten, and raped by the gang leader, Slim. When the police release her she commits suicide because she has fallen in love with Slim—clearly, a sadomasochistic product of a warped masculine imagination.

25. Queneau, *The Sunday of Life*, p. 65.

26. Ibid., p. 105.

27. Ibid, p. 83.

28. Raymond Queneau, *Le Vol d'Icare* (Paris: Gallimard, 1968), translated by Barbara Wright as *The Flight of Icarus* (London: Calder & Boyars, 1973).

29. Allen Thiher, *Raymond Queneau* (Boston: Twayne Publishers, 1985), p. 112. Thiher is aware of the fact that Queneau's writing is ambivalent and needs decoding. Thiher misses the mark when he finds no history in *Le Dimanche de la vie*, which he takes to be about *petit bourgeois* hedonism. He finds Kojève's interpretation of Valentin Brûas a Hegelian sage to be "strange" and has no idea what Hegel has to do with this novel.

30. Queneau, *The Sunday of Life*, p. 43.

31. Ibid., p. 94.

32. Kojève also considers the poet in the novel to be a Hegelian sage. See Raymond Queneau, *Loin de Rueil*, 1948, which is translated as *The Skin of Dreams* by H. J. Kaplan (New York: Howard Fertig, 1979).

33. G. Brée and M. Guiton, *An Age of Fiction* (New Brunswick: Rutgers University Press, 1957), pp. 169–79.

CHAPTER 8

1. Dominique Auffret, *Alexandre Kojève*, p. 359.

2. Raymond Queneau, "Première confrontation avec Hegel," in *Critique*, Nos. 195–196 (August/September 1963), pp. 694–700. This is a eulogy to Bataille that traces his intellectual preoccupation with Hegel. It

explains that Bataille's struggle to understand Hegel culminates in the acceptance of Kojève's version of Hegel. Queneau makes it clear that Kojève's lectures were of critical importance in Bataille's development, even though Queneau claims that Bataille sometimes dozed off during the seminar. However, a very thick and detailed pile of notes on Kojève's lectures testify to the contrary. See Denis Hollier's comments preceding Kojève's "Hegelian Concepts," in Denis Hollier (ed.), *The College of Sociology* (Minneapolis: University of Minnesota Press, 1988), p. 86.

3. See Denis Hollier (ed.), *The College of Sociology.*

4. Michel Foucault, "Hommage à Georges Bataille," *Critique,* Nos. 195–196 (August/September 1963), pp. 751–770. The essay is available in English translation as "A Preface to Transgression," in Foucault's *Language, Counter-Memory, Practice* (Ithaca: Cornell University Press, 1977), pp. 29–52; see also Jacques Derrida's essay on Bataille, "From Restricted to General Economy: A Hegelianism Without Reserve," in Derrida, *Writing and Difference* (Chicago: University of Chicago Press, 1978), pp. 251–277. In *Positions* (Paris: Editions de Minuit, 1972), p. 89, note 25, Derrida claims that his major texts are a reading of Bataille. Heidegger's accolades appear on the jacket of Bataille's *On Nietzsche,* translated by Bruce Boone with an introduction by Sylvère Lotringer (New York: Paragon House, 1992).

5. Quoted by Georges Bataille in *The Accursed Share,* Vol. II and III, translated by Robert Hurley (New York: Zone Books, 1991), Vol. II, p. 31. Vol. II is entitled *The History of Eroticism,* and Vol. III is entitled *Sovereignty.*

6. Of course, this analogy is not as good as Bataille thinks it is. The man who invites friends over for champagne also has some of the champagne himself.

7. Bataille, *The Accursed Share,* Vol. II, p. 43.

8. Ibid., Vol. II, p. 44.

9. Ibid., Vol. II, p. 28.

10. As Bataille explains, the sovereign or the "chief of men" is someone who has immense wealth at his disposal and who squanders it in an overtly conspicuous and spectacularly wasteful display. Bataille associates sovereignty with the "unproductive glory" of the past and contrasts it with the rational and utilitarian condition of our bourgeois world, which has "lost the secret" of living sovereignly or with splendor. *The Accursed Share,* Volume I, *Consumption,* translated by Robert Hurley (New York: Zone Books, 1991), p. 63; see also Volume III, *Sovereignty,* p. 197ff.

11. Ibid., Vol. I, pp. 29, 131.

12. Ibid., Vol. II, pp. 52, 94.

13. Ibid., Vol. II, pp. 70, 53, 61, 73.

14. Ibid., Vol. II, pp. 73–75.

15. Ibid., Vol. II, pp. 53, 56.

16. Ibid., Vol. II, p. 56.

17. Ibid., Vol. II, p. 57.

18. Bataille traces the earliest developments of human eroticism in *Les Larmes d'eros* (Paris: Jacques Puvert, 1961), translated by Peter Connor as *Tears of Eros* (San Francisco: City Lights, 1989). Bataille suspects that there might have been a "paradisaic aspect to early eroticism," which we find in the art of cave men,

but soon a certain "heaviness" sets in. Bataille finds this "heaviness" in the famous Lascaux cave where a man with a bird's head and an erect phallus stands before a dying bison. Bataille thinks that the image portrays an awareness of the connection of sex, sadism, death, and anguish.

19. Bataille, *The Accursed Share*, Vol. II. p. 17. Bataille was fascinated with eroticism; Vol. II of *The Accursed Share* is a *History of Eroticism;* Bataille's *Tears of Eros, Eroticism, Death and Sensuality*, as well as all his fictional works also deal with eroticism; as we shall see in the next chapter, Bataille's reflections anticipate Foucault's *History of Sexuality.*

20. Ibid., Vol. II, p. 76.

21. Ibid., Vol. II, p. 73.

22. Ibid., Vol. I, p. 38, where Bataille laments the loss of the real meaning of freedom and its replacement with a "lackluster" phenomenon subject to necessities like justice.

23. Bataille is right to point out that Islam means to surrender one's life to God and his will, and that the holy war is first and foremost a war against the self. See Ibid., Vol. I, *Consumption*, pp. 81ff.

24. Ibid., Vol. I, p. 110: Bataille understands Lamaism as violence turned inward. This is a classic Freudian understanding of all self-restraint as internalized forms of domination or violence. This same Freudian understanding of restraint is also apparent in the work of Foucault, and in my view, accounts for the inability to distinguish self-restraint from the internalization of power and violence.

25. Ibid., Vol. I, p. 54.

26. The expression belongs to Martin Heidegger, "The Question Concerning Technology," in *Basic Writings*, p. 315.

27. Bataille, *Accursed Share*, Vol. II, pp. 66, 71.

28. Ibid., Vol. I, p. 133.

29. See "The Psychological Structure of Fascism," and "Nietzsche and the Fascists," in Georges Bataille, *Visions of Excess: Selected Writings 1927–1939*, edited with an introduction by Allan Stoekl; Stoekl's excellent introduction focuses on Bataille's relationship to fascism.

30. This letter appears as an appendix to Bataille's *Guilty*, a translation of *Le Coupable* (Paris, Gallimard, 1961) by Bruce Boone, with an introduction by Denis Hollier (Venice, California: The Lapis Press, 1988), p. 124. A slightly fuller version appears in Bataille's *Oeuvres complètes* (Paris: Gallimard, 1970), Vol. 5, pp. 369–371.

31. Georges Bataille, "Hegel, l'homme et l'histoire," *Monde nouveau*, Vol. II, Nos. 96–97 (1956), Part II, p. 3. This essay reveals the extent to which Bataille's interpretation of Hegel is identical to Kojève's.

32. Bataille, *Guilty*, p. 123.

33. Bataille, *The Accursed Share*, Vol. II, p. 52.

34. Bataille uses this expression in his letter to Kojève that appears as an appendix to Bataille's *Guilty*, p. 123ff. See also Bataille's discussion of the end of history in *Accursed Share*, Vol. II, pp. 189–191.

35. See, for example, Bataille, "The Sacred Conspiracy," in *Visions of Excess*, p. 179.

36. Despite his criticism of the College, Kojève gave a lecture at the College entitled "Hegelian Concepts." See Hollier (ed.), *The College of Sociology*, pp. 85–93. This is the lecture in which Kojève declared that it was Stalin, not Napoleon, who was the culmination of history. Apparently, Kojève's "intellectual powers" as well as his conclusion left the members of the College "flabbergasted."

37. Ibid., pp. 12–23.

38. Ibid., pp. 13–14.

39. This may seem surprising in view of Bataille's love of art. For example, he wrote *Manet: Biographical and Critical Study*, translated by Austryn Wainhouse and James Emmons (Cleveland: The World Publishing Co., 1955). Bataille hails Manet as the first modern artist who had the courage to show things as they are. Bataille thinks that is precisely why his "Olympia" caused such an uproar—modeled on Titian's famous Venus, it was a painting of a female nude, not Venus, but a real live woman in this world, looking neither provocative nor shy, but simple and direct. Bataille praises Manet for having swept away the artistic splendor of days gone by because it was a lie that did not fit the banality of the bourgeois world. Bataille therefore praises Manet for not withdrawing into a world of fiction, which Bataille thinks artists are inclined to do.

40. Hollier (ed.), *The College of Sociology*, p. 15.

41. Ibid., p. 16.

42. Ibid., p. 22.

43. Bataille, *Accursed Share*, Vol. II, pp. 91–92.

44. Ibid., Vol. II, p. 77.

45. Ibid., Vol. II, p. 78.

46. Ibid.

47. Ibid., Vol. II, p. 73.

48. Hollier (ed.), *The College of Sociology*, p. 23.

49. Susan Sontag thinks that Bataille is the Wagner of pornography. She argues that pornography is a form of knowledge or truth that, like any other form of knowledge or truth, has its dangers. But the knowledge that is revealed by people like Bataille who experience their sexuality at an "unsettling pitch" is probably less dangerous to the community than other endeavors. She is aware of the fact that Bataille portrays death and killing as the height of erotic pleasure. But she refuses to take the violence in pornography seriously; instead, she maintains that it is like comedy—the characters always spring back fully healed. Nothing could be further from the truth. There is nothing comic about Bataille's lust for death; nor do the characters spring back fully healed. See "The Pornographic Imagination," in her *Styles of Radical Will* (New York: Farrar, Straus and Giroux, 1966), pp. 35–73.

50. See Bataille, "Base Materialism and Gnosticism," in *Visions of Excess*, pp. 45–52.

51. For an account of the necessary tension between the Apollonian and the Dionysian, see Nietzsche's *Birth of Tragedy*, translated by Francis Golffing (New York: Doubleday Anchor Books, 1956). Bataille was extremely enchanted with Nietzsche and he believed that Nietzsche's diatribes against Hegel were the result of having only the most superficial understanding of Hegel's thought. Had Nietzsche understood Hegel (the way Kojève did), he would have realized that his views were most compatible with his own. See Bataille's *Sur Nietzsche* (Paris: Gallimard, 1945), translated by Bruce Boone as *On Nietzsche* (New

York: Paragon House, 1992). In this work, Bataille tries to write like Nietzsche, with his "blood." He is convinced that the inner torments of his own psyche are the microcosm of the plight of Western civilization. His life, as well as the life of Western civilization, is characterized by a profound longing for a summit that is not there. He describes the psychic anguish involved in dealing with the dead end that Western civilization has reached. The history of the West is the tragedy of the human psyche itself. It is the anguish engendered by an extravagant and costly effort to reach a summit that is death. For all his veneration of Nietzsche, it must be admitted that Bataille's longing for ascetic mortification and his thirst for death and annihilation is radically contrary to the spirit of Nietzsche's "joyful wisdom."

52. This is the gist of Jürgen Habermas's essay "Between Eroticism and General Economics: Georges Bataille" in Habermas, *The Discourse of Modernity*, 1985, translated by Frederick Lawrence (Cambridge, Massachusetts: MIT Press, 1987), pp. 211–237. See also Habermas's discussion of the Dionysian cult that he rightly believes to be integral to postmodernity, Chapter IV of the same volume, especially pp. 83ff.

53. Bataille, *The Accursed Share*, Vol. II, p. 49.

54. See for example Denis Diderot's novel, *The Nun*, translated by Leonard W. Tancock (London: Penguin, 1974).

55. See for example Bataille's *Guilty*.

56. Georges Bataille, *Le Procès de Gilles de Rais* (Paris: Jean-Jacques Pauvert, 1965), translated as *The Trial of Gilles de Rais*, by Richard Robinson (Los Angeles: Amok, 1991).

57. Bataille, *The Trial of Gilles de Rais*, pp. 9, 12.

58. Ibid., pp. 58–60.

59. Ibid., p. 12.

60. Ibid., p. 42.

61. Ibid., p. 41.

62. Ibid., p. 57. Bataille's discussion of the importance of the public execution in the Middle Ages anticipates the ideas that were popularized by Foucault in *Discipline and Punish: The Birth of the Prison*, translated by Alan Sheridan (New York: Random House, 1979).

63. Ibid., p. 60.

64. Ibid., p. 58.

65. Georges Bataille, *L'Impossible* (Paris: Les Editions de Minuit, 1962), translated by Robert Hurley as *The Impossible* (San Francisco: City Lights, 1991).

66. Georges Bataille, *L'Expérience intérieure* (Paris: Gallimard, 1954), translated as *Inner Experience*, by Leslie Anne Boldt (Albany: State University of New York, 1988). See also Jean-Paul Sartre's review of the book in Sartre, *Situations*, Vol. I (Paris: Gallimard, 1947), pp. 143–188. Sartre doubts the sincerity of Bataille's desire to be lost in the totality and oneness of being (p. 174). In contrast, Sartre believes in the absolute separateness of the individual. Sartre also notices that Bataille is not a consistent atheist, and that his atheism requires God. He therefore compares him unfavorably to Nietzsche on that count (p. 178). What sets Sartre apart from Bataille is also what sets him apart from the postmodernism of Foucault, Lacan, or Derrida: Sartre rejects the idea that the individual's identity is constituted by the collectivity, except in bad faith. Unlike the postmoderns, he is much more confident in the capacity of the individual to transcend the formative forces of power and to find or create his authentic self.

67. Georges Bataille, *Eroticism, Death and Sensuality*, translated by Mary Dalwood (San Francisco: City Lights Books, 1986).

68. Jacques Lacan shares Bataille's view of mysticism and sexuality; see Juliet Mitchell and Jacqueline Rose (eds.), *Feminine Sexuality: Lacan and the ecole freudienne*, translated by Jacqueline Rose (London: Macmillan, 1982), p. 147.

69. There is no doubt that Bataille admired the stark dualisms of the Middle Ages—lords and ladies, castles and dungeons, nobles and peasants, sin and redemption, eroticism and celibacy. But his love affair with Christianity was very short-lived. He was converted to Catholicism in 1918 and spent some time in the Benedictine abbey on the Isle of Wight, where he seriously considered becoming a priest. By 1922, he had abandoned his faith for good, and in his typically paradoxical fashion espoused an atheistic theology. In the final analysis, Christianity did not lend itself to the cycles of taboo and transgression that Bataille associated with the vitality of the primitives. And even though Christianity permitted public executions, it prohibited animal sacrifices—something that Bataille regarded with special interest.

70. This is the reason that André Breton referred to him as the "excremental philosopher."

71. Bataille, *The Accursed Share*, Vol. II, p. 84.

72. Hollier (ed.), *The College of Sociology*, p. 21.

73. Bataille, *The Accursed Share*, Vol. II, p. 85.

74. Ibid., Vol. II, p. 84.

75. Nothing describes the perversity of Bataille's brand of atheism better than Nietzsche's "great ladder of religious cruelty." Man begins by sacrificing human beings to his god—usually the most loved, like the sacrifice of the firstborn. Then in the "moral epoch" man sacrificed his strongest instincts to God. Finally, when there is nothing left to sacrifice, but the desire to sacrifice is still great, God himself, the last comfort and joy, is sacrificed to the Nothing. This is the "final cruelty" and the colossal stupidity that Nietzsche attributes to his own generation. Bataille mistakenly believes that Nietzsche's "ladder" is an inexorable historical destiny that cannot be escaped. See *Beyond Good and Evil*, Part III, Sec. 55; Bataille quotes the passage at length in his *Inner Experience*, p. 131.

76. Bataille, "The Sacred Conspiracy," in *Visions of Excess*, p. 181. Bataille's journal *Acéphale* was named after the headless god and its intent was to urge man to abandon his head and not to be governed by his reason.

CHAPTER 9

1. Michel Foucault, *Discipline and Punish*, translated by Alan Sheridan (New York: Random House, 1977, 1979), p. 48.

2. Ibid., p. 49.

3. Ibid., p. 61.

4. Michel Foucault, *Power/Knowledge: Selected Interviews and Other Writings 1972–1977*, edited by Colin Gordon, translated by Colin Gordin, Leo Marshal, John Mepham, Kate Soper (New York: Pantheon Books, 1972), p. 104.

5. Ibid., p. 96.

6. Michel Foucault, "Governmentality," in *Ideology and Consciousness*, Nos. 6–9 (Autumn 1979–Winter 1981/82), p. 10.

7. Ibid. p. 21.

8. Michel Foucault, *History of Sexuality*, Vol. I, translated by Robert Hurley (New York: Random House, 1980), p. 144.

9. Ibid., Vol. I, p. 145.

10. Ibid., Vol. I, pp. 149–150.

11. Allan Bloom has similar forebodings. See my discussion in Chapter 2 of Part III.

12. See Foucault's introduction to *Hurculine Barbin: Being the Recently Discovered Memoirs of a Nineteenth-Century Hermaphrodite*, translated by Richard McDougal (New York: Pantheon, 1980). I am indebted to Lisa Warden for bringing this work to my attention.

13. See Foucault's introduction to *Hurculine Barbin*. Feminists who believe with Foucault that sexuality is a social invention are particularly fascinated with the story. For the best defense of the view that sexuality is a social invention, see Judith Butler, *Gender Trouble* (New York: Routledge, 1990).

14. Foucault, *History of Sexuality*, Vol. I, pp. 83, 89, 105, 151.

15. Michel Foucault, "A Preface to Transgression," in Foucault, *Language, Countermemory, Practice* (Ithaca: Cornell University Press, 1977), pp. 29–52. This is a translation of Foucault's "Hommage à Georges Bataille," which originally appeared in *Critique*, Nos. 195–196 (1963), pp. 751–770. This is an important essay in which Foucault pays tribute to Bataille. The essay makes it clear that Foucault saw no need to distinguish between writing in his own name and giving an account of Bataille's thought.

16. James Miller, *The Passion of Michel Foucault* (New York: Simon and Schuster, 1993). Even though I reject Miller's thesis, I think that he is quite right to point to the importance of the influence of Bataille.

17. Nietzsche, *Thus Spoke Zarathustra*, translated by Walter Kaufmann, (New York: Penguin, 1954), Prologue, Sec. 5; Heidegger, "Overcoming Metaphysics," and "Only a God Could Save Us," in Richard Wolin (ed.), *The Heidegger Controversy* (New York: Columbia University Press, 1991); Max Weber, *The Protestant Ethic and the Spirit of Capitalism*, translated by Talcott Parsons (New York: Charles Scribner's Sons, 1958), pp. 181–182; Alexandre Kojève, *IRH*, pp. 160–161.

18. Michel Foucault, *Madness and Civilization: A History of Insanity in the Age of Reason*, translated by Richard Howard (New York: Random House, 1965), p. 13.

19. Michel Foucault (ed.), *I, Pierre Rivière: A Case of Parricide in the Nineteenth-Century* (Lincoln: University of Nebraska Press, 1975).

20. Jean-Paul Sartre, *Saint Genet* (Paris: Gallimard, 1952). In this massive volume, Sartre pays tribute to Genet as the quintessential "outsider" in Camus's sense of the term, an existentialist and a divinely free man. He regards both his treacheries and his homosexuality as freely chosen and unfounded.

21. On the contradictory character of Foucault's philosophical position see David Couzens Hoy (ed.), *Foucault: A Critical Reader* (New York: Basil Blackwell, 1986), especially the essays by Michael Walzer, Jürgen Habermas, and Charles Taylor. See also Kenneth Minogue, "Can Radicalism Survive Michel Foucault?" in *Critical Review*, Vol. 3, No. 1 (Winter 1989), pp. 138–154; Charles Taylor and William Connolly, "Michel Foucault: An Exchange," *Political Theory*, Vol. 13, No. 3 (August 1985), pp. 365–385; Tom Keenan, "The Paradox of Knowledge and Power: Reading Foucault on a Bias," *Political Theory*, Vol.

15, No.1 (February 1987), pp. 5-37; Paul Bove, "Forward: The Foucault Phenomena: the Problematics of Style," in Gilles Deleuze (ed.), *Foucault* (Minneapolis: University of Minnesota Press, 1986).

22. Foucault, *Power/Knowledge,* pp. 93, 105, 106, 107; Foucault, *The History of Sexuality,* Vol. I, pp. 136–144; Michel Foucault, *Discipline and Punish,* translated by Alan Sheridan (New York: Vintage Books, 1979), p. 27.

23. Foucault, *Power/Knowledge,* pp. 92, 93, 94, 105.

24. Michel Foucault, "Nietzsche, Genealogy and History," in *The Foucault Reader,* Paul Rabinow (ed.) (New York: Pantheon Books, 1984), p. 80.

25. Friedrich Nietzsche, *The Use and Abuse of History,* translated by Adrian Collins, (New York: Library of the Liberal Arts, 1957), Sec. VI, p. 41.

26. Ibid., Sec. III, p. 19.

27. Ibid., Sec. III, p. 20.

28. See Foucault, "Nietzsche Genealogy, History," in Rabinow (ed.), *The Foucault Reader,* pp. 76–100.

29. Foucault, "A Preface to Transgression," pp. 41, 42.

30. This may explain why Foucault's histories contain a subtle nostalgia for the Middle Ages. It is not surprising to find James Miller pointing to Foucault's interest in the practices of sadomasochism; see his recent biography, *The Passion of Michel Foucault* (New York: Simon and Schuster, 1993). Miller's description of sadomasochistic practices, such as hanging from a meat hook while your blood drips to the floor, sounds like something that would happen to you in the dungeon of a castle in a Gothic novel. Alasdair MacIntyre is quite right to point out that what Miller takes to be examples of self-discovery (that supposedly lead to the freedom of self-mastery and self-restraint at the end of Foucault's life) sound more like self-indulgent fantasy. See the discussions of Miller's book by MacIntyre and others in *Salmagundi,* No. 91, (Winter 1993). Miller's biography is a fascinating chronicle of Foucault's life, but it is philosophically speaking very muddled. His main thesis is that Foucault was fascinated by cruelty, confinement, and death. All his books are autobiographies that document these fascinations. His participation in the sadomasochistic community in San Francisco was part of the same psychic preoccupation with death, torture, and other extreme or "limit-experiences"—hence his interest in Bataille and Sade. And even though Foucault repudiated the search for truth and denied that there is a subject unconstructed by power, Miller believes that Foucault's life testifies to the contrary. Indeed, Miller argues that Foucault's life and work can be understood as a "Nietzschean quest" to liberate himself from the dominant powers and become "who thou art." At the end of his life, he finally realizes that he cannot escape the truth about who he is. He comes face to face with the self he tried to discover, exorcise, and reinvent; he comes face to face with the desires and impulses that disciplinary power had dismissed as abnormal, ill, and perverse and whose "innocence" Foucault tried to establish in his books. At the end of his life, Foucault begins to "think differently" and feels compelled to "confess" the truth about himself. He returns to the classics—admittedly not Socrates, but Diogenes the Cynic. Miller maintains that Diogenes, like Socrates, devoted himself to the project of self-knowledge and to the discovery of the truth. Foucault is therefore a philosopher in the classic sense of the term as understood in the West—he is a seeker after truth who believes that self-knowledge is the key to this enterprise.
    As fascinating as this tale is, it is very puzzling and confused. First, although Miller is quite right to point to the connection between Foucault and Bataille (pp. 85–89), Miller has no philosophical appreciation of Bataille; he thinks of him simply as an "inhabitant of the *demimonde*" who is obsessed with morbid themes of death, cruelty, and human sacrifice. I have tried to show that Foucault learned much more from Bataille than a taste for death and cruelty—he learned his whole way of thinking. Second, Miller's biography is erected on the ashes of Foucault's philosophy. Miller's assertion that Foucault was involved in a lifelong quest for self-discovery, self-liberation, self-making, and the search for truth, can-

not make sense of Foucault's central philosophical claims—that there is no truth, that there is no sub-ject unconstituted by power, and that there is no hope of liberating ourselves from power (or as I have argued, no reason to do so). Third, Miller's central thesis regarding Foucault's Nietzschean quest is undeveloped. As MacIntyre has pointed out, the Nietzschean idea of freedom as self-making has noth-ing to do with the classical idea of freedom as self-restraint and self-mastery. But Miller blurs the two. Fourth, Miller's claim that Foucault rediscovered the obligation to tell the truth—an obligation that is at the heart of the Western philosophical tradition—strikes me as totally farfetched. As Miller acknowl-edges, it is not Socrates, but Diogenes the Cynic whom Foucault admires. It seems to me that the man who is famous for masturbating in the public square is not an icon of self-knowledge and self-restraint, but of transgression.

CHAPTER 10

1. James Nichols, translator of the *IRH*, was a student of Allan Bloom's. Other translations are also by Strauss's students or their associates. For example, Kojève's, "Hegel, Marx and Christianity," translated by Hilail Gildin, *Interpretation*, Vol. 1 (1970) pp. 21–42. See also Kojève's, "Death in the Philosophy of Hegel" translated by Joseph J. Carpino, *Interpretation*, Vol. 3 (1973) pp. 114–156. See also "Kojève-Fessard Documents," translated by Hugh Gillis, *Interpretation*, Vol. 19, No. 2 (Winter 1991–1992), pp. 185–200.

2. Kojève wrote his dissertation on Vladimir Soloviev under Karl Jaspers in Heidelberg, and published it in the form of two essays, "La Métaphysique religieuse de Vladimir Soloviev (1) and (2)," in *Revue d'his-toire et de philosophie religieuses* 14, No. 6 (1934), pp. 534–544, and Nos. 1–2 (1935), pp. 10–152, respec-tively. Strauss's early work was on Maimonides; see his *Philosophy and Law: Essays Toward the Understanding of Maimonides and His Predecessors*, translated from the German by Fred Baumann (New York: The Jewish Publication Society, 1987).

3. This is explained by Michael Roth, *Knowing and History* (Ithaca, New York: Cornell University Press, 1988), p. 95.

4. See Leo Strauss, *CORR*.

5. Michael Roth, *Knowing and History*, is a case in point. Stanley Rosen's *Hermeneutics as Politics* is an excep-tion. Rosen is the only one of Strauss's students to recognize the affinity between the two writers.

6. Leo Strauss, *OT*, pp. 78, 68.

7. Ibid., pp. 198, 26, 27, and 32, 25, 74.

8. Ibid., p. 57; see also Eric Voegelin's review of *On Tyranny* in the *Review of Politics*, Vol. 11, No. 2 (1949), pp. 241–244: Voegelin argues that Machiavelli's account of tyranny surpasses Xenophon's pagan account because it borrows the Christian conception of Caesarism. According to Voegelin, tyranny is to be distinguished from Caesarism because the latter is necessitated by the corruption and decadence of the people and is therefore a matter of historical necessity—it is needed to punish the people for their sins. For Strauss's response to Voegelin, see *OT*, esp. pp. 190–192, 195–197: Strauss rightly remarks that Voegelin's distinction is a very convenient excuse for tyranny.

9. Strauss, *OT*, pp. 45, 54, 78–79, 44, 50ff.

10. Ibid., pp. 99, 40, 42–43, 72–73 where Strauss makes distinctions between the wise man, the political man, the gentleman, and the vulgar; for other references to "gentlemen" and their "vulgar virtues" see the following books by Leo Strauss: *What Is Political Philosophy?* (Westport, Conn.: Greenwood Press, 1959), p. 113; *Natural Right and History* (Chicago: University of Chicago Press, 1953), pp. 142–143, 150 note 24; *City and Man* (Chicago: University of Chicago Press, 1964), pp. 27–28, 37; *Persecution and the Art of Writing* (Westport, Conn.: Greenwood Press, 1952), p. 154; *Liberalism Ancient and Modern* (New York:

Basic Books, 1968), p. 11; and *Studies in Platonic Political Philosophy* (Chicago: University of Chicago Press, 1983), pp. 43, 54, 66.

11. Strauss, *OT*, pp. 213–214.

12. Ibid., p. 212.

13. Ibid., p. 214.

14. Ibid., p. 213.

15. Ibid., p. 218.

16. Ibid., p. 215.

17. Ibid., p. 216; see also Strauss, *Natural Right and History*, p. 151.

18. Strauss, *OT*, p. 215.

19. On Strauss's glorification of pederasty, see Shadia Drury, review of Leo Strauss, *The Rebirth of Classical Political Rationalism*, edited by Thomas L. Pangle (Chicago: University of Chicago Press, 1989), *Political Theory*, Vol. 19, No. 4 (November, 1991), pp. 671–675. On why it is so important for Strauss to insist that the philosopher does not need love, see Shadia B. Drury, *The Political Ideas of Leo Strauss* (New York: St. Martin's Press, 1988), pp. 68–69.

20. Strauss, *OT*, p. 214.

21. Ibid., p. 220.

22. Kojève's letter to Strauss, July 1, 1957, in Strauss, *CORR*, p. 281: "knowledge = re-called [completed] history."

23. Strauss, *OT*, pp. 157–159, 198.

24. Ibid., p. 157.

25. Ibid., pp. 173, 176, 180, 182. Strauss wholeheartedly agrees with Kojève's elaboration of the issue, but he cannot help feeling a "nascent shock" at the "more than Machiavellian bluntness" with which Kojève expresses himself. The explicit and unceremonious style in which Kojève describes the philosophical enthusiasm for tyranny disconcerts one who is nourished on the "noble reserve" and "quiet grandeur" of the ancients (p. 198). In a letter to Kojève of August 22, 1948 (Strauss, *CORR*, p. 236), Strauss asks Kojève to review his book, saying that only Kojève and Jacob Klein are likely to understand it, adding that he (Strauss) refuses to go through an open door, when he can enter through a keyhole.

26. Kojève's letter to Strauss, September 19, 1950, in Strauss, *CORR*, p. 255.

27. Kojève's letter to Strauss, July 1, 1957, in Strauss, *CORR*, p. 281. See also my discussion in the section on "The Sage" in Chapter Four, Part I, of this book.

28. According to Raymond Aron, Kojève was the *éminence grise*, the power behind the throne, at the French ministry. He exerted a great influence on Olivier Wormser and Valéry Giscard d'Estaing. He took this role very seriously and was often angry when his suggestions were not adopted. See Raymond Aron, *Memoirs: Fifty Years of Political Reflection*, translated by George Holoch, with a foreword by Henry A. Kissinger (New York: Holmes and Meier, 1990), p. 67.

29. Strauss, *OT,* pp. 210, 211, 218.

30. Ibid., p. 163.

31. Ibid., p. 164.

32. Ibid., p. 176.

33. Kojève's letter to Strauss of September 19, 1950, in Strauss, *CORR,* p. 255; and Kojève, *ILH,* p. 39.

34. Kojève's letter to Strauss, September 19, 1950, in Strauss, *CORR,* p. 255.

35. Strauss, *OT,* p. 93: The wise man is described as a "stranger." Strauss also makes much of this in his interpretation of Plato's *Laws,* see Leo Strauss, *The Argument and the Action of Plato's Laws* (Chicago: University of Chicago Press, 1975). By the same token, Kojève is described as having a "white Russian" attitude toward the many; see Raymond Aron, *Memoirs,* p. 68.

36. Stanley Rosen is the only writer who has recognized the similarity between Strauss's and Kojève's ways of thinking. In *Hermeneutics and Politics* (Oxford: Oxford University Press, 1987), he argues that both Strauss and Kojève are "moderns" because they both believe in the primacy of the will, and they both regard philosophy as an act of will or a matter of propaganda intended to change the world or remake it according to the image conceived by the philosopher. Both of them thought of philosophy as propaganda, or the instrument for making the world. Both used interpretation or hermeneutics as a political vehicle. One posed as an interpreter of Hegel, the other as an interpreter of Plato. But their hermeneutical escapades are disguised propaganda, or ways in which they disseminate their ideas. According to Rosen, both Kojève and Strauss embarked on a personal quest to become gods surrounded by lesser deities. Kojève even made Merleau-Ponty his Apollo (apparently because he was handsome). I cannot speculate about their own personal quests to divinity, since I have not known either one. Rosen is in a position to make such claims since he knew both of them well. On the basis of their writing, I wholeheartedly endorse Rosen's claim that both Strauss and Kojève deified the philosopher, because they thought that ideas make the world. But Rosen also claims that they both thought something was true simply because it was intersubjectively shared, and this is why it was so important for them to amass converts—i.e., disciples who would validate their discourses and make them true. I have not found evidence to suggest that they thought of truth simply as intersubjectivity. I don't think that they thought of their ideas merely as propaganda, or a product of their own arbitrary will. I think that they really believed that genuine philosophers (and they thought of themselves as genuine) were in tune with reality or with the truth, and that they ought to shape the world according to the inner truth to which they alone have access.

Rosen makes all sorts of other claims, which I think are misleading. Rosen adopts the classic Straussian view of Kojève as the quintessential "modern," saying that his thought is particularly instructive because it displays the contradictory nature of the Enlightenment project. But Rosen thinks that Strauss too is a "modern"—not so much a Nietzschean as a Kantian. His reason is that Strauss shared the modern assumption that the will was primary and that truth was intersubjective—and *that* is the reason he was so eager to amass as many disciples as possible.

Rosen also maintains that Strauss was a "modern" because he was not sufficiently "esoteric"—anyone who writes as much as Strauss did about esotericism could not be all that esoteric. Nevertheless, the esoteric thesis was eccentric enough to produce the "infantry of troops" he needed for his divine project. Rosen goes so far as to suggest that there was no secret teaching, or if there was, then it was platitudinous, or that Strauss did not know what it was. But, unlike the less thoughtful Straussians, Rosen could smell a rat, and he had the courage to say that the emperor had no clothes, at the risk of being regarded as not having the "requisite subtlety."

Rosen makes a valiant effort to disentangle himself from the Straussian web, but he does not always succeed. And his wildly ingenious claims are sometimes quite unsubstantiated. I think that it is misleading to call Strauss a "modern," especially when Plato is also deemed to be a "modern" and Nietzsche is declared to be really a Platonist.

37. Strauss, *OT,* p. 214.

38. Ibid., p. 187.

39. C. S. Lewis, *The Abolition of Man* (New York: Macmillan, 1947) makes this argument brilliantly. George Grant makes a similar argument with less power and eloquence; see his *Technology and Justice* (Toronto: House of Anansi, 1986). Grant erroneously regards Strauss as an ally; see his "Tyranny and Wisdom: A Comment on the Controversy between Leo Strauss and Alexandre Kojève," *Social Research,* Vol. 31 (1964), pp. 45–72, also reprinted in George Grant, *Technology and Empire* (Toronto: House of Anansi, 1969). Grant and Lewis believe that technology facilitates the tyranny of the few over the many; Strauss's view is the reverse.

40. See, for example, Nicola Chiaromonte, "On Modern Tyranny: A Critique of Western Intellectuals," *Dissent,* Vol. 16 (March/April 1969), pp. 137–150. Chiaromonte argues that instead of being critical of the established order, Western intellectuals have become apologists of modern technocratic society. The latter assumes a scientific air by which they are too easily duped. Modern society forces individuals to give up more and more of their freedom in the name of augmenting the power of "generic Humanity" over nature. The result is a society characterized by increasingly autocratic but impersonal forms of organization. We live in a tyranny that poses as a democracy, but none of our intellectuals know it. Chiaromonte nods to Strauss as an ally. But Strauss does not criticize modernity because it diminishes freedom. This critique of modernity presupposes the modern appreciation of freedom, which Strauss does not share. While it is often obtuse, Chiaromonte's article contains some significant insights.

41. Strauss, *OT,* p. 224.

42. Ibid., p. 222.

43. Ibid., p. 226.

44. There is no doubt that Jane Austen was one of the greatest literary figures to have written in the English language. But I cannot help being suspicious of those who praise her too highly. It is often not so much her work that is being praised, but the fact that she was a "good woman" who knew her "place" and wrote nothing that would disturb the established order. Straussian literary critics find irony everywhere, but not in Jane Austen's novels.

45. Strauss, *OT,* pp. 198, 222.

46. This is the thesis of Strauss's *The Political Philosophy of Hobbes* (Oxford: Clarendon Press, 1936); see also Strauss's "Quelques remarques sur la science politique de Hobbes," *Recherches philosophiques,* Vol. 2 (1932–1933), pp. 609–622.

47. Strauss, *OT,* pp. 223, 26; see also Strauss's letters to Kojève, August 22, 1948, and September 11, 1957, in Strauss, *CORR,* pp. 236–239 and pp. 291–294.

48. Strauss, *OT,* p. 224.

49. Ibid., pp. 223–224.

50. Ibid., p. 224.

51. Ibid., p. 224.

52. Ibid., p. 203.

53. Ibid., p. 224.

54. Ibid., p. 224.

55. Ibid., p. 224.

56. Ibid., p. 224.

57. Ibid., p. 226.

58. I have profited immensely from Fritz Stern's book *The Politics of Cultural Despair* (Berkeley: University of California Press, 1961). The book deals primarily with Paul de Lagarde, Julius Langbehn, and Moller van den Bruck. Although these are less well known right-radicals than the ones I have mentioned above, the spirit is the same—dark, apocalyptic, and extremely seductive. Stern is right in thinking that these writers exploit the spiritual and psychological grievances of men—general unpolitical discontent. But they also touch on some of the true weaknesses of liberal modernity.

59. This is why Strauss's critique of Heidegger is disingenuous. See his "An Introduction to Heideggerian Existentialism" in Thomas L. Pangle (ed.) *The Rebirth of Classical Political Rationalism* (Chicago: University of Chicago Press, 1989) as well as my review of this collection in *Political Theory* (November 1991), pp. 671–675.

60. See my discussion of Strauss on Rousseau in Drury, *The Political Ideas of Leo Strauss*, pp. 152ff.

61. Leo Strauss, "The Liberalism of Classical Political Philosophy," *Review of Metaphysics*, Vol. XII (1958–1959), pp. 390–439. In the context of his examination of Eric A. Havelock, *The Liberal Temper in Greek Politics* (New Haven: Yale University Press, 1957), Strauss explains clearly his understanding of liberalism—egalitarian, technological, universalistic, humanistic, democratic, progressive, and optimistic—in short, the incarnation of Kojève's universal and homogeneous state.

62. For Strauss, America was the embodiment of the spineless liberalism of Weimar, which spawned Hitler. Many of Strauss's students are still under the impression that he was a friend of liberal democracy, or that his criticisms of it were mild and wishy-washy. Strauss's words lend support to this misconception, as when he says that "liberal or constitutional democracy comes closer to what the classics demanded than any alternative that is viable in our age" (*OT*, p. 207). This is the most complimentary statement Strauss ever made about liberal democracy. But Strauss's praise for liberal democracy must be understood in the context of the conditions of modern tyranny. Ancient tyranny shared the philosopher's concern for superiority—this is what Hiero and Simonides have in common. In contrast, modern tyranny is radically egalitarian, and this makes it, in Strauss's estimation, an enemy of philosophy. And what is worse, this antipathy to the superior few (i.e., the philosophers) is becoming a global phenomenon. It is only under these perilous conditions that Strauss praises liberal democracy, understood as a democracy that respects the rule of law. In other words, when the incompetent many rule supreme, the best thing to do is to make sure that their rule is limited by law. Liberal democracy is not second best; it is a necessary measure under desperate circumstances.

63. Allan Bloom, in "Responses to Fukuyama," *National Interest*, No. 16 (Summer 1989), p. 21.

64. Quoted in Terrence Ball and Richard Dagger, *Political Ideologies and the Democratic Ideal* (New York: HarperCollins, 1991), p. 152.

65. Fyodor Dostoevsky, *Crime and Punishment* (1866), translated by Constance Garnett (New York: Bantam Classics, 1958). See also the excellent introduction by Joseph Frank.

CHAPTER 11

1. Allan Bloom, *Giants and Dwarfs: Essays 1960–1990* (New York: Simon and Schuster, 1990). See "Teachers," pp. 235–273.

2. Ibid., p. 268, note.

3. To say this is not to undermine the book—for it is no mean feat to jazz up the ideas of Leo Strauss. There have been too many essays written on Bloom, most of which are not worth mentioning—being unfamiliar with the work of Leo Strauss, they totally miss the mark. Some of the more interesting essays have been collected in Robert L. Stone (ed.), *Essays on the Closing of the American Mind* (Chicago: Chicago Review Press, 1989).

4. See for example Richard Rorty, "That Old-Time Philosophy," *The New Republic* (April 4, 1988), pp. 28–37, also reprinted in Stone (ed.), *Essays on the Closing of the American Mind*.

5. Bloom's flirtation with Nietzsche has puzzled even veteran reviewers such as Kenneth Minogue, "The Graves of Academe," *Times Literary Supplement* (July 24, 1987), p. 786.

6. The expression is a mélange of Plato and Nietzsche, which is characteristic of Bloom's way of thinking.

7. "Commerce and 'Culture'" in Bloom, *Giants and Dwarfs*, pp. 277–294.

8. Allan Bloom, *The Closing of the American Mind* (New York: Simon and Schuster, 1987), pp. 187ff.

9. Bloom attributes the concept of sublimation to Rousseau. It was passed on to Kant, Schopenhauer, then Nietzsche—who actually formulated the term, which was then popularized by Freud. The idea of sublimation is to make the sublime out of the nonsublime. Rousseau thought that sexual desire was the sort of passion that, when properly managed, has a "singular effect on the soul." See Bloom's introduction to his translation of Jean-Jacques Rousseau's *Émile* (New York: Basic Books, 1979), p. 15; see also Bloom's "Rousseau on the Equality of the Sexes," in Frank S. Lucash (ed.), *Justice and Equality Here and Now* (Ithaca: Cornell University Press, 1986), pp. 68–88.

10. Bloom, *Closing*, pp. 187–88.

11. Ibid., p. 202.

12. Ibid., p. 192.

13. Ibid., pp. 37, 204.

14. Ibid., p. 37.

15. Ibid., p. 38.

16. Ibid., p. 37.

17. Bloom remarks that we need to be reminded that myth is, by definition, falsehood. This fact is apparently all too "often forgotten in our post-Nietzschean fascination with myth" (*Closing*, p. 207). It seems to me that it is Bloom who is most in need of reminding.

18. Bloom, *Closing*, pp. 37, 38.

19. Ibid., p. 203.

20. Ibid., p. 192.

21. Christianity was deleterious to culture because it led to the decay of love of the fatherland. Bloom admires both Machiavelli and Rousseau for having recognized this danger in Christianity. By promising a heavenly fatherland, Christianity "took away the supports from the earthly fatherland, leaving social men who

have no reason to sacrifice private desire to public duty." Bloom therefore considers modern philosophy to be the heir of Christianity. See Bloom's introduction to Rousseau's *Émile*, p. 5.

22. Bloom interprets the downfall of Othello to his faith in fictitious universalistic Christian principles. Because of his devotion to Christianity, Othello fights for a city only to the extent to which it stands for a truth that transcends all cities. Instead of thinking that this was Othello's best quality, Bloom criticizes Othello on the grounds that it is impossible to be a cosmopolitan man and a lover of honor at the same time, because in Bloom's view, honor is necessarily tied to absolute devotion to a particular city. Bloom surmises that the demise of Othello and Desdemona had nothing to do with the hostility of the world toward their love, but to their own failings, especially to Othello's flawed conception of honor. See his "Cosmopolitan Man and the Political Community," in Allan Bloom with Harry Jaffa, *Shakespeare's Politics* (New York: Basic Books, 1964), pp. 35–74.

23. Bloom, introduction to Rousseau's *Émile*, p. 5.

24. Ibid., p. 4.

25. Bloom, *Closing*, p. 193.

26. Ibid., p. 204.

27. Ibid., p. 51.

28. Ibid., p. 204.

29. Bloom associates this spiritedness with what Rousseau called *amour propre*, what Plato called *thymos*, and what Kojève called the desire for recognition. He thinks that Rousseau and Plato differ on the original nature of man. Rousseau thinks that in the absence of civilization, man was characterized by a natural and healthy self-esteem or *amour de soi*. But, thanks to the corruption of civilization, *amour de soi* is deformed into *amour propre* or pride. This latter is the source of anger, vanity, resentment, revenge, jealousy, competition, and other passions. *Amour propre* is not a natural or healthy self-esteem, but a desire for recognition, and a capacity to esteem oneself only when one is esteemed by others. It therefore leads to the desire for dominion and conquest. Rousseau thought this unnatural, but in Bloom's interpretation, Plato thought that it was part of the natural makeup of man that he called *thymos*, an integral part of the human psyche. This also fits the Kojèvean view that no animal can be insulted—being insulted is peculiarly human because it depends on the desire for recognition. Bloom sides with the latter view and regards Rousseau's attempt to banish *thymos* or *amour propre* as unwise. Instead of banishing it, Bloom thinks that culture should "tame this lion in the soul." This is to be accomplished by turning men into warriors, making them "cave dwellers" and supplying them with "noble myths." On the differences between Rousseau and Nietzsche, see Bloom's introduction to his translation of Jean-Jacques Rousseau's *Émile*, p. 12.

As we shall see in the next chapter, Francis Fukuyama inherits Bloom's idea that Plato's *thymos* is equivalent to Kojève's desire for recognition. I will argue that there are some very significant and interesting differences between the two concepts that Bloom's simple account does not reveal. I am inclined to side with Rousseau in thinking of *amour propre* as a deformity of soul. Nor do I think that Plato would disagree. But unlike Bloom, I do not wish to establish the rightness of a particular position simply by maintaining that it was held by the divine Plato.

30. Bloom, *Closing*, p. 201.

31. See Nietzsche's *Thus Spoke Zarathustra*, Part I, "On the New Idol," pp. 48ff.

32. Bloom, *Closing*, p. 190.

33. Ibid., p. 77.

34. Ibid., p. 68.

35. Ibid., pp. 74–75.

36. Ibid., p. 54.

37. Bloom is unable to appreciate anything distinctively American, such as jazz and blues, which spring from the suffering of the black Americans.

38. Kojève, *IRH*, p. xi. Apparently Bloom wanted the title of his book to be *Souls Without Longing*—a title that captures the essential characteristic of Nietzsche's last men.

39. One of these students describes his years with Bloom in terms that invoke the garden of Eden: see Michael Zuckert, "Two Cheers (At Least) for Allan Bloom," in Stone (ed.), *Essays on the Closing of the American Mind*, pp. 73–76.

40. In Rousseau's *Émile*, Émile is educated to be natural, free, and independent, especially of the conventions of his time. Ironically, he ends up being slavishly devoted to his tutor.

41. Bloom, *Closing*, p. 42.

42. Ibid., p. 42. The direct analogy Bloom makes between the two stories implies that the needs of university students differ little from the needs of a four-year-old.

43. Ibid., p. 89. Bloom complains that "these kids just do not have prejudices against anyone." They don't even hate the Jews or the Italians; and as a result, these groups no longer have an intense sense of what differentiates them—gone is the "solemnity of the interfaith or interethnic get-togethers" Bloom knew as a child. The best that America can be for Bloom is a microcosm of the Old World and its mutual hostilities. But, alas, the melting pot has worked (except where the blacks are concerned); and America has become a homogeneous and classless society of equal and prosperous men and women. The portrait of America as an egalitarian society sounds bizarre to a Canadian like myself who is not used to seeing so many beggars as when I am visiting America's most affluent cities.

44. Bloom, *Closing*, p. 51.

45. Ibid., p. 88.

46. Ibid., pp. 123, 125.

47. Ibid., p. 143.

48. Ibid., p. 212. Like Strauss, Bloom does not think that Nietzsche was anti-Semitic. Strauss's unpublished essay, "Why We Remain Jews," reads almost like an apology for Nietzsche. Strauss emphasizes a passage in which Nietzsche speculates that the Jews have the potential to be the sort of ruling elite that could lead Europe out of her decadence, if only they had not been so effeminized by their religion.

49. Weber classified political authority as traditional, rational, and charismatic. Weber believed that the domination of man by man was a necessary element of every culture. Without violence (that is what domination means), it is impossible for culture to emerge out of the chaos of nature. But violence cannot succeed in establishing and maintaining order unless it is camouflaged by legitimating myths that facilitate the willing submission of the dominated. Weber classified these legitimating myths in terms of his famous categories: traditional, rational, and charismatic. Traditional authority legitimizes coercion simply on the grounds that this is the way things have always been. Rational authority legitimizes coercion as the most effective means to the pursuit of rational self-interest. Charismatic authority has its legitimacy in the extraordinary grace of a single personality. Bloom thought that the concept of charisma

was the opposite of the rationalism of liberal democracy and that it referred to Nietzsche's cultural geniuses. See Max Weber, "Politics as a Vocation," in *From Max Weber: Essays in Sociology*, edited and translated by H. H. Gerth and C. Wright Mills (New York: Oxford University Press, 1958), pp. 77–128.

50. Bloom, *Closing*, p. 146.

51. Ibid., pp. 207–208.

52. Ibid., p. 208, see also pp. 201, 274, 277.

53. Two reviews that brilliantly document the contradictions and inconsistencies of Bloom's book are: Dan Latimer's review in *Textual Practice*, Vol. 2, No. 2 (Summer 1988), pp. 280–289, and Jean Bethke Elshtain, "Allan in Wonderland," *Cross Currents*, Vol. 36, No. 4 (Winter 1987–1988), pp. 476–79, also reprinted in Stone (ed.), *Essays on the Closing of the American Mind*.

Latimer argues that Bloom cannot choose between two dualities—on one hand, the serene, moderate, cosmopolitan, peace-loving rationalist who resembles the character of Adrian Leverkuhn in *Doktor Faustus* and that of Ahriman in *The Magic Mountain*, and on the other hand, the Teutonic *Blut und Boden* warrior, devoted to art, music, and the Kaiser, living on the edge, risking all and catching syphilis, like Serenus Zeitblom in *Doktor Faustus* and Ahura-Mazda in *The Magic Mountain*. Latimer provides ample textual evidence that makes his account of Bloom's contradictions rich and compelling. However, I believe that many, if not all, of these contradictions would disappear if we take into account the fact that Bloom believes in one set of standards for the few and another for the many. The *Blut und Boden* is an ideal necessary to sustain the cohesiveness of society; it should therefore be actively promoted by the philosopher, who is himself a cool and rational cosmopolitan. The trouble is, Bloom comes dangerously close to finding his own myths irresistible, and therefore betrays the coolness of his philosophic rationalism.

Elshtain points to the contradictory, inconsistent, and mutually exclusive ways in which Bloom uses the term *nature*. First, nature is that which is hidden by convention (i.e., that which is outside the cave). Second, nature is vulgar, cheap, and low; and thanks to Hobbes and Locke, this cheap and vulgar nature has come to be the foundation of American culture. Third, nature is something good and wholesome that has been defiled; and Bloom is nostalgic for a return to nature. But on the whole, Elshtain concludes that Bloom uses *nature* to pronounce the goodness of something without being aware of the contentiousness of the term. In short, Bloom uses the term *nature* "as a stick to beat his opponents with, and a magical wand to sprinkle the star dust of classicism, intelligence, right reason, . . . and high culture, . . . over the pages of his book." Elshtain also documents the corresponding ambiguities of his use of the terms *culture* and *convention*—sometimes as something high, sometimes as something low.

I hope to have explained the source of these inconsistencies and ambiguities. Elshtain implies that they are due to Bloom's lack of clearheadedness and his generally disorganized mode of expression. While I would not disagree entirely with this assessment, I believe that there is an inner coherence to Bloom's thought. Many of the inconsistencies revealed by Elshtain dissolve when the dual standard that Bloom takes for granted—one standard for the few and another for the many—is recognized. For the many, convention or culture and adherence to it is good—unless this happens to be American culture, which gives to the many what is appropriate only for the few. Only the few should be entitled to the openness that allows them to penetrate the reality beyond culture.

Other ambiguities in his use of the terms *nature* and *culture* are due to his unsuccessful attempt to straddle the positions of Plato and Nietzsche. When he is under the sway of Nietzsche, he speaks of culture as high and humanizing, but when he is under the sway of Plato, he thinks of culture as mere convention. He tries to blur the difference between the two positions, but his own language betrays him. It betrays the fact that Plato and Nietzsche begin from different premises; they do not simply reach different conclusions from the same premises, as he maintains.

Elshtain is right in thinking that nature remains a standard of sorts for Bloom. I have shown that Bloom believes that culture must be imposed against nature, and that nature cannot be the foundation of culture. Bloom thinks that culture should transform nature, but not subvert her. He does not explain this distinction. He simply assumes that the conventions he does not like are based either on unadulterated nature (e.g., American culture) or on the complete subversion of nature (e.g., feminism).

54. See Ernest Fortin's comparison of Strauss with the Pied Piper in "Dead Masters and Their Living Thought: Leo Strauss and his Friendly Critics," in *The Vital Nexus*, Vol. 1, No. 1 (May 1990), pp. 61–71; see also my reply to Fortin and others in Drury, "Reply to My Critics," in the same issue.

55. Bloom, introduction to his translation of Rousseau's *Émile*, pp. 5-6.

56. See Leo Strauss, *Socrates and Aristophanes* (Chicago: University of Chicago Press, 1966). Bloom is aware of the fact that waspishness is the sort of self-righteous indignation that leads to the killing of Socrates. But for him, as for Strauss, that is no reason to condemn it—Socrates was asking for it. See my discussion of *waspishness* as well as my discussion of Socrates in Shadia B. Drury, *The Political Ideas of Leo Strauss* (New York: St. Martin's Press, 1988), Chapter four. See also Bloom's "Interpretive Essay," in Bloom's translation of the *Republic of Plato* (New York: Basic Books, 1968). Bloom echoes the views of Strauss on Socrates. He does not deny the charges—he thinks that Socrates is guilty: Athens had "good reason to accuse him" (p. 309). Moreover, Bloom thinks that the *Republic* subtly explains why Socrates was guilty, by explaining the subversive nature of philosophy, or its capacity to undermine faith in the city's gods and its laws. Bloom's point is not that Socrates's ideas undermined the beliefs of a particular city, but that philosophy undermines the beliefs that make *any* civil society possible (p. 307). On the whole, Plato is made to sound like Nietzsche pontificating on the necessity of wholehearted attachments to culture and its myths. So much so that Plato is portrayed as endorsing Polemarchus's view of justice as being good to friends and evil to enemies. Bloom complains that moderns cannot appreciate the "dignity" of the perspective of Polemarchus, and the unswerving loyalty to "one's own" that it involves (p. 318).

57. This is an example from C. S. Lewis, which I've politicized; see his excellent *Broadcast Talks* (London: The Centenary Press, 1942).

58. Bloom, *Closing*, pp. 109, 114.

CHAPTER 12

1. Francis Fukuyama, *The End of History and the Last Man* (New York: Free Press, 1992). Fukuyama's book was preceded by his widely publicized article, "The End of History?" originally published in *The National Interest*, No. 16 (Summer 1989), pp. 3–18, with responses from Allan Bloom, Gertrude Himmelfarb, Irving Kristol, and others.

2. Fukuyama has complained about the "literal-minded way that people treat ideas," in Jonathan Alter, "The Intellectual Hula Hoop," *Newsweek*, October 9, 1989. Some reviewers believe that Fukuyama is saying that the good guys have won, and that evil has been vanquished once and for all; see for example, Strobe Talbott, "The Beginning of Nonsense," *Time*, September 11, 1989. James Crimmins, in "World Remains a Conflict of Ideas," *Globe and Mail*, December 28, 1989, understands the thesis as the triumph of a single ideology at the level of ideas, not practice. Fukuyama upholds the latter interpretation, saying that the end of history does not mean the end of world events, but "the end of the evolution of human thought" about the first principles governing social and political organization. See his "Reply to My Critics," *National Interest* (Winter 1989–1990), pp. 21–28.

3. Ray Conlogue, "The End of History: Is It Bunk?" *Globe and Mail*, December 28, 1989, develops the environmental criticism.

4. Many reviewers of Fukuyama's book have noted the darkness of the book, but have been at a loss to explain how so much gloom could go hand in hand with the "celebration" of the victory of liberal democracy around the globe. Reviewers have dismissed the book as confused and contradictory; see for example Stephen Holmes, "The Scowl of Minerva," *The New Republic* (March, 23, 1992), pp. 27–32. John Dunn, "In the Glare of Recognition," *Times Literary Supplement*, April 24, 1992, p. 6, dismisses the book as the product of a puerile, inconsistent, and inconclusive mind, which has, to make matters worse, suffered the slings and arrows of a Straussian education. Pierre Hassner finds more Nietzsche than Hegel;

see "Responses to Fukuyama," *The National Interest*, No. 16 (Summer 1989), pp. 22–24. James Atlas notices the "veiled contempt for the very culture whose triumph in the political sphere it purports to celebrate," in "What is Fukuyama Saying?" *New York Times Magazine*, October 22, 1989. Strobe Talbott, in "Terminator 2: Gloom on the Right," *Time*, January 27, 1992, p. 32, explains the darkness of the book in terms of the general gloom that has descended on the American Right in the wake of the collapse of the Evil Empire. The picture of the "Terminator" attached to the article is more appropriate than the magazine or the author is aware. It was included as a way of saying that America is the "Terminator" who has brought down all these other competing regimes. But to my mind, the "Terminator" represents the perversity of the decadent American conception of valor, which, as I will show, animates Fukuyama's book. Jeffrey Simpson, "Is This the Pot of Gold at the End of History?" *Globe and Mail*, April 4, 1992, wonders why a celebration of triumph reads like *The Waste Land*.

5. Daniel Bell, *The End of Ideology: On the Exhaustion of Political Ideas in the Fifties* (New York: Free Press, 1960), and Seymour Martin Lipset, *Political Man: The Social Basis of Politics* (New York: Doubleday, 1959).

6. Charles Taylor, "Neutrality in Political Science," in *Philosophy and the Human Sciences: Philosophical Papers*, Vol. 2, (New York: Cambridge University Press, 1985).

7. Fukuyama, *End of History*, p. xix.

8. Ibid., p. 182.

9. Ibid., p. 183.

10. *Megalothymia* can also have collective manifestations. Nationalism is a collective version of *megalothymia* that leads an entire nation or group to insist on the superiority of their own ethnic and cultural uniqueness vis-à-vis other peoples. In its most belligerent manifestations, it leads to wars of conquest, as in Nazi Germany. It is the claim of a group or collectivity to conquer others on the ground that they are racially and culturally superior. In its more benign manifestation, it insists on separatism and the exclusion of other ethnic and cultural groups from its proclaimed borders. Fukuyama believes that nationalism has been effectively "defanged" by modernity, and increasingly appears only in its benign manifestation. Religion can also be a collectivist manifestation of *megalothymia*, as when religious groups insist that others recognize their gods as supreme. The wars of religion in Europe were a case in point. Ibid., pp. 270–272.

11. Ibid., p. 147.

12. Ibid., p. 147.

13. Ibid., p. 148.

14. Ibid., p. 156, my italics.

15. Ibid., p. 147.

16. Ibid., p. 156. I have often heard young students trained by the Straussians say that the black people in America must live with the consequences of the cowardly "choice" made by their ancestors.

17. Ibid., p. 181–182.

18. Leo Strauss has argued this at great length in his *The Political Philosophy of Hobbes*, translated by Elsa M. Sinclair, (Chicago: University of Chicago Press, 1952).
19. Fukuyama, *End of History*, p. 157.

20. Ibid., p. 185.

21. Ibid.

22. Ibid.

23. Ibid., pp. 160, 185.

24. Ibid., p. 190.

25. Ibid., p. 185.

26. Ibid., p. 159.

27. Ibid., p. 157.

28. Ibid., p. 186.

29. Ibid., p. 185.

30. Ibid., p. 187.

31. Ibid., p. 188.

32. Ibid., p. 193.

33. Ibid., p. 148.

34. Ibid., pp. 199, 197.

35. Holmes, "The Scowl of Minerva," pp. 27–33.

36. Jon Elster, *Sour Grapes: Studies in the Subversion of Rationality* (Cambridge: Cambridge University Press, 1983), p. 98. Elster criticizes Arendt, saying that she regards "politics as the plaything of an already-educated elite, rather than as an educative process."

37. Fukuyama, *End of History*, p. 178.

38. Fukuyama's understanding of sex as "conquest" just slips out. Ibid., p. 176.

39. In Kurt Vonnegut, Jr., *Welcome to the Monkey House* (New York: Dell Publishing Co., 1950), pp. 7–13.

40. I am indebted to my colleague the classicist Martin Cropp for the understanding of spirit as spunk.

41. Fukuyama's insistence that *thymos* is an "innate sense of justice" flies in the face of his own claims about *thymos*. It flies in the face of *megalothymia*, as well as *isothymia*. The former, which is the desire to dominate others, cannot, by any stretch of the imagination, be said to spring from an innate sense of justice. Fukuyama does not even try to make the connection. But he does think that *isothymia* is closely related to, if not identical with, our sense of justice. His reasoning is that *isothymia* is the expression of the anger and indignation that people feel when others do not recognize their true worth. Justice is giving each his due, as Fukuyama acknowledges. However, *isothymia* is the demand for equal and mutual recognition, independent of merit. And this cannot be identical with a sense of justice.

42. Fukuyama, pp. xvi, 165.

43. Fukuyama's reading of the Platonic psychology is altogether outrageous. He thinks that *desire* moves men to want things, and *reason* tells them the best ways or the most efficient way to do it. This is so false that it cannot be called a misreading. See for example, p. xvii.

44. Plato, *Republic*, translated by Richard W. Sterling and William C. Scott (New York: W. W. Norton & Co., 1985), 440A.

45. Fukuyama, *End of History*, p. 151.

46. Ibid., p. 151.

47. Ibid., p. 190.

48. Ibid., p. 148.

49. Ibid.

CHAPTER 13

1. Gilles Deleuze and Félix Guattari, *Anti-Oedipus: Capitalism and Schizophrenia* (Minneapolis: University of Minnesota Press, 1983).

2. Strauss, *What is Political Philosophy?* (Westport, Conn.: Greenwood Press, 1959), p. 32; see also Strauss, *The Argument and the Action of Plato's Laws* (Chicago: The University of Chicago Press, 1975).

3. This is the thesis of Benjamin Barber in "Jihad Vs. McWorld," *The Atlantic*, Vol. 269, No. 3 (March, 1992), pp. 53–63.

S·E·L·E·C·T·E·D B·I·B·L·I·O·G·R·A·P·H·Y

BY KOJÈVE

Kojève, Alexandre. *Introduction à la lecture de Hegel.* Edited by Raymond Queneau. Paris: Gallimard, 1947. Most of this work is available in English as *Introduction to the Reading of Hegel,* edited by Allan Bloom and translated by James H. Nichols, Jr. New York: Basic Books, 1969.

Kojève, Alexandre. *Essai d'une histoire raisonnée de la philosophie païenne,* Vol. 1, *Les Présocratiques.* Paris: Gallimard, 1968. Kojève explores his views of Pre-Socratics such as Heraclitus and Parmenides in an effort to develop a Hegelian system of knowledge that begins with the philosophical love of wisdom and ends in its possession.

Kojève, Alexandre. *Kant.* Paris: Gallimard, 1973. Kojève emphasizes the Kantian dualism between man and nature, which is an important aspect of Kojève's own thought.

Kojève, Alexandre. *Le Concept, le temps et le discours.* Paris: Gallimard, 1991. Kojève attempts to show that wisdom is possible only in the fullness of time.

Kojève, Alexandre. *Esquisse d'une phenomenologie du droit.* Paris: Gallimard, 1981. Originally written in 1943, but published posthumously. Kojève compares the aristocratic conception of right with the bourgeois one.

Kojève, Alexandre. "Reviews." A series of book reviews in *Recherches philosophiques,* Vol. 2 (1932–33), pp. 470–486, and Vol. 3 (1933–1934), pp. 428–431.

Kojève, Alexandre. "La Métaphysique religieuse de Vladimir Soloviev (1)," and "La Métaphysique religieuse de Vladimir Soloviev (2)," *Revue d'histoire et de philosophie religieuses,* Vol. 14 (1934), pp. 534–554 and Vol. 15 (1935), pp. 110–152, respectively. Based on Kojève's dissertation, this was written under the supervision of Karl Jaspers. Kojève focuses on the mystical union of man and God in Jesus Christ.

Kojève, Alexandre. "Hegel, Marx et le christianisme," *Critique,* (August/September 1946), pp. 339–366. English translation by Hilail Gildin, "Hegel, Marx and Christianity," *Interpretation,* Vol. 1 (1970), pp. 21–42. Kojève argues that Hegel's dialectic is atheistic, not theistic and that the God of Christianity is nothing other than humanity in its historical evolution. He declares that all post-Hegelian thought is a dispute between the theological views of the Right Hegelians and the secular views of the Left Hegelians. And since ideas make history, all such writings are "propaganda" that is part of a program of struggle intended to determine the shape of the world.

Kojève, Alexandre. "Christianisme et communisme," *Critique,* Nos. 3–4 (1946), pp. 308–312. This is a review of a book by Father Gaston Fessard, who was a Right Hegelian. An English translation by Hugh Gillis is available, along with correspondence between Kojève and Fessard, and Fessard's "Two Interpreters of Hegel's Phenomenology: Jean Hyppolite and Alexandre Kojève," in "Kojève-Fessard Documents," *Interpretation,* Vol. 19, No. 2 (Winter 1991–92), pp. 185–200. Fessard thought that Hegel's dialectic culminated in divine salvation. He regarded Kojève as an existential Marxist because he emphasized man's finitude, but could not see that Hegel's dialectic began with finitude and culminated in the infinite. He regarded Kojève as a stimulating and engaging interpreter of Hegel, especially when compared to Hyppolite, whose interpretation of Hegel was similar to Kojève's, but not as well expressed.

Kojève, Alexandre. "L'Idée de la mort dans la philosophie de Hegel," Appendix II of Kojève's *Introduction à la lecture de Hegel,* described above. English translation by Joseph J. Carpino, "The Idea of Death in the Philosophy of Hegel," *Interpretation,* Vol. 3, Nos. 2 and 3 (Winter 1973) pp. 114–156. Amply illustrates Kojève's debt to Heidegger, which is discussed at length in Part I, Chapter 5 of this book.

Kojève, Alexandre. "Les Romans de la sagesse." *Critique*, Vol. 60 (1952), pp. 387–397. A review of three of Raymond Queneau's novels. He regards Queneau's protagonists as sages living at the end of history. I believe that Kojève provided the deepest reading of Queneau, and I elaborate on it in the chapter on Queneau above.

Kojève, Alexandre. "Le Dernier monde nouveau." *Critique*, Vol. 12, No. 2 (1956), pp. 702–708. Kojève regarded Sagan's novel as symptomatic of the eclipse of manhood at the end of history. See my discussion of this in Part I, Chapter 4, the section entitled "The Eclipse of Manhood."

Kojève, Alexandre. "Origine chrétienne de la science moderne," *Science*, Vol. 31 (May–June, 1964), pp. 37–41. Kojève argues that Western science could only have emerged in the context of a Christian culture because Christianity, unlike other religions, transcends the duality between man and God in its conception of the incarnation of Jesus Christ. This idea opens the way to the scientific efforts to perfect the human world. But even though Christianity gave birth to Western science, science no longer needs Christianity.

Kojève, Alexandre. "The Emperor Julian and his Art of Writing," *Ancients and Moderns: Essays on the Tradition of Political Philosophy in Honor of Leo Strauss,* edited by Joseph Cropsey (New York: Basic Books, 1964), pp. 95–113. The essay is written in jest as a parody on the Straussian art of writing. Kojève argues that the Emperor Julian, like every philosopher, was an atheist living in the "age of slavery" which was dominated by faith in a god who could alleviate the slavish anxiety about death. Being so out of step with his time, Julian resorted to esoteric writing. Kojève then explains that the esoteric style of writing is a very useful invention since it (1) satisfies the desire for playfulness, (2) allows philosophers to recognize one another more readily, (3) enables philosophers to edify the masses with lies, (4) provides comforting myths for the slavish who are unable to face death and need to believe in immortality, (5) lends stability to the status quo, and (6) is convenient for the philosophers who cannot really defend their beliefs to anyone who is not already convinced by them.

Kojève, Alexandre. "Entertien avec Gilles Lapouge: 'Les Philosophes ne m'intéressent pas, je cherche des sage,'" *La Quinzaine littéraire*, Vol. 53 (1–15 July 1968), pp. 18–20. Expresses some of his eccentric views on Napoleon, the end of history, the sage, Japan, and the *négativité gratuite*.

Kojève, Alexandre. "Pourquoi concret." Wassily Kandinsky (1866–1944), *Ecrit complets: La Forme*. Paris: Denoël Gonthier, 1970, Vol. 2, pp. 395–400. Kojève regards his uncle's innovative abstract art as the art of the universal and homogeneous state. See my discussion of this essay in Part I, Chapter 4, the section entitled "Kandinsky's Art."

Kojève, Alexandre. "Capitalisme et socialisme: Marx est Dieu, Ford est son prophète," *Commentaire*, Vol. 9 (Spring 1980), pp. 135–137. Argues that history will culminate in capitalism and not in communism as Marx had maintained. The reason is that twentieth-century capitalism has overcome the difficulties that Marx identified so clearly, and is now in a position to accomplish the very goals of history that Marx thought only communism could achieve.

ON KOJÈVE

Aron, Raymond. *Memoirs: Fifty Years of Political Reflection,* translated by George Holoch, forward by Henry Kissinger. New York: Holmes & Meier, 1990. See especially pp. 65–99, 465–466. He describes Kojève as the *éminence grise* at the French Economic ministry. Thinks that the reason Kojève went to work at the French ministry is that he wanted to be like Plato and advise a tyrant, but also because he believed that regional markets like the European Union would precede the universal empire. Aron noted that Kojève had a "white Russian" attitude toward the many. Aron was convinced that Kojève's books did not reflect his genius. But despite his intellectual admiration for Kojève, Aron did not follow in his footsteps—he shunned heroic politics.

Aron, Raymond. "Interview." *Encounter*, Vol. 41, No. 6 (1973), pp. 81–84. Describes Kojève as the most intelligent man he ever met.

Auffret, Dominique, *Alexandre Kojève: La Philosophie, l'état, la fin de l'histoire*. Paris: Bernard Grasset, 1990. Auffret focuses on Kojève's work at the French Ministry and tries to link it to his intellectual life. The book also contains a complete bibliography of Kojève's work. She regards Kojève as a right-wing Marxist who was as enigmatic as he was brilliant.

Bertman, Martin A. "Hobbes and Xenophon's *Tyrannicus*." *History of European Ideas*, Vol. 10, No. 5 (1989), pp. 507–517. Bertman maintains that Kojève's universal and homogeneous state is the logical conclusion of Hobbes's preoccupation with self-preservation. But he does not see any of the dark aspects of the universal and homogeneous state, nor does he think it would necessarily be a tyranny.

Desanti, Jean-T., "Hegel, est-il le père de l'existentialisme?" *La Nouvelle critique*, No. 56 (1954), pp. 91–109. Desanti thinks of Hegel as a stepping stone to Marx and Lenin. He is skeptical of Kojève's interpretation of Hegel, which he rightly understands as existential. Very cognizant of Kojève's dualistic ontology as a significant departure from Hegel.

Descombes, Vincent. *Modern French Philosophy*. Translated by L. Scott-Fox and J. M. Harding. Cambridge: Cambridge University Press, 1980. Scholarly and insightful. An excellent source. Kojève figures very prominently in his account. Describes Kojève as having a "terrorist conception of history." Descombes is well aware of the extent of Kojève's influence on existentialism as well as postmodernism. Points to the fact that Kojève's ominous "death of man" was echoed again and again by those who came after him.

Goldford, Denis J. "Kojève's Reading of Hegel," *International Philosophic Quarterly*, Vol. 22 (1982), pp. 275–294. A superb essay containing a penetrating critique of Kojève that admirably reveals the differences between Kojève and Hegel.

Gourevitch, Victor. "Philosophy and Politics, I" and "Philosophy and Politics II." *Review of Metaphysiscs*, Vol. 22, No. 1 (September 1968), pp. 58–84, and Vol. 22, No. 2 (December, 1968), pp. 281–328, respectively. Gourevitch was a student of Strauss who also studied with Kojève. Gourevitch gives a very detailed account of the debate between Kojève and Strauss. Takes a more balanced view of the debate than Strauss's students are inclined to do. He is rightly critical of Strauss for having no understanding of love, and for his view of the philosopher as a stranger.

Grant, George. "Tyranny and Wisdom: A Comment on the Controversy Between Leo Strauss and Alexandre Kojève." *Social Research*, Vol. 31 (1964), pp. 45–72. Grant believes that he is already living in the universal and homogeneous state, and the thought of it makes him ill. He is a Christian thinker who never understood Strauss, but who admired him and adopted his rhetoric and his melancholy about modernity. His commentary on the debate is not illuminating.

Heckman, John. "Hyppolite and the Hegel Revival in France," *Telos*, No. 16 (Summer, 1973), pp. 128–145. Very informative, particularly of the political and intellectual climate in France at the time that Hyppolite and Kojève were writing.

Kelly, George Armstrong. "Notes on Hegel's Lordship and Bondage," in *Review of Metaphysics*, Vol. 19, No. 4 (June 1966), reprinted in Alasdair MacIntyre (ed.), *Hegel: A Collection of Critical Essays*, (New York: Doubleday, 1972), pp. 189–217. An excellent essay on the master-slave dialectic. Regards Kojève's interpretation as an extreme distortion.

Lilla, Mark. "The End of Philosophy: How a Russian émigré brought Hegel to the French." *Times Literary Supplement* (April 5, 1991), pp. 3–5.

Pippin, Robert P. "Being, Time, and Politics: The Strauss-Kojève Debate." *History and Theory,* Vol. 32, No. 2 (1993), pp. 138–161. A conventional reading, like that of Michael Roth and others.

Poster, Mark. *Existential Marxism in Postwar France: From Sartre to Althusser.* Princeton: Princeton University Press, 1975. Poster emphasizes the intellectual importance of Kojève in the development of Sartre's existential Marxism and thinks that Kojève came close to "veering toward fascism" (p. 12).

Riley, Patrick. "Introduction to the Reading of Alexandre Kojève." *Political Theory,* Vol. 9, No. 1 (February 1981), pp. 5–48. Riley argues that Kojève distorts Hegel's philosophy. Regards Kojève's universal and homogeneous state as the realization of the Kantian ideal of universal respect for all persons as ends in themselves. Points to some important differences between Kojève and Hegel.

Roth, Michael S. *Knowing and History: Appropriations of Hegel in Twentieth-Century France.* Ithaca and London: Cornell University Press, 1988. Roth's study contains discussions of Jean Wahl, Alexandre Koyré, Jean Hyppolite, Alexandre Kojève, Leo Strauss, Maurice Merleau-Ponty and others. It is very scholarly, but uninspired, with a good bibliography. Roth takes a typically Straussian position on the Kojève-Strauss debate and sides with the "ancient" wisdom of Strauss.

Roth, Michael S. "A Note on Kojève's Phenomenology of Right." *Political Theory,* Vol. 11, No. 3 (1983), pp. 447–450. A review of Kojève's *Esquisse d'une phenomenologie du droit* (Paris: Gallimard, 1981).

Roth, Michael S. "A Problem of Recognition: Alexandre Kojève and the End of History." *History and Theory: Studies in the Philosophy of History,* Vol. 24, No. 3 (1985), pp. 293–306. Emphasizes Kojève's "turn" as a dramatic change of heart. Paints Kojève as a modern philosopher who finally recognizes the errors of his ways.

Rosen, Stanley. *Hermeneutics as Politics.* Oxford: Oxford University Press, 1987. See especially Chapter 3, which is a detailed discussion of Kojève and Strauss. Rosen is the only student of Strauss who recognizes the close affinity between the two writers. He studied with both of them and has a great deal to say about their style and their character.

Rosen, Stanley. Review: Kojève, *Essai d'une histoire raisonnée de la philosophie païenne,* Vol. 1: *Les Présocratiques* (Paris: Gallimard, 1968). *Man and World,* Vol. 3 (1970), pp. 120–125. Rosen rightly argues that Kojève's conception of wisdom is indistinguishable from the silence of the pre-philosophical.

RELATED WORKS

Anderson, Walter Truett. *Reality Isn't What It Used To Be.* San Francisco: Harper & Row, 1990. Delightfully postmodern, without surrendering to meaninglessness, or resorting to stupefying profundity.

Bell, Daniel. *The End of Ideology.* New York, Free Press, 1960. See my discussion in Part III, Chapter 3, section entitled "End of History Vs. End of Ideology."

Benda, Julien. *The Treason of the Intellectuals,* translated from the French by Richard Aldington. New York: W. W. Norton & Co., 1928. Benda argues that the intellectuals should be above the political fray. He laments the passing of the good old days when philosophers had to be dragged kicking and screaming into the cave.

Chiaromonte, Nicola. "On Modern Tyranny." *Dissent,* Vol. 16 (March/April, 1969), pp. 137–150. A brilliant essay. An all-out attack on the alliance of tyranny and wisdom in the modern world. Castigates the intellectuals for having become apologists of power, content to play the role of prince's advisors.

Ferry, Luc, and Alain Renaut, *French Philosophy of the Sixties: An Essay on Antihumanism.* Amherst: University of Massachusetts Press, 1985. An excellent work. Ferry and Renaut argue that French postmodern philosophers have an antipathy to everything universal, including ethical norms and human rights. But this fact is concealed by their wholesale commitment to duplicity. The "death of man" is one of those duplicitous themes that refers simultaneously to the reification of man by the human sciences as well as to the death of the subject in postmodern thought.

Hegel, Geog Wilhelm Friedrich. *Phenomenology of Spirit*, (1807). Translated by J. N. Findlay. Oxford: Oxford University Press, 1977.

Hegel, Geog Wilhelm Friedrich. *Lectures on the History of Philosophy*, 3 Vols. (1840). Translated by E. S. Haldane (London: Routledge & Kegan Paul Ltd., 1892, 1955).

Hegel, Geog Wilhelm Friedrich. *Philosophy of Right* (1821). Translated by T. M. Knox. Oxford: Oxford University Press, 1967.

Heidegger, Martin. *Being and Time* (1927). Translated by John Macquarrie & Edward Robinson. New York: Harper & Row, 1962.

Heidegger, Martin. *An Introduction to Metaphysics* (1953). Translated by Ralph Manheim. New York: Doubleday & Company Inc., 1961.

Heidegger, Martin. *Basic Writings.* Edited with an introduction by David Farrell Krell. New York: Harper & Row, 1977. Includes Heidegger's "Letter on Humanism" and "The Question Concerning Technology."

Hyppolite, Jean. *Genesis and Structure of Hegel's Phenomenology of Spirit.* Translated by Samuel Cherniak and John Heckman. Evanston: Northwestern University Press, 1974.

Marcuse, Herbert. *One Dimensional Man.* Boston: Beacon Press, 1964. Deplores the connection between progress and the one-dimensionality of existence.

Merleau-Ponty, Maurice. *Humanisme et terreur: essai sur le problème communiste.* Paris: Gallimard, 1947. Translated by John O'Neill as *Humanism and Terror.* Boston: Beacon Press, 1969. Merleau-Ponty agonizes over whether the terror of the Communist Party under Stalin is necessary to realize the goal of history or whether it is merely gratuitous. If the party succeeds, then its terror must be deemed necessary and justified—but that is difficult to know in advance. This is thorny problem that Kojève dispensed with since he thought that history had already ended.

Nietzsche, Friedrich. *Thus Spoke Zarathustra* (1892). Translated by Walter Kaufmann. New York: Penguin Books, 1982. The first Part, section 5, contains the famous description of the last man.

Nietzsche, Friedrich. *The Use and Abuse of History.* Translated by Adrian Collins. London: Macmillan, Library of the Liberal Arts, 1957. A classic in the philosophy of history.

Nietzsche, Friedrich. *Beyond Good and Evil.* Translated by Walter Kaufmann. New York: Random House, 1966.

I·N·D·E·X

9 780312 120924